D0026931

VALKYRIE

AN INSIDER'S ACCOUNT OF
THE PLOT TO KILL HITLER

HANS BERND GISEVIUS

TRANSLATED FROM THE GERMAN BY
Richard and Clara Winston

FOREWORD BY Allen W. Dulles
INTRODUCTION BY Peter Hoffmann

Da Capo Press
A member of the Perseus Books Group

Library of Congress Cataloging-in-Publication Data

Gisevius, Hans Bernd, 1904-1974.
  Valkyrie : an insider's account of the plot to kill Hitler / Hans Bernd
Gisevius ; translated from the German by Richard and Clara Winston ;
foreword by Allen W. Dulles ; introduction by Peter Hoffmann.—1st Da
Capo Press ed.
      p. cm.
  "This Da Capo Press paperback edition of Valkyrie is an abridged edition
of the full edition of *To The Bitter End* first published in Cambridge, Mas-
sachusetts in 1947 and republished by Da Capo Press in 1998 with a new
introduction by Peter Hoffmann. Originally published in German as *Bis
zum bittern Ende* in 1946"—T.p. verso.
  Includes index.
  ISBN 978-0-306-81771-7 (alk. paper)
  1. Hitler, Adolf, 1889-1945—Assassination attempt, 1944 (July 20) 2.
Schenk von Stauffenberg, Klaus Philipp, Graf, 1907-1944. 3. German—
Politics and government—1933-1945. I. Gisevius, Hans Bernd, 1904-
1974. Bis zum bittern Ende. English. II. Title.
  DD256.35.G53 2009
  943.0860   2008034713

First abridged edition published by Da Capo Press 2009

Published by Da Capo Press
A Member of the Perseus Books Group
www.dacapopress.com

Da Capo Press books are available at special discounts for bulk purchases in
the U.S. by corporations, institutions, and other organizations. For more
information, please contact the Special Markets Department at the Perseus
Books Group, 2300 Chestnut Street, Suite 200, Philadelphia, PA 19103, or
call (800) 810-4145, ext. 5000, or e-mail special.markets@perseusbooks.com.

To the Memory of
HANS OSTER
*Who was killed on April 9, 1945
in the death camp at Flossenburg*

Contents

Author's Preface to the Original Edition

THIS BOOK is not intended as a history of the Third Reich. The author has selected a few prominent incidents out of the confusion of contemporaneous events and has attempted to use these as points through which to trace the broad curves of the historical process.

The account is not drawn from hearsay; all of it comes from the author's experience. At the age of twenty-nine, when the Brown dictatorship was initiated, I intended to make a career of the civil service; the circumstances of the times plunged me at once into the midst of the revolutionary turbulence. I was buffeted on all sides by the mounting waves and many times came close to going under. Now I believe that the time has come when, for the sake of my dead friends and for my own sake, I ought to set down the most important experiences and impressions of this period.

I have no wish to apologize either for my approach or for my present point of view. There are some who are proud of having kept aloof from the rapid changes of these past twelve years, who have learned nothing new during those cataclysmic years, and who now would like to take up again the attitudes and habits that were so suddenly interrupted. I have learned a good many important things. Those years have provided a discipline without which I should probably have clung to many errors and prejudices. On the other hand, I am not ashamed to declare frankly that I formerly stood on the Right, and that, in spite of all unsavory experiences, I have not abandoned my conservative point of view.

From 1929 on, it became more and more apparent that the

leaders of our Left and Center Parties were incapable of holding the masses in line. It seemed quite reasonable to hope that the rising flood could be stemmed by the Right and safely guided into evolutionary channels. In any case, the attempt had to be made; otherwise the plunge into the Brown Revolution would be inevitable. Conservatism is not synonymous with social reaction or retrogression. The circle of "young Rightists" (the last militant representatives of whom we shall meet again among the tragic victims of July 20, 1944, twelve years later) considered themselves far more progressive and European-minded than the clique of parliamentary leaders who governed from 1918 to 1929. The latter group consisted almost entirely of persons who had facilely made the shift from the Kaiser's Germany to the allegedly "new" republican system. The faces might not have been all the same, but the mentality of imperial Germany was everywhere in evidence.

The fact that our Stahlhelm and our German nationalists did not succeed in carrying out the mission that had fallen to their lot is no argument against our experiment. But it is an indication that we were gravely deficient in real inner conviction and in the will to resist. The tragedy of German history before 1933 was not that so many Germans swung to the Right; the real tragedy consisted in the fact that for more than fifty years there had been no real conservatives on the Right. Government circles under Kaiser Wilhelm, who later, after the First World War, became imperial nationalists, had only a spurious conservative outlook to offer. It is they who were most to blame for the general feeling in Germany that conservatism was irreconcilable with social progress and democracy.

But let us not deceive ourselves. Both German liberalism and German Marxism must bear a considerable measure of guilt for the disaster of Nazism. More than any other intellectual movement of the nineteenth century, liberalism, with its overemphasis upon individualism, contributed greatly to the dissolution of religious and ethical principles. Similarly, liberalism's mechanistic idea of centralization helped to obstruct any step toward a healthy kind of federalism. The speed with which centralism can deteriorate into extreme nationalism is something that we Europeans, who have felt the worst blows of nationalism, have experienced not only in Germany but in the rest of Europe. As far as Marxism is concerned, the slogans of "the dictatorship of the proletariat" and "the mobilization of the masses" also gave a fateful turn to the whole subsequent course of history. When the younger generation vigorously rejected political institutions which shaped, not a living democracy, but a caricature of democracy, they were impelled by motives deeper than political immaturity.

The things that were swept away in 1933 were by no means all good or worthy of being preserved. Not every politician whose constituency turned against him can plume himself on the soundness of his former policies because the Nazi regime turned out to be so dreadful. It would hardly be of any use to bring about a restoration of those who perpetually insist that they were in the right. History has proved that all of us Germans were so terribly in the wrong that it simply won't do to pillory only registered members of the National Socialist Party and the SS, or to condemn as pro-fascist everyone who stood on the Right before 1933. We must fight our way forward to new forms of life, over ground pitted with graves and ruins. In so doing, the more thoroughly we free ourselves from the spell of the immediate past—but also from the specters of the more distant past!—the more clearly and resolutely we shall perceive that we must begin again at the beginning. We must realize that not only have our institutions become heaps of rubble, but their yellowed mortgages are also worthless; no matter what forces and traditions of the nineteenth century underlie these deeds, they are now no more than scraps of paper.

The occupation powers have allowed the Communists, who were the most consistent opponents of the German political system that prevailed between 1918 and 1933, a significant share in the work of reconstruction. This policy implies that the powers do not consider open opposition to the principles, customs, and legal codes of the Weimar Republic a damning fault. One can have opposed the Weimar Republic and still be entitled to work for the establishment of a real democracy—which the German people have not yet been privileged to experience. Therefore, I hope that after this period of utter ideological confusion on the part of the Right, new conservative forces will in time arise. In a true democracy, the groupings that spring up out of party politics cannot be limited to the strict Center. Precisely because ours is a revolutionary age, there is a real need within Germany for sincere advocates of a new legitimacy, for a courageous anti-collectivism and a supra-national point of view. Such a conservative movement must not only put nationalism far behind it, but must have the intellectual alertness to draw the significant lessons from the downfall of all three German empires of the past: the Hitler dictatorship, the Bismarckian reign, and the Prussia of Frederick the Great.

So much for my political philosophy. In the following chapters I shall give an account of my principles and my activities during the period from [1939] to July 20, 1944. Since so many important witnesses and almost all the secret collections of documents have been destroyed, I feel it my duty to enlarge on matters which may be of interest to future historians as well as to our wearied contemporaries. For historians will one day try to discover why no one was on hand to avert the catastrophe in time.

—H. B. G.

Foreword to the Original Edition

HANS BERND GISEVIUS is one of the few survivors of the group of Germans who actively plotted to do away with Hitler. In the early days of the conspiracy he was at the center of activities in Berlin. Then he became one of the foreign envoys of the conspirators, and that is how I came to know him in Switzerland.

We met there early in 1943. I was then in charge of the work in Switzerland of the Office of Strategic Services and attached to the American Legation in Bern. Gisevius was ostensibly a German vice-consul in Zurich. In reality, he belonged to a small circle of men in the German counter-intelligence service, the Abwehr, who, under Admiral Wilhelm Canaris and General Hans Oster, were working against the Nazis. Our first secret conference took place in January of 1943, after I had taken careful soundings about the man I was to meet. Sources I trusted thoroughly had told me in strict confidence of the work he was doing, and that he was the one person in Switzerland who could tell me the inside story of the German underground.

He did that, and much more. As soon as mutual confidence was established Gisevius let me into the secret of the conspiracy, led by General Beck and Carl Friedrich Goerdeler.

Even before I met him Gisevius had completed roughly one half of his present book. It is interesting to note that he had done this writing before the German defeat was apparent, in fact, when Germany was riding roughshod over Europe. After I had known him a few months he gave me the bulky German manuscript and asked my help in getting it translated, as even in those days he was looking forward to the time when he could make available to the English-reading world the story of what went on behind the scenes of Nazi Germany. Also, he wished the manuscript to be in safe hands in the event that he did not live to finish it.

Gisevius's philosophy can be summed up in a few words. To him, a victory for Hitler meant the end of Christian civilization, and of Western culture in Europe and possibly in the world. He proposed to do his bit to prevent it, and felt that in doing so he was only carrying out his duty as a German. Quite rightly, he did not consider that he was working against his country; he felt he was working for it. But he wanted the Allies to hurry, to destroy Hitler before all the foundations on which a better Germany could be built had been demolished. He wanted to prevent Hitler from carrying on the fight "to the bitter end."

This was not to be, but not because Gisevius and his fellow conspirators lacked courage or the determination to risk everything in the attempt. Fate had ruled that Hitler was to carry on until Germany was in ruins.

It is hard to say whether or not it is better that the plot should have failed. If Hitler had been killed, German resistance would have collapsed and the war would have ended in 1944. But possibly the crimes of the Nazis were so great that nothing short of total destruction could have sufficed, despite the cost to the Allies and the loss to Germany of a group of men who are sorely needed now in the task of German reconstruction. At least one thing is clear. We have the evidence that there were some Germans who were willing to make the attempt to do away with Hitler and his régime, even though they received no encouragement from Hitler's enemies, and even though it was clear that if their effort was successful it would mean the total military defeat of Germany.

When Gisevius left Switzerland on July 11, 1944, to join

in the final phases of the last plot, he took his life in his hands. The Gestapo had been trying to get him for a long while, and when the plot failed I hardly expected to see him again. Through underground channels he finally succeeded in getting word out to us that he was safe and in hiding in Berlin, and after careful preparation we were able to find a way to get through to him false papers, on which he traveled unmolested to the Swiss frontier. Thus he was able to write the last dramatic chapters of his book, and to add another touch of drama to a life already crammed with adventure.

In April 1946, Gisevius appeared as a witness at the Nuremberg Trials and during three days on the witness stand confronted Goering and his cohorts with damning evidence to add to the accumulated record of their crimes. In the course of his cross-examination of Gisevius, Mr. Justice Jackson described him as "the one representative of democratic forces in Germany to take this stand to tell his story."

It is in this book that he really tells his story. It is one of deep human interest and of historical importance—the inside story of what went on within Germany among those who plotted against the Nazis.

—ALLEN W. DULLES
New York, 1947

Introduction to the 1998 Edition

BY PETER HOFFMANN

HANS BERND GISEVIUS, the son of a Prussian high-court judge, was born in Arnsberg in Westfalia, Germany, on June 14, 1904, and died in Switzerland on February 23, 1974.[1] After attending high-school in Berlin, he became a student of law and received a doctorate in 1929. In the same year he joined the *Deutschnationale Volkspartei* (German National Peoples Party, DNVP), a rightist conservative party, and the *Stahlhelm* veterans' organization. When he was articling in the judicial system in Berlin, he also took part in the Right's campaign against the Young Plan, which rescheduled German reparation payments. His political activity resulted in his punitive transfer to Düsseldorf in May 1930, and in libel suits against him, with one brought by Chancellor Heinrich Brüning. Gisevius lost them all, although they provided him with prominence as well as notoriety: by the end of 1931 he had been elected to membership in the national council of the DNVP. In the autumn of 1931 Gisevius had formed under his leadership a young DNVP group (*Arbeitsgemeinschaft junger Deutschnationaler*) that involved itself in the party's internal struggles. He advocated cooperation with the *Nationalsozialistische Deutsche Arbeiterpartei* (National Socialist German Workers Party, NSDAP). In 1933 he was leader of the *Deutschnationaler Kampfring Westen* (German National Combat Ring West) in Düsseldorf-Ost and a member of the national executive board of the DNVP. But on June 11, 1933 the NSDAP daily newspaper *Völkischer Beobachter* reported—on its front page under banner headlines—the sensational resignation of Dr. Gisevius and two other DNVP executive-board members, and quoted

them for "their commitment to National Socialism" as the sole
support of the German state.

In July 1933 Gisevius passed his second law examinations
and in August he entered the Prussian civil service as an asses-
sor in the Political Section of the Prussian Interior Ministry.
He aspired to the position of chief of the Prussian *Geheime
Staatspolizei* (Secret State Police, for short, Gestapo[2]) which
soon became the national Secret State Police. He joined forces
with the head of the executive department of the Prussian
Secret State Police, Arthur Nebe, and intrigued with him
against the successful candidate, Rudolf Diels, whom they
denounced as a Communist. As a result, Diels was temporarily removed. When he returned after a short absence, he
accused Gisevius of reactionary subversion and had a warrant
issued for his arrest. Gisevius escaped through postings to positions without authority, such as observer at the trial of the
Reichstag arsonist in Leipzig, and as a government counsellor in
Münster and Potsdam.

Notwithstanding his application of November 15, 1933, to
join the NSDAP[3]—two weeks *after* the Gestapo warrant for
his arrest had been issued—Gisevius did not become a National Socialist. Whether or not he had made his application sincerely or for his own protection, there is no record to indicate
that he later withdrew it. There was a moratorium for new
memberships from May 1, 1933 to May 1, 1937,[4] and since
Gisevius was in some disgrace with the authorities, it was not
likely that an exception would have been made for him. When
the moratorium was lifted, his eligibility had not improved.

His attempt to crash the gates to power had failed; his
career had become derailed. He was in and out of postings in
the Prussian and Reich interior ministries, appearing as Berlin
Police Chief Wolf Count von Helldorf's permanent deputy on
the police staff for the 1936 Olympiad, only to be dismissed

upon the intervention of Reinhard Heydrich, the new chief of the Gestapo and of the Security Police and SD.

The alternative to advancement within the National Socialist establishment appeared toward the end of the 1930s. At Hitler's announcement in November 1937 of his plans for war, both Field Marshal Werner von Blomberg, the war minister, and General Werner Baron von Fritsch, the commander-in-chief of the army, raised objections. By the end of January 1938 they had become tainted by scandal and were dismissed. During this crisis the conspiracy against Hitler began to form itself around the chief of the General Staff of the army, General Ludwig Beck, and the former Reich Prices Commissioner and mayor of Leipzig, Carl Goerdeler. It included the chief of the Abwehr (military intelligence), Admiral Wilhelm Canaris; Canaris's right hand, Major Hans Oster; Helldorf; the former Reich Economics Minister Hjalmar Schacht; Nebe; and Berlin's Deputy Chief of Police, Fritz-Dietlof Count von der Schulenburg. Having made Oster's acquaintance, Gisevius attached himself to the conspirators. He specialized in observing the Gestapo and in using his connections to keep the conspirators informed and to help them plan a coup d'état. Oster and Gisevius were the most active conspirators.

Since the Gestapo had based the accusations against Fritsch on a false identification, Gisevius saw an opportunity to do battle against the agency that had rejected him and that he perhaps still hoped to head. Gisevius's ambition became a catalyst that helped to assemble the forces of the resistance movement that culminated in the abortive July 20, 1944 insurrection. By the late summer of 1938—after Beck had resigned in protest against Hitler's threat of war against Czechoslovakia, and after General Franz Halder had succeeded him as chief of the General Staff—the conspiracy aimed at overthrowing Hitler. Oster and Schacht now referred Halder to Gisevius for

matters concerning the deployment of the police in a coup d'é-
tat. The Berlin military district commander, General Erwin
von Witzleben, employed Gisevius as a liaison between himself
and the Oster group, and provided him with a cover name and
an office on the pretext that he was sorting through family
papers.

When war broke out, Oster arranged for Gisevius to be
drafted into the Abwehr, and in 1940 installed him as an intelligence agent, disguised as a vice-consul, in the German consulate-general in Zurich, where he had no duties and no office.
While there, he helped establish foreign contacts for the resistance. He worked for the Abwehr, and also collaborated first
with British intelligence (who soon suspected him of being a
double-agent), and from January 1943 (after the arrival of
Allen W. Dulles in Bern as head of the Office of Strategic
Services bureau there in the autumn of 1942) with American
intelligence.[5] He helped to channel reports on SS atrocities
into Hitler's leadership staff—onto the desk of the Chief of
Armed Forces Supreme Command (OKW), Fieldmarshal
Wilhelm Keitel—by disguising them as foreign intelligence
material.[6] He risked his life with his double role, in the interest of ending the war and the crimes that were being committed under the cover of war.

During these years Gisevius persuaded Oster to use
Abwehr money to establish a fund in Switzerland that would
be available to a post-Hitler resistance government. In the
autumn of 1942, Hans von Dohnanyi—with the aid of Oster,
Canaris, Helmuth James Count von Moltke, and Dietrich
Bonhoeffer—helped a number of Jews escape to Switzerland.
Gisevius withdrew from the fund $100,000 as partial compen-
sation for the assets which the refugees had to leave behind in
Berlin, and as security against the émigrés becoming wards of
the Swiss state, which the Swiss government demanded as a

condition for granting the necessary entry visas. Gisevius got into difficulties with the OKW accounting section that supervised the financial transactions of the Abwehr, which was also a section of OKW. Some of Gisevius's appropriations from the fund had not followed prescribed procedure. The OKW accounting section investigated and found Oster, Gisevius, and others to be involved in unauthorized transactions. At the same time, the Abwehr chief in Bern, Commander Hans Meisner, had become suspicious of Gisevius's many contacts with enemy representatives in Switzerland, and accused Gisevius of collaboration with the enemy. The OKW accounting section demanded the repatriation of the fund in the summer of 1942. Gisevius at first resisted its repatriation, since his ability to use it had given him considerable status, but he relented toward the end of the summer of 1942.[7] He returned briefly to Germany in the summer of 1943, escaping just before he was to be arrested.

Gisevius continued in his double role in Switzerland until July 1944, receiving from Abwehr couriers information that he passed on to Allen Dulles, such as information on the development of what later became the V-1 and V-2 rockets and ballistic missiles, and as Dulles wrote in recommending Gisevius as a witness for the Nuremburg War Crimes Trial, "clues which later helped toward the spotting of the German testing station at Peenemunde."[8]

On July 11, 1944, having been informed by his German contact in the conspiracy that the coup d'état was about to occur, Gisevius travelled to Berlin in order to participate in it. After it failed, he went into hiding until he was able to escape to Switzerland on January 23, 1945, with the aid of a passport that belonged to Carl Deichmann, a brother of Helmuth James Count von Moltke's wife. The passport had been doctored through the offices of Dulles, and Georg Federer in the German Legation in Bern helped to provide the necessary visa.[9]

ii

Gisevius began his book in Germany in 1938 but completed most of it in Switzerland during the war. He continued writing it while helping Allen Dulles's assistant Mary Bancroft and her friends Mary Briner and Elizabeth Scott-Montagu prepare a translation, which was transmitted to OSS headquarters in Washington.[10] In fact, Dulles had initiated the translation as a method of unobtrusively but frequently debriefing Gisevius in the interest of American intelligence. But Gisevius was most anxious to have his book published as soon as possible, believing that it would launch him into the prominence that had eluded him in the years from 1929 to 1934, and again, through the failure of the coup d'état of July 20, 1944. But with the war over, he was now a *formerly* useful informant, and his attempts to gain an official or otherwise respectable position met with embarrassed or indifferent rejection by the beneficiaries of the information he had earlier transmitted.

To the Bitter End was first published in a German-language edition in Switzerland (1946) and in an English translation in Britain and in America (1947). The Swiss publishers had been reserved in light of rumors about Gisevius's association with the National Socialist dictatorship, but were eventually persuaded by testimonials from unimpeachable sources. The book was very successful in Switzerland and in Germany and was reprinted, with some revisions, several times. After Gisevius had testified at the Nuremberg War Crimes Trial in 1946, he was able to choose from among eight offers from American publishers.[11]

When I met Gisevius in Lausanne and St. Légier in Switzerland in 1971 and 1972, To the Bitter End had been subjected to criticism for 25 years. He said at once that he had written his book "in a subjective form, not as a book for historians."[12] Indeed, Gisevius had not intended to offer a memoir of life in Hitler's Third Reich, but rather a serious analysis of the National Socialist dictatorship and a history of the resistance to it. He had only thrown in the firsthand episodes to enliven the more serious aspects. He later made some changes, eliminated repetitious passages, and gave the text more of the appearance of a firsthand account. Although much of what he had related has been confirmed by other contemporary sources—often in crucial detail—the accuracy of numerous points has been disputed on the basis of other sources and of internal evidence.

iii

One of Gisevius's most grievous errors in judgment concerns Colonel Klaus Count von Stauffenberg. Gisevius's description of Stauffenberg, the leader of the July 20, 1944 insurrection, reveals less about the colonel than about Gisevius's own political orientation, and about his resentment of a rival who did not seem to appreciate Gisevius's contribution to the resistance.

Gisevius met Stauffenberg for the first time in Berlin on July 12, 1944, eight days before the colonel's last assassination attempt against Hitler. Much of what Gisevius relates about Stauffenberg, however, came to him not mainly from his only conversation with Stauffenberg before July 15 and 20, 1944, but, as he himself relates, from conspirators such as General Friedrich Olbricht and General Ludwig Beck, and most of all, from Canaris's successor as head of the Abwehr, Colonel Georg Hansen.[13] In view of Gisevius's own record as a transmitter of historical information for which he had displayed strong personal feelings, and in light of what is known about both Gisevius's alleged sources and Stauffenberg himself, Gisevius's account is at best questionable hearsay.

Gisevius disliked Stauffenberg. He sensed that this dynamic leader would be an obstacle to his own far-reaching ambitions and intrigues. In his book he mocked Stauffenberg as a presumptuous and ignorant amateur (p. 134): "As chief of staff to the commander of the home army he wanted me to 'inform' him about phases of the situation with which he was not acquainted. I came from Switzerland where all sorts of information was available. Would I give him my impressions?"

When Stauffenberg had joined the conspiracy in the late summer of 1943, he had begun quickly to take matters into his own hands, to organize and coordinate the preparations for Hitler's overthrow. In the matter of foreign contacts he relied on Helmuth James Count von Moltke, Adam von Trott zu Solz, and Otto John whom he knew, and who were able to travel abroad (to Turkey, Sweden, Switzerland, Spain), rather than on older diplomats such as Ulrich von Hassell or Friedrich Werner Count von der Schulenburg, the former ambassadors in Rome and Moscow respectively, who were no longer in a position to travel to neutral countries.[14] Stauffenberg must have been informed of Gisevius's background, and it cannot have inspired his confidence. Gisevius was understandably upset by Stauffenberg's attitude toward him. He had spent years establishing a usable contact for the resistance abroad, with the undertaking to Allen Dulles that every communication from General Ludwig Beck, the presumptive post-Hitler head of state, was coming only through Gisevius himself. He had revealed military information to Dulles in order to establish his own credibility, only to find that Stauffenberg seemed to regard him merely as an incidental source of background information.[15]

In his book Gisevius reduced Stauffenberg to a frustrated

cripple:[16] "I sensed at once that this unfortunate man must renounce the hope of attracting masses of people to his cause. His effectiveness must henceforth be confined to small groups. It was as if a pitiless destiny had deliberately planned to thrust him into the role of a conspirator." He described Stauffenberg as rude and boorish, and judged that "consciously or unconsciously, he was trying to overcompensate for the inferiority feelings engendered by his mutilation." Gisevius considered Stauffenberg "a swashbuckler," "typical of the 'new' class of general staff officers: the kind of man best suited to Hitler's purposes—or to purposes of assassination" (which in the context must suggest a Nazi murderer), who "in the final analysis was fighting for the continuation of Nazi-militaristic 'legality.'"[17] And: "Stauffenberg was motivated by the impulsive passions of the disillusioned military man whose eyes had been opened by the defeat of German arms."[18] Stauffenberg "had shifted to the rebel side only after Stalingrad."[19] With patronizing insincerity, Gisevius—so he himself reports—personally expressed to Stauffenberg during their interview that night in July his respect for Stauffenberg's courage to carry out the assassination.[20]

When he declares Stauffenberg "boorish," Gisevius's air of offended refined sentiments is not convincing in light of his insulting and inaccurate description of the man who dared to kill Hitler. Gisevius was not aware that throughout 1942 Stauffenberg had attempted, singlehandedly and against overwhelming odds, as a lowly major in the General Staff, to convince senior commanders on the eastern front to overthrow Hitler. Nor did Gisevius know Stauffenberg's inclination of taking the opposite side in any conversation for the sake of acting as *advocatus diaboli*.

There appears to have been a clash of views when Gisevius explained his anti-Communist and pro-American positions.

Stauffenberg replied (according to Gisevius's account of the conversation—the only one that exists) that very likely it would be necessary to negotiate with the Soviet Union, since it was probably "too late for the West," and the Red Army would reach the gates of Berlin within a few weeks. If this is an accurate account of what Stauffenberg said, the basis of it was the fact that German forces were unable to halt the rapid advance of the Red Army, which was about to occupy east and central Germany. Numerous attempts of the resistance to arrange for a separate cease-fire had been rejected by the western powers, so that it was impossible for German forces to withdraw unilaterally without being thrown into chaos by the pursuing enemy. There was no alternative to negotiating with, or surrendering to, the Soviet Union as well as to the western powers.

But Gisevius himself believed, as he told Beck the next day, that the western powers had no inclination at all to treat with any German government, and, according to Gisevius, Stauffenberg had not said that he sought to negotiate *only* with the Soviet Union.[21] In fact, it is not clear from Gisevius's account what exactly Stauffenberg had said. Gisevius describes his own summary of what Stauffenberg said as "only an approximation of what he said, for he contradicted himself in the same breath."[22]

There are two other sources by which one may gauge Gisevius's account. Firstly, Allen Dulles was convinced of the necessity to offer assurances to the German and German-occupied peoples that America would prevent the Soviet Union from "imposing their brand of domination on Europe," and soon after his arrival in Bern, he had urged his government, in a dispatch dated December 6, 1942, to implement the necessary policies.[23] This was his view *before* he met Gisevius in January 1943. Gisevius took the same position and sought to convince him that America must defeat not only Nazi Germany but the Bolshevik world revolution as well, and that therefore America needed to conclude a separate peace with Germany after the resistance had overthrown Hitler. Secondly, there is a memorandum that Gisevius left behind for Dulles in Zurich before travelling to Berlin on July 11, 1944. Herein Gisevius advocated—before he had ever met Stauffenberg—an arrangement to have western Germany occupied by the western powers, and here he claimed, before Stauffenberg had allegedly suggested it, that many Germans believed their country could come to an arrangement with Russia if Germany accepted a Bolshevik government.[24] The implicit threat to the western powers' postwar position is obvious. These views were part of the basis on which Gisevius and Dulles collaborated.

After Gisevius had escaped to Switzerland, he reiterated and apparently expanded his predictions and warnings. They are reflected in Dulles's January and February 1945 cables to Washington, in which Dulles sought to induce his government to offer terms to German military leaders who surrendered in one or all of the western theaters of war. Dulles was already pursuing a secret contact with the German Supreme Commander West, Fieldmarshal Gerd von Rundstedt, and he had established such a contact with the German Supreme Commander Southwest, Fieldmarshal Albert Kesselring in Italy.[25]

It appears, therefore, that the conclusions Gisevius claimed to have drawn from his conversation with Stauffenberg were views he had held before he had ever met Stauffenberg, and which coincided with those of Dulles.

Finally, there is a further dimension to the immediate rift between Stauffenberg and Gisevius: the latter's personal ambition strongly suggested that he must have a role in the dispositions of the western powers for Germany. If these dispositions were made as he suggested them to Dulles, Gisevius would gain standing. It was really too late for all of this since Germany could now only surrender unconditionally, and the victorious powers would see no need to honor any commitments. But Gisevius tried desperately to stay in the game. He had told Mary Bancroft just before leaving Zurich in July 1944 that he claimed for himself the position of foreign minister in the future German government.[26] When he mentioned the question of a post-coup position for himself to Stauffenberg, the colonel had not said anything but had merely smiled.[27]

In a report for Dulles in February 1945, Gisevius went even further. He claimed that the resistance conspiracy of July 1944 had planned, immediately following upon a successful coup d'état, to put in place a directory of five that was to hold all executive power. Three days afterward, a cabinet was to have been formed under the authority of the new head of state, General Ludwig Beck. There were to be a chancellor, a vice-chancellor, and ministers of the interior, economics, justice, cultural affairs, finance, foreign affairs, and war. But all civil executive authority was to be turned over to Gisevius.[28]

To the end of his life Gisevius believed that Stauffenberg had been "left-leaning," mostly under the influence of the Social-Democrat Julius Leber. He believed this equally about several others such as Fritz-Dietlof Count von der Schulenburg.[29] Perhaps having lived abroad for so long, and with his background as a right-wing die-hard conservative in the *Deutschnationale Volkspartei* and in the *Stahlhelm*, Gisevius was hypersensitive to any hints of an association with socialist forces.

As the political animal Gisevius was, he evidently misread Stauffenberg's idealistic views. He sensed in Stauffenberg the hidden agenda of the Secret Germany of the disciples of Stefan George and thought that this involved "the continuation of

Nazi-militaristic legality."[30] Stauffenberg, for his part, understood Gisevius's potential for mischief when he threatened, no doubt in jest, to have the book that later became *To the Bitter End* suppressed.[31]

iv

What Gisevius's book does offer is an authentic atmosphere, a firsthand flavor of life in that dictatorship, and of life at a rather high level. Gisevius has obviously overblown the substance and importance of the interviews he managed to have with eminent persons. But his account of the conspiracy to overthrow Hitler is important because it is, to a large extent, a rare firsthand account, detailed, and chronologically close to the events, although it is colored by Gisevius's flamboyance and resentments.

A substantial amount of the contents is valuable, and on the whole, not necessarily less reliable than other autobiographical works. The reader needs to approach the book critically, and to keep in mind whether or not Gisevius was describing his own personal experiences or those of others, and was thus depending on other firsthand witnesses, or on hearsay, or on official correspondence, or on newspapers and the radio. A researcher wishing to use this book as a primary source would in any case have to look for corroboration in other primary sources before accepting anything as fact.

Whatever the weight of Gisevius's ambitions and career orientation, his commitment to destroying Hitler is undeniable, and it led him to take extraordinary risks with his life. Still, questions remain. For example, it is unclear why Gisevius erected a monument for his friend Nebe and made excuses for Nebe's function as commander of *Einsatzgruppe* B, which was responsible for the murder of more than 100,000 Jews in Russia. Did Gisevius really believe that his friend Nebe was not responsible for mass murder? Did Gisevius really lack the knowledge of what the *Einsatzgruppen* had done?[32]

In the end the reader must decide for himself whether this is the book of an aspiring statesman unjustly frustrated in his righteous ambition, or the work of someone whose personality clashed with his ambition.

—PETER HOFFMANN
Montreal
February 1998

PETER HOFFMANN, William Kingsford Professor of History at McGill University in Canada, is the author of the acclaimed *The History of the German Resistance 1933–1944, Hitler's Personal Security,* and *Stauffenberg: A Family History, 1905–1944.*

Notes to the Introduction

1. This biographical sketch is based mainly on Gisevius's own book (*To the Bitter End*, Houghton Mifflin Company, Boston, 1947); on his testimony at the Nuremberg War Crimes Trial (*Der Prozess gegen die Hauptkriegsverbrecher vor dem internationalen Militärgerichtshof Nümberg 14. November 1945–1. Oktober 1946*, vol. XII, Sekretariat des Gerichtshofs, Nürnberg, 1947); on Allen W. Dulles's postwar accounts (Allen Welsh Dulles Papers, Firestone Library, Princeton, N.J.); on Dulles's cables from Bern in the National Archives; and on Allen Welsh Dulles, *Germany's Underground*, Macmillan, New York, 1947. The most important sources for Gisevius's biography besides his own book are his extended testimony during the Nuremberg War Crimes Trial; his personnel file in the Berlin Document Center; his papers in the Archiv für Zeitgeschichte in the Eidgenössische Technische Hochschule in Zurich; the records of the German Foreign Office, particularly the files of the legation in Bern; the records of the American Office of Strategic Services (now in the National Archives in College Park, Maryland); and my interviews with Gisevius in 1971 and 1972. Numerous works dealing with wartime intelligence and resistance contain references to Gisevius. See also Rudolf Diels, *Lucifer ante portas*, Deutsche Verlags-Anstalt, Stuttgart, 1950, *passim* and p. 342; Susanne Strässer, "Hans Bernd Gisevius—Ein Oppositioneller auf Aubenposten,'" in Klemens von Klemperer, Enrico Syring, Rainer Zitelmann, eds., *"Für Deuuchland."* *Die Männer des 20. Juli*, Ullstein, Frankfurt/M.-Berlin, pp. 56–70.
2. Gisevius, *End*, pp. 133–138.
3. Hans-Bernd Gisevius, Aufnahme-Erklärung, Berlin, November 15, 1933, BDC Parteikanzlei-Korrespondenz.
4. Hans Volz, *Daten der Geschichte der NSDAP*, A. G. Ploetz, Berlin, Leipzig 1943, p. 54.
5. Dulles to Justice Robert Jackson, March 27, 1946, Library of Congress, R. H. Jackson Papers, Box 102, file "Gisevius, Hans Bernd"; Anthony Cave Brown, *The Last Hero: Wild Bill Donovan*, Vintage Books, New York, 1982, pp. 288, 290.
6. *Prozess* XII, pp. 292–293.

7. Winfried Meyer, *Unternehmen Sieben. Eine Rettungsaktion für vom Holocaust Bedrohte aus dem Amt Ausland/Abwehr im Oberkommando der Wehrmacht,* Hain, Frankfurt am Main, 1993, pp. 322, 325–329, 332.
8. Dulles to Justice Robert Jackson, March 27, 1946, Library of Congress, R. H. Jackson Papers, Box 102, file "Gisevius, Hans Bernd."
9. Hans Bernd Gisevius, *Wo ist Nebe? Erinnerungen an Hitlers Reichskriminaldirektor,* Droemer, Zurich, 1966, *passim;* Gisevius's dedication in Federer's copy of the German edition of *To the Bitter End;* author's interview with Federer, March 29, 1977; Dulles to Donovan, January 28, 1945, OSS records, National Archives, Washington, D.C.
10. Cf. Mary Bancroft, *Autobiography of a Spy,* William Morrow and Company, Inc., New York, 1983, pp. 164–170; Mary Bancroft papers.
11. Mary Bancroft, "The Story of a Book," typescript, n.p., n.d. [ca. 1946/47], Mary Bancroft papers.
12. Author's (Hoffmann) interview with Gisevius, August 4, 1971.
13. Mary Bancroft papers; interviews with M. Bancroft, December 16, 1980; March 16, 1985.
14. Gisevius said this in a letter to Dr. Ferdinand Sauerbruch on April 1, 1947, in which he encouraged the famous surgeon to publish his reminiscences about Stauffenberg, particularly, as he had told Gisevius, that Stauffenberg was physically unsuited for his role as assassin and coup-d'état leader. According to Gisevius's letter, Sauerbruch based this on his observation of Stauffenberg when Stauffenberg recovered in Sauerbruch's hospital from the wounds he had sustained in Tunisia. In his reply to Gisevius, Sauerbruch mentioned only "long observation" upon which he based his view of Stauffenberg. Copies of both letters are in the author's possession, the originals are presumably in the Gisevius Papers. In fact, Stauffenberg did not recover in Sauerbruch's hospital, the Charité in Berlin, but in the First General Military Hospital in Munich; Peter Hoffmann, *Stauffenberg, A Family History, 1905–1944,* Cambridge University Press, Cambridge, New York, Melbourne, 1995, pp. 181–185, 187, 190. In 1972 Gisevius named Hansen as his main source for his views on Stauffenberg, and additionally Olbricht, Beck, and Goerdeter: interview with the author, September 8, 1972.
15. Hoffmann, *Stauffenberg,* pp. 213–224.
16. Gisevius, interview, September 8, 1972.
17. Gisevius, *End,* p. 507.
18. Ibid., pp. 508, 510–511.
19. Ibid., p. 510.
20. Ibid., p. 512.
21. Ibid., p. 510.
22. Ibid., p. 518.

23. Ibid., p. 509.
24. Allen Welsh Dulles, *From Hitler's Doorstep: The Wartime Intelligence Imports of Allen Dulles, 1942–1945,* Neal H. Petersen, ed., Pennsylvania State University Press, University Park, Pennsylvania, 1996, p. 25.
25. H[ans] B[ernd] G[isevius], Memorandum for A[llen] W[elsh] D[ulles], typed, n.p., July 1944, Mary Bancroft papers.
26. *Foreign Relations of the United States. Diplomatic Papers. The Conferences at Malta and Yalta 1945,* United States Government Printing Office, Washington, 1955, p. 957; Dulles to Donovan No. 4077, January 25, 1945, OSS records, National Archives, College Park, Maryland.
27. Bancroft to Dulles [May 11, July 11, 1944], Mary Bancroft papers.
28. Interview, August 4, 1971.
29. H[ans] B[ernd] Gisevius, Bericht [to Mary Bancroft for Allen Dulles], typed, (Zurich), February 1945, Princeton University Library, Allen W. Dulles Papers, Box 20, p. 31. There is a more subdued reference to this proposed arrangement in the first German edition of Gisevius's book *(Bis zum bittern Ende,* Fretz &C Wasmuth, Zurich, 1946, vol. H, pp. 304–305, 325); it is part of numerous passages that are omitted in the English edition.
30. Interview, August 4, 1971.
31. Gisevius, *End,* p. 511; author's interview with Gisevius, August 4, 1971; Gisevius in interview with Joachim Fest (1971); Hoffmann, *Stauffenberg,* pp. 243–247, 293–295, and *passim.*
32. Gisevius, *Nebe,* pp. 240–253; cf. Raul Hilberg, *The Destruction of the European Jews,* revised and definitive edition, Holmes & Meier, New York, London, 1985, p. 1,214.

1

Toward the Catastrophe—
September 1939 to July 1944

The First Feelers

AT THE NUREMBERG TRIALS it was asserted that Hermann Goering had made a last desperate attempt to save peace during the three days that intervened between Hitler's invasion of Poland and the Anglo-French declaration of war. The question was examined with minute care, but it was clear then and it is clear now that a world conflagration could have been avoided only by Hitler's withdrawal from the Polish adventure. That is all that need concern the historians in regard to those three days.

On the other hand, psychologists will find much interesting material in the secret history of those three days. Who could have dreamed what is now proved fact—that up to the last moment Hitler refused to believe that the British would declare war? Who would have imagined the terrible state of depression that the news of the British declaration produced in the chancellery? "What are we going to do now?" For the clairvoyant, the man who behaved with the "sureness of a somnambulist," was completedy stunned, and his uneasiness was communicated to his entire entourage. Everyone around him was confused and numbed.

On the eighteenth day the Russian troops—"in order to safeguard the complete neutrality of Soviet Russia"—invaded eastern Poland. That, of course, decided the fate of the country. As a matter of fact, the Poles fought much more bravely than they at first seemed to have done. In the light of the feeble resistance offered by some of the countries that were later invaded, the Polish stand was admirable indeed. Had their valor been fully appreciated, who can say that the liberty of Europe might not have been won then and there? But for that a similar performance on the part of the Western Powers was necessary. The fact that it was not forthcoming, in spite of all the Allied promises, is a second reason for not overestimating the German accomplishment in that first campaign; for the victory that Hitler won there was nothing but gambler's luck.

We know that Hitler staked everything on the belief that the British and the French would not advance. Neither his clairvoyance nor his superior strategy, but simply and solely the incompetence of the West provided him at that fateful moment with an antagonist—perhaps collaborator would be the better word—of the temper of General Maurice Gamelin [commander of the French forces in 1940]. Gamelin was precisely the type of opposing commander that the dictator needed; a general of the old school, dragged down by memories of the wearing, endless battles of 1918. Gamelin feared nothing more than an attempt to break through heavily fortified lines of defense. He was the type of European who had remained untouched by a dynamic epoch; who detested risks and wanted only to wait; who was dead-set against recognizing that it might be necessary to take the offensive in order to defend peace.

Because Gamelin refused to risk a fight, Hitler won his gamble. We Germans have no right to cite the military and political sins of the other side as excuses for ourselves; but for all Europeans the clear recognition of their onetime reluctance to fight can be transformed into a source of creative power, just as the honest admission of their guilt can redeem the Germans.

Poland lay shattered; the Warsaw victory parade was over; and now Hitler's generals were overcome by fear. Was it absolutely necessary for the war to go on to the end—or was some compromise still possible? Outwardly Germany appeared to be standing tense and firm, taking a deep breath before plunging headlong into the un-plumbed abysses of a great war. In reality fearful confusion reigned in all authoritative quarters.

Hitler brooded and tormented himself. He instinctively felt that he himself must take the active role, but he knew that the decision involved total war, irrevocable, all-destructive war. Once he gave the signal, the only remaining alternatives would be victory or ruin. He remembered very well what had happened in 1918, when the human and material resources of America came to the rescue of the hard-pressed Allies. Germany must not again be outstripped by time. Because he felt this pressure of time, he conceived the idea of striking an unexpected blow, violating the neutral countries and trying for a surprise triumph on the widest possible front. Who can say how often his restless mind had already traveled that bloodstained military route that led from Holland into the Belgian flank and from there straight across France to the Pyrenees?

Although Hitler dreamed of an incomparable triumph, his generals were alarmed. They knew how perilous that road was. In October and November 1939, they still had inhibitions about entrusting their personal lives and their country's destiny to the unbalanced visions of "the greatest military leader of all time." They were still afraid both of what would take place if the revolutionary Fuehrer won and what would happen if he lost. At last they had come face to face with the question of whether an outright overthrow of the government would not be cheaper than the otherwise inevitable carnage.

A savage struggle began—between the unhappy generals

and their Fuehrer; between the worried civilians and the military demi-gods; between the generals' own doubts and irresolution and their longing for glory. For weeks the decision hung by a thread. More than once it appeared that the outcome of the war would be decided, not on the battlefield, but among the cliques of conspirators in the *Oberkommando der Wehrmacht*.

At that time our group of friends put out the first tentative feelers to determine whether and how we could act in unison with the "enemy." I use the word "unison" deliberately because I want to avoid any misunderstanding. In these first peace feelers, as in all others, we never wanted to produce a victorious peace for Hitler or for Nazism. We knew if Hitler survived any peace that was concluded, the practical result would be a stabilization of his system and a justification of his unscrupulous foreign policy.

We were aiming at something entirely different, but for the present we had to discover whether it would be at all possible to deal with the Allies. We wanted to take precautions against the new "stab-in-the-back" legend to the extent that the opposing armies would not fall upon Germany at the moment we opened our civil war. Above all, we wanted to prove to the wavering generals that there was another recourse besides plunging blindly ahead, that it would be possible to put an end to the war honorably—although we would undoubtedly have to make the concessions that the Allies would justly demand in order to guarantee that they would not be dragged into another military adventure within a few years.

Our previous experience had shown that all pleas to the generals were in vain as soon as Hitler set a fixed date on which the armies were to march. Then, they held, it was no longer time to be concocting seditious plans. Therefore, we had to anticipate Hitler. We must so fortify the opposition among the generals that the intuitive Hitler would not dare to set the critical date. To do this we had to show General Werner von Brauchitsch [commander-in-chief of the German army] and General Franz Halder [current chief of the German General Staff] that there were tangible chances for peace if they would precipitate the occasion by refusing to obey Hitler's order to take the offensive.

Once more General Hans Oster [chief of staff of Abwehr] took this responsibility upon himself. With the outbreak of the war he had been promoted and had become one of the four department heads within the Abwehr. Within an intelligence service many things can be managed so that they escape the eyes even of so ubiquitous an espionage organization as the Gestapo. Oster proved this during his first weeks in his new post by cautiously establishing certain foreign ties. Doctor Joseph Mueller took his first trip to the Vatican. The inquiries he made there and the answers he received gave us the right to assure Halder and Brauchitsch that all bonds had not been severed and that there were still understanding people on the enemy side who were willing to collaborate toward an honest liquidation of the Nazi system.

But was it not likely that the generals would reply that they knew nothing officially about such offers? At last we decided to take a carefully considered step. Our generals would certainly pay attention if the President of the United States intervened and personally guaranteed that a just peace would be concluded with a denazified Germany. Therefore, Hjalmar Schacht sent a letter to America in the hope that the recipient, Leon Frazer, former president of the Bank of International Settlements, would bring it to the attention of President Roosevelt.

What we had in mind was to restrain Hitler until the opposing forces could gather strength. At the same time we planned on more than action by the generals. Since it seemed to us more and more dubious that they would ever act, we had decided to strike at the critical point of Nazi rule: the temper of the people. Up to the very last year of the war, Hitler was singularly tremulous about the psychological reactions of the masses. It was a curious phenomenon, contrasting strongly with his usual brutality. Did he know intuitively not only that he affected the masses suggestively, but that he was also borne along by the popular mood?

The dictator's caution in this respect went so far that until shortly before July 20, 1944, he could not bring himself to proclaim total war; he did not go even so far as the British had gone long since. Up to the last months of the war the principal exponents of the popular temper, the women, were not drafted. It was out of the same concern for safeguarding this source of mystic strength that he ordered the Party propaganda system to spread all sorts of peace rumors in the fall of 1939.

We thought we could trap the Nazis in the net of their own peace talk. We would seize their slogans; we would, so to speak, try to extract some truth out of the propagandist lies. The Nazis at the time were mysteriously hinting that Hitler was engaged in vital diplomatic negotiations, that things were not half so bad as they seemed, and that the war declaration was merely a matter of form. What we wanted was to launch a real peace offensive. In short, we wanted to point out to the Germans which persons were merely pretending and which were actually ready to negotiate.

Before the Polish invasion the dictator had tricked his generals by proffering an "ironclad" guaranty that the war would not spread. It was clear, now that the Western Powers had not taken the invasion of Poland lying down, that any further action would ignite the world conflagration. All that was needed now was three or four months of public discussion in which Hitler would be forced to declare himself. Otherwise the 'phony' war would do us no good. Unless it were accompanied by a propaganda offensive its effect would necessarily boomerang: because the Germans would no longer take the war seriously their concern about peace would lapse. The German people must be told that they were letting themselves into a life-and-death struggle. The Nazis' "divisive" propaganda must be counteracted. The ideal person to do this was the president of the United States. He was still considered non-partisan, and his name was highly respected in Germany in spite of—or perhaps because of—the Nazi slanders against him.

Roosevelt had, of course, already made several sincere appeals without eliciting any response but a mocking echo. It was perhaps asking too much to request him to mediate once more. He might well make the obvious objection that first the Germans themselves ought to bring about some fundamental changes. It was to this that Schacht was alluding when he wrote:

> My feeling is that gaining time will help a great deal at the present moment.... There are people who think it might be too early to discuss plans before certain conditions have taken place. I am starting from another point. My feeling is that the earlier discussions should be opened, the earlier it will be to influence the development of certain existing conditions.

I smuggled this letter to Switzerland; Oster arranged a trip for me especially for this purpose. Unfortunately, it was all in vain. No reply came from across the Atlantic. Inwardly, Roosevelt had already made his decision. He had resolved to burn the Nazi canker out, root and stalk. Consequently, there was only one course left open to him. Gradually he drifted farther and farther from the role of mediator, until at last he was able to throw the decisive power of America openly into the scales.

Three Critical Weeks

DURING THE LATTER PART OF OCTOBER 1939, while I was in Zurich, I received a telegram recalling me to Berlin. Somewhat reluctantly I took the next train to the capital. By then I was all too familiar with those alarms which at first awakened high hopes and ended in depressing disillusionments. My premonitions were correct; Schacht and Oster were already regretting having sent the telegram. For a time, they told me, it had appeared that something was in the air. Hitler had flown to Berchtesgaden a few days before to retire into his usual brooding silence. Then he had surprised the drowsing generals with a revised plan of campaign. By mid-November at the latest he wanted to begin the offensive in the West, but no more had come of this than a brief shock. Upon the urgent representations of Brauchitsch and Halder the dictator had given ground. For some days now he had communicated with no one. Apparently he was ready to renounce this latest notion; consequently, any chance for a *Putsch* also had to be postponed.

A thousand rumors were flying around Berlin, but it still appeared utterly fantastic that Hitler should launch an attack against the Western Powers. It would be much more sensible for him to wait on the defensive behind the Siegfried line. A brutal invasion of Belgium and Holland seemed equally inconceivable. In time we became accustomed to such violations of neutrality, but in 1939 our conception of international law had not yet been blunted, so that even the generals were tormented by scruples.

On October 30 the spell was broken. We learned that Hitler had finally resolved to strike and had set November 12 as the date for the offensive. For us this news initiated a period of intense activity. We were determined to exert all the strength we had; to implore, argue, and cajole.

During this period I made some notes which I concealed inside of some innocent-looking atlases. I hid them so well that later on I was no longer able to find some of the notes. Others may have become a bit mixed up. I can, therefore, offer no more than rather inadequate recollections of a vital period in world history.

In a sense my casual diary may be said to reflect only the undercurrents, for it deals with the mental distraction and the condition of incessant civil war of nerves, rather than with the drama of political and strategical decisions that were made—or rather not made—at the time. In the first place, it makes clear how hotly contested the great turning-point of the war actually was. In the second place, it is clear that the internal situation in Germany in the fall of 1939 and the spring of 1940 was basically different from what it was conceived to be by those in the enemy and neutral camps. Thirdly, it proves once more that in times of historic upheavals the fate of nations depends not so much upon the resolution or the daring of the great brigands as it does upon the irresoluteness and cowardice of those who are called—but not chosen—to defend freedom.

During [the first three weeks of] that November 1939 the usurper skated by disaster three times. The first was when he rushed out of the Munich beer hall five minutes before the bomb exploded. The second was when he wore out the generals, who had at last summoned up the energy to act, by repeatedly postponing the offensive. Finally he had let his "Providence" persuade him to wait. In the chaotic conditions I have described a sudden concrete order to launch the offensive might, after all, have evoked an uprising of the generals—certainly not a planned action, but some unpredictable, unforeseeable act of desperate self-defense. Even if this had not taken place, the unpopular offensive, if it had been launched six crucial months too soon, would certainly have meant the military end of Hitler.

In November 1939, Hitler did not yet possess those "secret weapons" with which in May 1940, he surprised the Dutch and Belgians and, in fact, the general staffs of the rest of the world. In November 1939, a dense autumnal fog covered the muddy and impassable fields of the Western Front. In November 1939, above all, the "phony" war had not yet gained much ground for the Nazis. The French soldiers had not yet gone through that enervating wait in and behind the Maginot Line while the Nazi loudspeakers blasted them with well-calculated defeatist propaganda.

November 1939—what tremendous potentialities still existed at that time for Germany, for Europe, for the whole world! But the time was not yet ripe for Hitler's downfall. First the destiny of Europe's North and West had to be fulfilled. Even then the stormy waves of the Revolution would surge on and on, southward to the Mediterranean, eastward almost to the Nile, until at last they mingled with the blood-stained stream of the Volga, until they broke against the myth-ridden mountainous wall of the Caucasus and at last gradually ebbed to nothing upon the endless reaches of the Russian steppes.

The Zither Player

MUCH OF THE SECRET HISTORY of the Third Reich remains to be revealed. In the brief period since the collapse we have had time only to skim through the many documents of that history. Our brief glimpse, however, has served to establish one remarkable fact: that Nazi reality was far more sober, far more banal, than the rumor-peddlers in all countries were willing to believe. Fundamentally, there are not too many secrets to come to light.

For example, how numerous were the alleged attempts at assassination that were "reliably" reported? Again and again attacks on prominent Nazis—Himmler, Ley, Goering, Hitler most of all—were rumored. When all these tales came to nothing, the outside world found a simple explanation: there were no assassins; there was no opposition; eighty million Germans were submitting passively to tyranny.

Today we know that there were in fact very few attempts at assassination, but on the other hand, that the resistance to Hitler was incomparably stronger than outsiders assumed. Are these two facts contradictory? Surely it is hard to comprehend how millions of Germans could see a terrible catastrophe gathering to overwhelm them and yet do nothing to stave it off; but have we not witnessed similar paralysis of will and inability to react in earlier times and under other systems of terror? At most we can say that in our mass age the sum of suffering has been raised to a higher power, and that in collective living individuals' sensitiveness to psychic and physical demands upon them has been dulled. The same mystery of submissiveness is illustrated by the four or five million murdered Jews who for years could have had no doubts as to their fate and who yet, even on the final march to death, did not attempt to take a few of their murderers with them into the next world. There is the even clearer example of the twelve million foreign laborers who lived in the Third Reich during the last years of the war. Virtually unguarded, or at any rate numerically and in united strength far surpassing their guards, they did not rise up until after the collapse. Night after night explosives were secretly dropped over Germany by planes for the use of this strongest of all fifth columns. The only one who made use of them was a German: Stauffenberg.

No one would wish to assert that all of these millions were cowardly or lacking in resolution. That is not it. Rather they simply did not have the opportunity to attempt an assassination. True enough, Hitler often drove more or less unprotected through crowds of people without being attacked; but spontaneous assassinations are very rare in history, and dictators prefer to make their public appearances a surprise. Whenever the Nazi leaders made a previously announced appearance, the measures taken for their protection were on a tremendous scale.

Since the end of the war, we have had many descriptions by "insiders" of the protective cordon that even an army officer resolved on assassination would have to penetrate. After the war began, no civilians had any chance to come into Hitler's presence, except the highest state functionaries—who were Nazis. It was even more difficult to obtain an effective explosive. When these hurdles had been overcome, there still remained the indispensable political preparations; for what was the good of a successful assassination if afterward Goering or Himmler should take over—and of course launch a merciless purge and an intensified reign of terror?

An assassination without a simultaneous *Putsch* would be senseless. Responsible political men could not go in for anything of the sort. Therefore, it was not by chance that on November 8, 1939, a solitary fanatic and not an oppositional group ventured the great gamble.

The last mention I have made of this attack was Oster's informing me on November 9, 1939, of the incredible announcement that "Lubbe Number 2" had been arrested.* For

---

* Gisevius is referring to a meeting with Oster following the Munich bombing of a Nazi memorial meeting. Hitler had left the meeting before the bomb went off and escaped injury, but seven others died and sixty-three were injured. Following the bombing, a "certain Herr Elser," a carpenter, was arrested on the flimsiest evidence. "Lubbe Number 2" is a reference to Marinus van der Lubbe ("Lubbe Number 1"), who was executed for setting the famous Reichstag fire in 1938. The evidence against Lubbe was circumstantial, at best. Lubbe was posthumously pardoned in 2008. *(Editor)*

days afterward we heard nothing at all. This intensified our suspicions. Ordinarily the Gestapo was very quick to supply "explanations." There were always some Jews, Bolshevists, reactionaries, priests, or other "enemies of state" on hand when the Black hangmen needed to get themselves out of an embarrassing situation. Whether they organized their incidents themselves or waited for some pretext, the SS was never at a loss about striking back hard and fast.

Why was nothing happening this time? Did the SS intend to make particularly careful preparations for its counter-blow against the Opposition? We breathed easier when the newspapers reported that Arthur Nebe [head of *Kriminalpolizei (Kripo)*] had been appointed to head the investigating committee. Now we should find out what was going on. Moreover, it was ground for feeling a good deal safer, since Nebe either would make the investigation come to nought if any danger threatened us or deliberately lead it into a false track. On the other hand, we wondered a good deal about this appointment. It was highly unusual for the Gestapo to be barred from an investigation that was obviously a matter of highest politico. There must be cogent reasons for this.

Once again we had to wait patiently for days. No more exciting arrests were announced. The Gestapo maintained impenetrable silence. The most startling aspect of the affair was that even Goebbels, so ready with tongue and pen, refrained from making any threats at all.

When the results of the investigation were at last published, we burst into laughter. We would not have credited even the Nazi propagandists with such crude lies. Every line of the account seemed to prove that the Nazis were so upset by the truth that they had by mistake taken an overdose of their usual mendacity. It seemed obvious to us that Himmler or some other active Nazi of the group of "old fighters" had been virtually convicted.

The very manner in which the news was presented stamped it as a fabrication of the propaganda ministry. All the newspapers were required to publish the sensational news on the first page and with every sentence in the same order. Two columns were placed side by side. In the first was the picture of "Lubbe Number 2," along with the details of how he had installed the bomb. His alleged employer was also unmasked: Otto Strasser, who was then living in Switzerland. In the adjacent column the arrest of two high functionaries of the British secret service was also reported. In the early morning hours of November 9, Colonels Best and Stevens had been lured to the German-Dutch border near Venlo, on the pretext that they were to meet members of the German Opposition. The two British colonels had then been kidnaped. A Dutch intelligence officer who had served as intermediary had been killed in the course of the kidnaping. The Dutch government was demanding the return of his body. Hitler now boasted to his generals that he had proved that the Dutch were violating their neutrality by collaborating with the British.

This search for a pretext for violating Dutch neutrality was, in fact, one of the chief reasons for the staging of this incident. Not even Goebbels dared to assert that there was any connection between the attempted assassination and the presence of the two British agents. The correlation was too improbable; the British would certainly not have met anyone to discuss the prospects of assassination if they had just instigated an unsuccessful attempt, but the appearance of the two stories in adjoining columns suggested to the innocent newspaper reader that an inner connection between them did exist.

As soon as Nebe returned from Munich, I asked him whether anyone in the chancellery or the Gestapo believed his detective story. His reply astonished me. Naturally, he said, neither Otto Strasser nor the British colonels had anything to do with the attack. "Lubbe Number 2" was the actual assassin. Self-taught in planting bombs, he could well boast of having achieved a masterpiece.

At first the Gestapo had jealously tried to prevent any interference in the investigation by Nebe. As early as the morning of November 9, Heydrich had determined the plotters—not by name, of course, but roughly speaking. Himmler presented his Fuehrer with a list of forty—exactly forty— Bavarian legitimists whom he wished to have shot at once as agents and accomplices, in order to set a terrible example; but to Heydrich's and Himmler's alarm, Hitler had refused to approve any mass executions. Instead, he had demanded a more convincing explanation, and when, after three days, the investigation continued to revolve around these forty legitimists, the Fuehrer had bluntly ordered the criminal police to work on the case.

Nebe told me that his first reaction had not been different from ours. He too had suspected that the conspirators were to be found in the *Oberkommando der Wehrmacht*, but his first glance at the evidence had relieved his mind considerably. It was quite obvious that the bomb, of which fragments remained, had not come from a military arsenal; unquestionably it had been put together by some private person. He quickly found another cause for satisfaction. Hundreds of confidential denunciations and affidavits had been turned in—and all of them accused Munich "old fighters" or the SS.

Nebe had also discounted the report of the capture of our "Lubbe Number 2." Consequently, he let several days go by before paying any attention to the arrested man. Other clues had seemed to him far more promising. It was not until quite late in his investigation that he interrogated Herr Elser. Then he concluded that Elser had in fact attempted the assassination. He claimed to have done it all alone. There was every reason to doubt this assertion. Nevertheless, the detectives finally were convinced that it was true. Elser's description of the construction and installation of the bomb was correct in every point. Moreover, from the psychological point of view Nebe found his story entirely credible. Here was a fanatical Communist who had resolved to kill the tyrant and who had done what numberless other determined enemies of Hitler had not been able to do: that is, he had found an answer to the crucial preliminary question of how precisely to calculate the right moment. A native of Munich, Elser had reflected that once a year Hitler always stood at the same spot at the same hour and always for the same length of time. This took place on the occasion of his traditional address in the Buergerbraeukeller on the evening of November 8. This reasoning was perhaps the assassin's finest achievement.

The most amazing feature of the bomb was the time fuse, which could be set ten days ahead of time. This was something that even experts had not yet accomplished. Otherwise, it was a rather primitive infernal machine. Nevertheless, its success indicated that even such old-fashioned *objets d'art* can produce, when well placed, tremendous explosive effects. After the explosion the hall was a shambles.

Still the question remained, Where and how to place the bomb? Elser found a place that was both effective and easy to work on unobserved—a column directly behind the speakers' desk. Under the guise of innocent beer-drinking, he utilized the quiet hours before closing time to drill his holes. Ten days before—that is, at a time when the police were not yet guarding the building—he concealed himself in the place one evening and within a few night hours completed the installation of the bomb.

Immediately afterward, Elser wanted to flee to Switzerland. His plan was to arrive early enough so that he could confide to someone his world-shaking secret. Naturally no one would believe him, but afterward no one would be able to deny that he was the author. It was for this reason that he equipped himself with the postcard picture of the beer hall with the marked column, the card that was afterward found on his person. But when he arrived at the border, he turned back. Shaken by doubts, he rode back to Munich, went to the Buergerbraeukeller once more and applied his ear to the column. He was relieved to hear his apparatus still faintly ticking. Unfortunately he had lost so much time that it was not until the night of November 8 that he was able to attempt his illegal crossing of the border.

Once captured, "Lubbe Number 2" had to fight as bitterly for his fame as sole author of the attempt as had his predecessor Marinus. Himmler and Heydrich were infuriated. How dare anyone claim that one man alone had created so much noise and disturbance? Impossible!

But they finally had to admit reluctantly that this Communist had been, if not the sole assassin, at least one of the chief agents. This destroyed their case against the forty Bavarian legitimists. Another story had to be invented into which the figure of this simple fanatical worker might credibly be fitted. The police had determined that the time fuse had been constructed out of an alarm clock of Swiss origin, and Elser had intended to flee to Switzerland. Both facts pointed to Otto Strasser, that bitter enemy of Hitler, to whose group the assassin might well belong ideologically. A month of torture began for the confessed assassin in the attempt to squeeze out of him a story he was simply unable to tell.

Himmler, jealous for his reputation as a bloodhound, refused to publish anything so slender and incredible as the authentic account. Similarly, Goebbels as a concocter of fairy tales trembled for his fame. The propaganda minister indignantly rejected Nebe's final report, even with the Gestapo addition of a mythical case against Otto Strasser. Undoubtedly to their own extreme surprise, the two British colonels found themselves linked with the Munich plot. Perhaps the English were not altogether unhappy about the charge.

The two colonels were not sent to a prisoner-of-war camp for officers. Instead, they were locked up in a concentration camp and for two full years in solitary cells they wore heavy chains day and night. The gentleman-criminal who had kidnaped them and was now "caring for" them was a man who managed to look like a wide-eyed innocent with disarming good manners. As with so many of these gangsters, the man's utter vileness is demonstrated more vividly by some "triviality" than by dozens of greater crimes. In their tormenting loneliness the two prisoners longed for news from their families. Their kidnaper expressed his regrets. Sympathetically, he gave Colonel Stevens his "word of honor" that everything had been done to establish contact, but unfortunately all the letters had been in vain. "You see"—he snapped his briefcase open—"here I have four letters for your comrade Colonel Best, but there hasn't been any mail at all for you." Then he went to see Best, a few cells farther down the row. Again the same kindly look, the same word of honor, the same snapping open of the briefcase—only this time he showed the prisoner five letters for his comrade Colonel Stevens.

The name of this cavalier, who founded his career by abusing the confidence of two British officers and making them victims of his private taste for refined sadism, soon became well known indeed. It was Schellenberg.

Elser was never tried, nor was he executed out of hand. Instead, he was taken to Dachau as a private prisoner of the Fuehrer. He was placed in the wing that housed the other guests of honor at Dachau, among them Martin Niemoeller and—later on—Best and Stevens as well. An SS guard stood constantly before the door of Elser's cell. Remarkably enough, he was no longer tortured. He had two rooms for himself, in one of which a cabinet-maker's shop was set up so that this inventive fellow could work on new ideas. Another pleasure that was permitted him was his zither, on which he played mournful songs.

Naturally, he soon became a legendary and mysterious figure. Why had he been allowed to live? The inhabitants of Dachau soon concluded that the zither player had planted his bomb on orders from Himmler and Hitler or from one of the pair. This seemed to be the only explanation for his curious immunity; but would Himmler have permitted a man to live if that man had been a tool of his on such an assignment? Or, if the incident had been prearranged, would Hitler have stood under a ticking time fuse which might easily have made the bomb go off a few minutes too early? If it had been done on orders, where was the follow-up? Himmler had not used the bombing as a basis for a Gestapo round-up, nor had Hitler twisted it to his own purpose. As we have seen, two weeks later the proposed offensive was definitely postponed until much later.

The original explanation holds: Elser had independently tried to play the part of Providence: not only tried, but succeeded; for every unsuccessful assassination produces an effect diametrically opposed to its intention; and this attack, too, constituted a gain for Hitler. Once again Providence had saved him. He himself believed it. In the midst of his speech, he declared, an inner voice had repeatedly told him: "Get out! Get out!" For a few minutes he had tried to shout down this voice; then he had obeyed it. Abruptly, he had broken off his address.

The generals and a large part of the populace were now no less ready to believe in this Providence of his. Six dead and sixty-three severely injured—in truth only a miracle had saved the Fuehrer.

So tangled were the obsessive ideas to which Hitler was subject that it is quite possible that he condemned Elser to his shadow existence because he seriously imagined that anyone who had prepared an assassination with so much imagination and skill must be capable of producing an ingenious invention. More likely the superstitious Hitler felt, on the basis of some astrological oracle, that his own life was inseparably linked with the destiny of "his" assassin, so that he must not condemn him to death prematurely. There seems to be no other explanation for the special treatment that was accorded Elser in the very last days of the Third Reich, for later on, a secret order was found in Dachau "from the very highest authority" that Elser was to be killed—and reported as "a victim of an air attack."

When the Gestapo men killed on their own account or on direct orders from Himmler, they did not require such complicated instructions and Hitler's orders for the liquidation of unwanted persons were not usually phrased in so tactful a manner. When the last notes of the Nazi *Goetterdaemerung* were sounding and the curtains were falling thunderously on the last moments of the Nazi thousand years, Hitler suddenly recalled the existence of "the zither player'; and fearfully, as if possessed by a sudden and inexplicable shame, this murderer of millions attempted to conceal his execution of an assassin who had long since been forgotten by the world public.

The Opposition

THE WINTER OF 1939-40 has gone down in the history of the war under the name of the "phony war," the *drôle de guerre,* as the French so piquantly called it. Would the mockers have chosen that appellation if they had had the gift of seeing into the future?

The malignant deceptiveness of that winter consisted precisely in the fact that nothing happened. Once more the revolutionary philosophy of the "as if," that perennial philosophy of our thousand years, took its toll. Because the terrors did not fall at once, because the insatiable revolutionaries paused to take a deep breath before they plunged into new violence, all our worried contemporaries sighed with relief and decided that now the worst was over and everything would turn out well. In the recent past they had not perceived the clash of arms in the midst of peace; now they were completely unable to comprehend this uncanny calm before the storm of "real" war.

"General Time" was on Hitler's side in this first stage of the war. True, the Western Powers were arming; but they did not plug the gap at Sedan and they continued to barricade themselves psychologically as well as physically behind the Maginot line. They refused to seize the initiative from the dictator, although the war in Finland was suggestive enough to make them reflect on the positive and negative importance of the Norwegian bases.

Hitler's actions, to be sure, also lagged. Obviously he was infected by his generals' skepticism. He continued to dream of great victories, but the conception that before midsummer he would have subjugated all of France and would possess jumping-off bases on the Channel may well have seemed bold even to him. Certainly he had not thought out all the political and strategic consequences of such an outcome. Otherwise he would have regeared his war machinery; he would have begun by the spring of 1940 at the latest what was already too late in the fall of 1940: the assemblage of every available ship, barge, and raft for the great leap which Napoleon had failed to take.

There was only one group that profited by this "strange" winter. The military bureaucracy in all the belligerent countries and even in the neutral lands began to seize the whole life of those countries in the grip of its coercive administration. Military censorship, military justice, military laws, and so-called military necessities became the canon binding upon all and sundry, and the uniformed bureaucrats became from then on, more and more inexorable and arbitrary. It was not only the extension of total war to the civil population, but also, and in fact above all, this extreme military schematization and mechanization that climaxed the dreadful process of "leveling" which has been the most prominent mark of our revolutionary epoch.

It is remarkable how slowly all of us—men all too accustomed to the excesses of this machine age—realized the power that a military machine can exert, the despotic tendency inherent in it, and the cold-bloodedness with which it operates. The fact that its gears and pinions were composed of men of flesh and blood did not make it any the less mindless and soulless. Quite the contrary. The technical limits of all precision machinery can be nicely calculated, but here the imagination and the intellect of millions of individual particles labored incessantly upon this anonymous "thing" to discover and close up every gap, every avenue of escape, from the grip of the military machine.

At first many persons thought that such excesses on the part of the military, such arrogant self-assurance and insensitivity, were possible only within the framework of the Prussian military caste; but it soon turned out that other nations were to suffer the same development. In a sense we Germans had in our misfortunes the saving grace that two bureaucracies rivaled one another. Because the Party and the state or the Waffen-SS and the Wehrmacht were fighting a constant underground battle, each side attempted to put forward the milder face.

The explanation for this mechanized zeal cannot be found in viciousness or in individual exploitation of unexpected power. This stubborn adherence to the new idol, "orders," emerged quite naturally from the very stuff of war; and it is significant that at the end of the war a military tribunal had to struggle to define where, in this circular distribution of authority from top to bottom and from bottom to top, the responsibility begins and ceases, and who is most answerable—he who gives the order or he who carries it out.

May humanity be spared any more wars! But if this wish should prove illusory, then may sensible men in all lands at least take timely precautions to make sure that next time the military machinery does not become even more all-encompassing, so much so that it atomizes human society before even the first atom bomb is dropped. Only those who have come in contact with a military machine—it is sufficient to have touched the invisible and impenetrable nimbus that surrounds it like a protective layer—can judge what it means to practice opposition or obstruction.

The German Opposition was hard hit by this change from "ordinary" Gestapo terror to the inflexible severity of military laws. In 1933 and 1934 the unions and political party organizations had been shattered. For years thereafter no tightly knit opposition groups had been formed—at least none that could be considered well-defined centers of resistance. Basically, there existed only individual oppositionists around whom groups of like-minded people formed. It was only after the alarming events of 1938 that the resistance front began to form anew. It grew at first in a hesitant fashion on a local scale; groups with the same point of view rarely submitted to a central leadership and even more rarely sought contact with other resistance groups; but just about the time these promising beginnings had progressed to the point where a gradual merging of these various circles and groups could be hoped for, the psychological and material changes of wartime threatened to undo all that had been accomplished.

The Opposition had to consider its stand in the new situation. A man might have fought bitterly against Hitler's insane war policy, but now the war was there. How was he to react toward it? As an oppositionist? As a patriot? As a European? Or as none of these, but quite simply as a soldier whose business it was to obey orders?

Let us not forget that totalitarianism and opposition are two mutually exclusive political ideas. In a democracy it is possible to practice opposition, but dictatorship permits no antagonists; it does not even put up with the lukewarm and the skeptical. Whoever is not for it is against it. Oppositionists must keep silent, or they must decide on underground activity.

Underground resistance and opposition are again two different matters. Opposition is struggle against an existing regime; it is an attempt to bring about a shift in course or a change in personnel, without directly overthrowing a system. Opposition, therefore, recommends a more prudent policy, offers reasoned advice, tries to reform by appeals to the common sense of the rulers and attempts to win the favor of the voters; but the oppositionist under a totalitarian system must not try to reform at all. His good advice would only help the tyranny; any intelligent recommendation would support the reign of terror.

Perhaps the penance for a nation that through folly or trickery has become subject to a dictatorship is precisely that it is left only with the alternative of exchanging tyranny for the yoke of the conquered. Or else the people of the nation must take upon their conscience the tremendous burden of devoting all their imagination and zeal to the purely destructive activities of underground work.

In such ambivalent situations the tempter approaches, and his shrewd arguments sound very good indeed. People say to themselves that they must not try to play God; the Lord knows what he intends to do. People who express themselves less piously say that now everyone is in the same boat. Others assert that in wartime a good citizen can do only one thing: patriotically fulfill all his obligations to the government, whether or not he likes that government.

This latter objection must be taken more seriously than people outside Germany, especially the German exiles, have done. The question could have been settled with relative ease had the attitude of obedience and loyalty arisen only out of fear of the Draconian wartime laws; for there is no excuse for a nation whose leaders have criminally started a war; at whatever cost the nation must refuse to abet the guilt or its leaders. If the prime question, however, appears to be, what consequences will a lost war have?—then oppositionists may well ask themselves whether there ought not to be a limit to their opposition and obstruction. Should they not co-operate with their government—even at the risk of preserving the reign of terror—in order to keep not only their own country, but the community of nations from the consequences of a disastrous collapse? What good European today will not regret the fact that when the Third Reich came to an end all state power ceased to exist in Germany, so that the victor powers found no valid authorities at all to serve them in the difficult task of occupation?

There was an additional element that grew in importance the longer the war lasted. The air attacks reinforced the people's sense of belonging to a community for good or ill. The bombs fell alike upon the just and the unjust. This instructive example on the home front led logically to the conclusion that this time the outraged enemy would be "tougher" than he had been in 1918. Twenty-five years before, the Germans had been firmly convinced that they were not guilty of the outbreak of world war, but with this war of Hitler's they could no longer evade their war guilt. Moreover, every day new and unique crimes were being committed. Perhaps the populace was not aware of the full extent of these, but enough reports trickled through the wall of silence to create a tremendous sense of guilt, and this guilt influenced all decisions.

With every new crime the Nazis deliberately cut off their lines of retreat. During the days of victory the corrupt sub-leaders boasted cynically of their diabolic system of involving themselves and others in so much guilt that there could be no turning back, only a colder and more ruthless pursuit of the war to its end.

The non-participants, those who really fought the Nazis and who demonstrably had done none of the killing, felt equally implicated. The "collective guilt" which is nowadays so indignantly repudiated was not invented by any armchair psychologists. The decent people of Germany were aware of it and suffered from it, and some, precisely because of this sense that they were fatally involved in guilt, advanced the thesis that only Hitler and Himmler were in a position to keep the avengers off German soil. The desire to stand together with one's fellows in times of distress cannot be condemned out of hand as immoral. It springs from a universal natural impulse, and we should not dismiss as trifling this phenomenon of the guiltless turning guilty because of their sense of shared responsibility.

Another fundamental difference between oppositional methods in a democratic and a totalitarian state must be noted. In a democracy the opposition can and in fact must work openly. Under totalitarianism it is only possible to obstruct and oppose if one is in some manner "on the inside." But how far can a man participate in a hated system without selling his soul? The more the Opposition came to recognize that the Nazi rulers could be defeated only by their own methods, the harder it was for them to solve the problem of conscience. It became more difficult for them to avoid objective as well as subjective guilt. Undoubtedly many paid too dear a price for the sake of having one or both feet "inside," and many others were unjustly accused of opportunism.

I recall my first encounter with Ulrich von Hassell shortly after his dismissal in 1938 [as ambassador to Rome]. I congratulated him for having successfully got himself kicked out; for it was well known that highly placed officials found it virtually impossible to resign when they wanted to. It took a great deal of skill to espy an opportunity to jump off the bandwagon. Even when one did break away, the dictator's whims were wholly unpredictable. Hitler often availed himself of an official's temporary unemployment to promote the man, to entrust him with a special commission, or to extort a public declaration of loyalty from him.

Hassell gave me a look of surprise. He could not understand that I really meant my congratulations. Then he advanced a thesis that gave me much to think about for years afterward. An oppositionist under a dictatorship must defend his official post with tooth and claw, he said, and if dismissed he must strive to get into the government again. Even an unpretentious post on the inside, Hassell urged, afforded an opportunity for exerting influence.

Carl Goerdeler, too, had much the same view and repeatedly tried to get "on the inside" again. He had all the more reason for wanting this, since his constant traveling inside Germany and abroad was possible only if he enjoyed some official or semiofficial protection.

The foolish talk of So-and-So's being "paid" by Hitler is evidence of the grotesque misunderstandings of the Opposition's true situation. Running through the list of the dead of the July 20 plot, I find that almost all of them were "inside" and "paid." Were the officers and officials who wanted to overthrow the Nazis to abandon the key positions they had acquired with such difficulty and maintained so tenaciously, merely in order to give possible moralistic critics no grounds for complaint? Or should they not rather take the stand that the money they received—from the state treasury, not from Hitler—was paid gladly by millions of taxpayers, who paid their taxes without wanting to subsidize Nazism, and who, though they might be prosperous business men or wage-earners, did not feel themselves inwardly corrupted by Hitler?

As far as I myself was concerned, I made the attempt in 1936—on an irrational and sentimental basis—to escape this "being paid by Hitler" by transferring to the "free" business world; but in 1937 a special federal law forbade officials to leave the civil service—another point that is passed over by critics. Thus, in the early part of 1939, I had to return to my former bondage; but even in retrospect I do not feel troubled in my conscience for having rejoined the class of salaried state employees.

The potentialities for effective opposition were directly proportionate to an individual's inclusion or exclusion from the Nazi governmental machine. Why else was it that the principal figures in the history of *putsches* from 1938 to 1944 were military officers, government officials, or industrial leaders, while the Left never participated, not even in an unsuccessful partial action? The organizations of Left and Right and Center had been destroyed by the end of 1934; but politically and socially, the members of the Center and the Right were closer to the generals and the high government officials; and that was what counted once the chance for an uprising from below had been lost.

The Resistance in the occupied countries had a clear task to perform: to get rid of the foreign conqueror. On this basis it was possible for the most diverse political and ideological groups to unite—although their unity did not outlast the war. In Germany no such clear issue existed, nor could it exist.

Communists, Social Democrats, liberals, conservatives, and Christians, all drew their own conclusions from the experiences of past and present. They were agreed mostly on the negative plank: that Nazism must go; but their positive aims were diametrically opposed. Some wanted socialism; others considered it the root of all evil. Some affirmed collectivism; others believed that we were already so deeply immersed in collectivism that we must do everything possible at least to ameliorate its ill effects. Some desired a centralized Germany, others a federal union. All were concerned with the question of educating the youth, but what a diversity of opinion there was on the problem, for example, of Christianity in the schools!

How, in such a situation, could there arise an Opposition leader, an "anti-Fuehrer" who would tower above all and unite the dissenting groups? How could there be any common lines of activity when the various groups could not even agree on the methods to pursue in their negative struggle? Running directly across all the oppositional groups from Right to Left was a dividing line between those who wanted immediate action and those who thought that honest opponents of Nazism must wait patiently, exercising great alertness but even greater restraint. The latter were convinced that those activists who were pressing for a *Putsch* or an assassination might well prove to be conscious or unconscious pacemakers for a new and even more dangerous type of nationalism.

Consequently, any attempt to classify the German Opposition must necessarily fail. Basically, there were only oppositionists. Each of these or less strong personalities had a group of friends who agreed with him. Each of them sought to extend his influence and therefore tried to establish contact with other groups and circles. This resulted in those many intersecting and tangential lines which so fused the picture. None of these men could possibly appeal directly to the masses. Never were they able to issue common slogans. So long as the reign of terror raged, they could do no more than prepare a shadow coalition of men of goodwill. For the rest, these upright men, though filled with the great urge to take their stand publicly, had to bear up under a heavy mental burden for which the Bible provides permission, but at the cost of inner peace: that is to say, they had to be as "wise as serpents."

Oppositional Circles

IF I REMEMBER RIGHTLY, it was in November 1939, that Wilhelm Leuschner, the leader of the Social Democrats, and Jakob Kaiser, the leading personality of the former Christian Union heads, put out their first cautious feelers to the *Oberkommando der Wehrmacht* and got in touch with the Abwehr groups. These two were perhaps the only ones—outside of Oster— who could claim to represent sharply defined circles.

In contrast to groups, which gathered around single strong personalities, I shall speak of circles only in connection with someone who had at his disposal a broad network of functionaries and who was technically in a position to maintain contact with these men. Leuschner and Kaiser, and for a long time Oster as well, had the good fortune and skill to conceal their shadow organizations from the eyes of the Gestapo until July 20, 1944.

Wilhelm Leuschner had formerly been minister of the interior in Hesse. In 1933 he was sent to a concentration camp. After his release he decided not to emigrate, but to continue the struggle from inside Germany. After some groping he founded a small business, not without assistance from certain "capitalists," men who had been his opponents in political life, but who were convinced of the need for a Social Democratic Opposition. His purchasing organization was splendidly adapted for camouflaging political work. Leuschner was a careful politician; his nickname "Uncle" indicated that some of his friends thought he could have used a little more passion and firmness. On the other hand, he was a very clever tactician and fully realized that in underground work it would not do to butt one's head against the wall. There were dozens of personal and political idiosyncrasies that had to be tolerated in order to prevent needless friction, for the ultimate outcome of internal dissension was unpleasant attention from the alert Gestapo. In retrospect we may well say that the Black bloodhounds almost never had any success so long as a group held together in a disciplined fashion. It was only when intrigues were being woven or something else was "out of tune" that the discords were picked up by the microphones in the Prinz Albrechtstrasse, which were peculiarly sensitive to every note of disharmony.

It is to Leuschner's credit that he put by all personal ambitions and gave Carl Goerdeler the precedence as soon as he came to know him better. A number of Leuschner's Party friends criticized this as a weakness in him, and some of them tried to outwit him. They succeeded only in harming themselves and the common front. Leuschner's retiring behavior cannot be ascribed to any "wait-and-see" policy, of which he has recently been accused. Rather, he recognized the conclusive importance of the military in any uprising, and he was selfless enough to respect and honor Goerdeler's position as the real instigator of a generals' *Putsch*.

Jakob Kaiser perseveringly reorganized the Christian Unions, without, however, forgetting the functions that accrued to him as a former Reichstag deputy of the Center. (Since the end of the Hitler regime he has again become prominent in parliamentary affairs.) Like Leuschner, with whom he had come to a broad agreement on matters of future social policy, Kaiser refused to be seduced from his allegiance to Goerdeler.

Oster, too, had formed a circle around himself, although he was so utterly without personal ambitions that he never sought the position leader; but he utilized the potentialities of the Abwehr so cannily that he was able to establish a whole network of confidential agents. His strength consisted in the fact that most people were ignorant of the extent of his influence. This unpretentious man was not fond of good notices especially in the grapevine press of the Opposition. He pursued his undeviating path, just as he had secretly marked it out for himself years earlier, and every day he had to cut his way anew through the tangle of oppositional problems or suspicions. Never did he participate in political negotiations. He deliberately avoided all so-called preliminary conferences in which good intentions or daring plans were often talked threadbare and which always ended merely in the prayer for *the* general to come to the rescue. The goal Oster had set for himself was to find that general and to place his apparatus at his disposal.

In fact, probably no oppositional approaches to generals were made except under Oster's guidance. Perhaps it might have been better if he had made use of or extended these connections on his own behalf; but this ran contrary to his nature. Accustomed to take a subordinate role, he left the military connections to Beck and political affairs to Goerdeler. Once he had arranged a conference for these men, he concentrated on his own work. "You must understand that my secondary occupation happens to be that of chief of staff in the Abwehr," he used to say to me as he sat at his desk writing out his instructions. He preferred to give orders in writing in order to save himself superfluous conversations; but while he worked, he would keep his ears cocked to note any news or incidents. He had worked very hard to consolidate his position. He would have risked all he had achieved if he had ever permitted any flaw in the daily conduct of his official work.

It was Wilhelm Canaris's [chief of Abwehr] great achievement to raise this virtually unknown major to the position of power which Oster held as a colonel and major-general during the war. Again and again the admiral extended his protecting hand over this controversial officer whose waiting room sometimes resembled a pigeon coop, filled as it was with mysterious persons—civilians among them!—for Oster seemed to be organizing an intelligence service of his own within the counter-intelligence service, although, as chief of the organizational division, he presumably should not have kept any agents of his own; and this aroused suspicion. Nowhere does professional jealousy produce so much inquisitive gossip as in an intelligence service. Not only the Nazified zealots, of whom there were a great many in the Abwehr, but quite respectable, unpolitical, and even opposition-minded officers endangered Oster's life by gossiping about the number of irons he evidently had in the fire.

Protection by a patron is never sufficient to cover a man. Under tense circumstances—which occur daily in underground work—the protégé must be able to demonstrate his competence. Oster did just this. Neither the personal and professional temptations inherent in military intelligence work nor the inescapable trickery of underground activity had any adverse effect upon his character. The onlooker sensed that this difficult and devious subsidiary occupation left the man quite untainted. Cheerfully he began and ended his day's work. Irritating circumstances could not confuse him; disappointments did not make him lose heart. He remained firm within himself, and this firmness sprang from his unshakable trust in God.

"To our last breath we all remain upstanding men, as we

were taught to be from childhood and in our soldierly discipline. Come what may, we fear only the wrath of God that will fall upon us if we are not clean and decent and do not do our duty." These were the words he wrote to his son from prison on his last birthday, and these were the principles he followed all his life.

How did Oster make use of his key position? One of the most important of his activities was to install his own confidential agents in the most diverse positions. These men did not necessarily have to be in on the conspiracy. It was sufficient if he knew he could depend on them in a crisis. This requirement alone made the choice of agents extremely difficult, for the officers assigned to the Abwehr were selected by the army personnel office, which considered qualifications from a viewpoint somewhat different from Oster's.

Aside from Nebe, who was eternally on the alert, Oster was almost always the first to hear about it when someone was threatened by the Gestapo, whether the person was a friend or stranger. Showing apparent abstraction, he would listen attentively to all conversations about new "cases." Now and then— of course merely out of curiosity—he would inquire about particulars or involve the officers in charge of the matter in an innocuous conversation. Oster managed to encircle the German Opposition with a cordon of silence. Naturally he was not always successful. With deep bitterness he often had to look on helplessly while the Gestapo and alas, even his own Abwehr, seized some unfortunate, but in general he succeeded for years on an astonishing scale. Even today many persons do not know that they owe their lives to him.

This was by no means all he did. A secret-service organization naturally is equipped with a great many steel safes. Oster became the archivist of the Opposition. The collection of documents that we had started back in 1933 swelled to considerable proportions with the passage of time. Almost daily Oster sent his loyal chauffeur, Jakobs, to Beck with a secret portfolio containing foreign newspapers or the latest military news or reports on Gestapo crimes. At the same time he operated as a kind of secret post office. He sent countless letters to the front or abroad, successfully evading the Gestapo censorship. In this regard he was especially glad when he could be helpful to the churches. The journey that Joseph Mueller made to the Vatican gave Oster great satisfaction. The work of Doctor Schoenfeld and Dietrich Bonhoeffer with the ecumenical movement in Geneva would not have been possible without his assistance.

But all that he did was done silently. Although he was one of the best-informed officers in the OKW, although even field marshals in their hunger for information sent emissaries to him, he preferred to play dumb. Only his very closest friends were aware of his underground activities. Toward the end he no longer spoke at all about his negotiations with the generals. This prompted many persons who were constantly seeking news about prospective *putsches* to declare that he was tired and resigned. The high-strung intellectuals within the Opposition who were concerned only with "politics" began to doubt his wisdom. I recall that on the afternoon of July 20, 1944, Beck, who badly missed this most loyal and best of assistants, talked to me about all this foolish gossip. Probably it was precisely his exaggerated selflessness that brought Oster into ill repute among the dashing young colonels of the Opposition, Beck said. "Now his greatest virtue, his ability to keep his mouth shut, is costing him his reputation."

To some extent Oster deliberately strove to remain colorless to the eyes of those outside of his immediate circle. He depersonalized himself; he made an effort to impress people as an emotionless and matter-of-fact administrator. He once described to me in one sentence his own conception of his function within the Resistance Movement. He was standing at his desk looking down pensively at the four or five telephones whose secret circuits connected him with the most diverse authorities. "This is what I am," he said. "I facilitate communications for everyone everywhere." Nevertheless, he was far more than a human switchboard, and his work went beyond those telephone conversations in which he repeatedly gave brusque warnings to generals and field marshals in their distant headquarters. He was the driving force, not merely the technician, of the Opposition. How wonderfully he had worked for us became clear to everyone when he was at last driven from office.

For the sake of his task, Oster renounced the chances for commands at the front with their possibilities of very swift promotion. This does not mean that he was not a soldier in heart and mind, and a soldier in the best sense of the word. He suffered greatly from the moral and professional collapse of his class. His alienation from the generals went so far toward the last that even on important occasions he could scarcely be persuaded to wear his uniform. He always wore his unpretentious civilian outfit, no matter how much Canaris protested—and Canaris had an extremely formalistic point of view about such matters. Nevertheless, he had a profound sense of what an officer's honor should be; it existed for him, although it had no connection with the stars and decorations of our other brass hats. There was no contradiction between his rejection of the uniform and the statement that I made at the Nuremberg Trials with my eyes on Keitel and Jodl: "In the midst of a German inflation in field marshals and generals that utterly devaluated those titles, Oster was really—a general."

The so-called Oster circle was treated inside the Abwehr with suspicion and often with open hostility. The other officers spoke contemptuously of the "civilians," by which they meant not so much the external matter of dress (since most of Oster's men were in military service) as the manner in which we worked together with a challenging disregard for epaulets and stripes.

Nevertheless, there were a large number of officers in the circle, among them such outstanding military men as General Erwin von Lahousen. Although Lahousen did not count himself a member of the innermost Oster Circle, it was he who supplied the explosives needed for the attempt on Hitler's life. Colonel Georg Hansen was one of the oldest oppositionists within the Abwehr. Until the maelstrom of July 20, 1944, swallowed him up, he held to a clear, undeviating line. When Canaris was forced to leave, Hansen succeeded for almost a year in guiding the remnants of the badly shaken organization with such adroitness that the Gestapo, which had had a failure of nerve, was prompted to let it alone.

Lieutenant-Colonel Heinz and Colonels Count Rudolf Marogna-Redwitz and Rudolf Schrader returned to military service when the reserve officers were reactivated. The war brought in naval Captain Liedig, Captain Gehre, and Count Ulrich von Schwerin. Heinz played an important part as a wise adviser and aide up to the very last. Unfortunately, he never got a chance to participate in a more active fashion, although he had temporarily taken command of a section of the Brandenburg sabotage regiment in the hope that he would be able to use it in the *Putsch*. Oster carefully installed Schrader as an Abwehr officer in headquarters where his zeal and energy found excellent application. He gathered information, performed courier service, and practiced espionage against his own counter-espionage organization. After the failure of the *Putsch* on July 20, 1944, he made the courageous decision to commit suicide rather than endanger his friends.

Count Marogna, an old Austrian officer, was stubbornly

shielded by Oster in his position as chief of the Abwehr branch in Vienna, although Marogna was engaged in a perpetual guerrilla war with the Gestapo. He too was murdered after July 20, 1944. Some day, when the history of the Austrian liberation movement is written, his name will take one of the first places. There will be many witnesses in the countries of southeastern Europe to testify to the devotion which this splendid man, a true European, lavished upon the cause.

The chief provost marshal of the army, Ministerial Director Doctor Ernst Sack, was more or less the connecting link between the military men and the civilians. In spite of his high military rank he remained a civilian to the core who never departed from simple decency in spite of all the pomp, the clicking of heels, and the barking of orders that surrounded him. Inexorable in his judgments, unrelenting even toward friends, Doctor Sack worked under tremendous difficulties— for he was Keitel's subordinate. He had to find the mean between the requirements of the Opposition and the general dissolution of moral concepts. This mean was often extremely elusive, for quite frequently criminals or freebooters alleged that they were oppositionists in order to profit by the general social decay. Sack was able to ward off intervention of the Gestapo in a large number of cases by quickly instituting a "severe" investigation by a court-martial and then winding up the affair after his own fashion. Some charges he was able to quash at once.

Among the civilians, I mention in first place *Reichsgerichtsrat* [supreme court justice] Doctor Hans von Dohnanyi, who from the beginning of the war was Oster's closest associate. An unusually clever man, he had scarcely passed his majority when he took the leap from *Oberregierungsrat* in the ministry of justice to his position in the supreme court. As personal assistant to Minister of Justice Franz Guertner he persuaded the minister to intervene in a vast number of cases. With his inflexible

sense of justice and his fervor, he repeatedly took over the reins
from his phlegmatic chief. During the Fritsch crisis* he joined
up with Oster, and from then on he was part and parcel of the
history of that circle. Dohnanyi became the judicial expert of
the Abwehr in all cases where something had to be "fixed." It
was he who undertook the drafting of secret political reports,
applying to them the clarity of intelligence and diction that
characterized all his work. Dohnanyi had a share in every
protest on the part of Canaris, every aid rendered by the
Abwehr, every illegal action on the part of the Oster circle during those years.

I need say nothing about Dietrich Bonhoeffer, the brother-
in-law of Dohnanyi. His name has gone down in the history of
the militant Church. Bonhoeffer contrived, from his vantage
point in the Abwehr branch at Munich, to provide Joseph
Mueller with effective protection.

Before 1933 Joseph Mueller had been one of the leaders of
the Bavarian People's Party. A praiseworthy exception, he had
vehemently resisted the general capitulation to the Nazis of the
bourgeois parties in his area. Very soon he began to engage in
underground work. The beginning of the war brought him in
contact with Oster, who entrusted him with using his connections in the Vatican to broach conversations on the possibilities
of peace. Mueller accomplished his task with remarkable
adroitness, and this cleverness stood him in good stead after
1943, when he had to justify his activities to the Gestapo. He
withstood interrogations in such a manner that the Nazis
decided that he was one of their most valuable hostages, whom

---

* In early 1938, Werner von Fritsch, commander-in-chief of the army, was
falsely accused of scandalous behavior by Goering and Himmler. Although
he was eventually acquitted, his reputation was destroyed, and he resigned.
Hitler used the affair to reorganize Germany's armed forces and replace
several generals. *(Editor)*

they hoped to use in some kind of exchange. Together with other prominent prisoners, he was liberated in South Tyrol.

Were I to name all the gallant opponents of the Nazis, the list would run on and on. But I must give a special place to Elisabeth and Theodor Struenck.

I had been friendly with the couple for a long time. Toward the end of 1937 I introduced them to Oster. From that time on, they were part of his intimate circle. When the war broke out, Oster installed Struenck, who was at the time director of a large insurance firm in Frankfurt-am-Main, in the Abwehr headquarters. In view of Struenck's low military rank—he entered the service as a lieutenant of the reserve and died a captain—it was difficult to find an occupation for him that was commensurate with his abilities. He had a strong and self-willed personality and did not wish to idle away his time. In the Abwehr, as throughout the OKW, there was a swarm of colonels and naval captains whose arrogance was all the more boundless for their possessing no other qualifications outside of their insignia of rank. Finding a place for Lieutenant Struenck was all the more difficult because his work in the Abwehr was in reality to be merely his subsidiary occupation; his main task was to perform special missions for Oster. Oster worked out an adequate solution which his successor Hansen was to perpetuate, so that Struenck was able to hold his position and play his important role of intermediary up to the last few days before the *Putsch* of July 20, 1944.

The Struencks had rented a modest little apartment in Berlin which remained listed under the name and telephone number of their landlord. It was definitely known to be unobserved and was therefore a splendid meeting-place in the center of the city for members of the Opposition. It is unfortunate that Frau Struenck was not able to keep a guestbook; it would be something she could exhibit with pride today, for a great many men of the Opposition met in her apartment. It was there that the first meeting between Goerdeler and Stauffenberg took place. In fact the Struencks' apartment in Nuernbergerstrasse 31 was virtually Goerdeler's headquarters whenever he stayed in Berlin. Sometimes he visited there three times a day. He was fond of discussing the strenuous and only too often depressing negotiations he conducted and he liked to forge new plans among his close friends. The Struencks were not only patient listeners, but candid advisers and counselors as well. I should judge that there was scarcely a single letter or memorandum that Goerdeler wrote during those years, scarcely a single conference in which he engaged, or a single tour of investigation that he undertook, which were not thoroughly discussed before and after with the Struencks.

After a while it became customary for every friend of the household to bring along his friends. The result was that things were at times rather lively in the tiny two-room apartment. It was quite a feat to prevent the various visitors from encountering one another. This tactic, upon which Nebe repeatedly insisted, was a precaution against the possibility of Gestapo espionage. Later events were to prove its fatal importance, at least in respect to many other persons. Struenck himself could not be saved. The Nazis treated his brave wife more viciously than they had the wives of any of the other conspirators of July 20, but she was rescued just before they were about to put her to death. Struenck himself traveled the last bitter road together with Oster and Canaris; he died fearlessly in his faith, a good comrade, a true friend.

Groups and Individuals

THE SCHULZE-BOYSEN GROUP cannot be called a circle, although nearly a hundred men affiliated to it went to their deaths and the group had established an extensive espionage network. The discovery by the Gestapo of the numerous secret radio transmitters they had set up developed into the biggest espionage trial of the war. The organization was guided by convinced Communists and worked for the Russian secret service.

The Schulze-Boysens, both husband and wife, were fanatical Communists who knew exactly for whom they were working. This was not true of most of the persons on the list of victims. The majority of them were adherents of the Left, but they had no suspicion that they were members of a Communist organization guided from Moscow; they first learned about these connections in court. Schulze-Boysen occupied a key position in the air ministry. Thus he had a large number of acquaintances with whom he could continually exchange oppositional information. It took some time before we were able to find out most—not all—of the particulars about this tragic case and ascertain which members belonged to the inner Communist circle, which ones merely wanted to give expression to their oppositional sentiments, and which were dragged into a fatal situation through lack of caution.

Hitler was extraordinarily agitated by this espionage case. For years the Nazis had been engaged in a spy-hunt because it seemed apparent from radio messages that were picked up that there must be Russian spies inside German headquarters, and somewhere near the very top. Everyone suspected everyone else, until sheer chance exposed the real spies. Then it was Goering's turn to rage. He had long since retired from active conduct of the war to spend his time at Karinhall with his banquets and his collection of paintings; but this scandal dealt a severe blow to the reputation for special reliability that his air ministry had cultivated. Therefore, he was sedulous in his backing of Hitler when the Fuehrer refused to confirm the Reich military tribunal's verdict condemning "only" fifty persons to death. Goering and Hitler insisted upon another forty-five death sentences, mainly for the wives of the chief defendants. When the presiding judge of the court refused to assent to this improvement on justice, he was forced to resign, but since anything was possible in the Third Reich, the judge who had just been dismissed for being over-lenient was given the post of chief military prosecutor. In this capacity the first important case that he conducted—not too benevolently—was that of Oster and his comrades.

Another group that did not comprise a circle according to our strict definition consisted of members of the churches. Everyone knows how many fighters and patient oppositionists there were in the ranks of the churches, but nothing would have suited the Nazis better than to convict important representatives of the Catholic or the Protestant churches of political conspiracy. It is important to note this in order to understand the complex problem of the Opposition in a totalitarian state. Good churchgoers had to be, or to become, convinced oppositionists. Their loyalty to their churches forced them into this intellectual position; but this effect of the churches was precisely the reason for cheating the Gestapo of its desired pretext for annihilating these centers of resistance. On the other hand, the bishops and other leaders of the churches must not compromise themselves by political concessions. It was very difficult indeed to find the proper course between these dilemmas; and we regret to note that a good many church leaders contented themselves with the far too worldly solution of steering an intact organization and bureaucracy through the turbulent waves.

Men like Ambassador Ulrich von Hassell, Freiherr von Hammerstein [the former commander-in-chief of the army who retired in 1934], Nikolaus von Halem, and even Martin Niemoeller cannot be assigned to any circle. Either out of stubbornness or deliberate intent these anti-Nazis remained independent.

In 1939, Hammerstein had considered arresting Hitler when the Fuehrer made a visit to the Western Front. Before the plan could be carried out, his intuitive master deprived him of his military command. From then until his premature death in 1942, the recalled general issued warning after warning. When Hitler plunged into the Russian adventure, the former commander-in-chief made the terrifying prophecy: "Of the army that is now marching against Russia not a single man will come back." We know now what hecatombs of human lives were to follow those first hundreds of thousands whom "the greatest general of all times" sent marching to their deaths on June 22, 1941. But who among the generals was willing to listen?

Ambassador Hassell was highly esteemed by Beck and by almost everyone else in the Opposition. With his trenchant humor, his diplomatic finesse, and his unshakable political principles, he was one of the most distinguished figures of the German Opposition Movement. He devoted his diplomatic talents to mediating among individuals of extremely diverse temperaments and opinions.

Nikolaus von Halem, in a sense a bohemian in the Opposition, was a man whose ingenuity was more marked than his genius; but he possessed a superb mind and was the best kind of cosmopolitan European. In his restlessness he drifted from one circle and group to the next. Everywhere, he sought an assassin who would kill Hitler—until at last he found the wrong one: Beppo Roemer. Arrested in 1942 together with Legation Councilor von Mumm, von Halem went to his death after July 20, 1944, with magnificent courage.

Around Johannes Popitz, the Prussian minister of finance, there gathered a group of men who were striving toward the same goal. In 1933, Popitz had offered his services to the Nazis, which was an astonishing act for a man who had served as under-secretary under Hilferding, the Social Democratic minister of finance. For years Popitz maintained that the only way to keep some curbs on the Revolution was to play off Goering against Hitler and Himmler. In order to make the sybarite of Karinhall amenable, Popitz used the Prussian state treasury to bribe Goering heavily, but by 1938 he realized where the Nazi express was headed. From then on his oppositional attitude solidified more and more. In the end he became one of the extremists. His application for membership in the Opposition, however, met with strong objections. Popitz's case seemed to be far more crass than the "ambiguous" case of Hjalmar Schacht. Although his intelligence was prized and although his profound acquaintance with the machinery of state was almost indispensable, he had shared too long in building up the Nazi dictatorship to be readily accepted. I myself was one of those who vetoed him most strongly, but when I at last met the man personally, I was deeply impressed by his manifest sincerity. He suffered greatly from the catastrophe that had befallen Germany and Europe, and in a sense he tried personally to atone for it. Year after year his pleas to generals and civilians, his struggles to win them over, became more anguished and more affecting. He may well have felt his death on the gallows as a release.

If it is to become a principle of international law that men who make the mistake of contributing toward totalitarianism can never turn back (the totalitarians hang them as traitors; the other side condemn them as accomplices), some may be deterred; but such a principle would profit chiefly the statesmen of disaster like Hitler. If such politicians should succeed again in involving their followers, associates, or fellow travelers in guilt, they would be able to confront those they had tricked with an ultimatum: henceforth there was only one way to redeem themselves internationally—to drag other nations down with them or—to *win* a war.

Professor Peter Jessen, who was a close friend of Popitz, also came out of the Nazi Movement—and split with it all the more emphatically. He was a member of the activistic wing of the Opposition.

Under-Secretary Erwin Planck, the brilliant son of the famous physicist, had moved from the army to his office in the chancellery under the chancellorships of Bruening and Schleicher. From 1933 on, he unswervingly opposed the Nazi system. In 1942 he abandoned all hopes of a *Putsch,* but this did not save him from the gallows.

Attorney Carl Langbehn, who chanced to be personally acquainted with Himmler, also wanted to play off the Gestapo against Hitler. He and Popitz worked together on this danger-ous ruse. Himmler said neither yes nor no; he played along until after July 20, 1944. Then he struck savagely.

There was another group in the foreign office. The strongest and most resolute personality in this group was the later ambassador, Erich Kordt. Kordt was one of the few early advocates of assassinating Hitler. He was in the fortunate posi-tion of being admitted to the secret parleys in the chancellery, and as early as 1939 he offered to set off the bomb. At that time it was not feasible to procure the necessary explosives for him behind the backs of the generals. In 1941, Ribbentrop more or less exiled Kordt by shipping him off to Tokyo.

The names of the legation councilors, Hans Berndt von Haeften and Adam von Trott zu Solz, are very well known. When the war broke out, Trott was sent off to a diplomatic post in East Asia. On the way there and back he formed many important ties. Until 1944 he served as an emissary of the cul-tural department, in which capacity he was able to travel fre-quently to Switzerland and Sweden. He never missed an opportunity to put out feelers. But his real oppositionist activ-ity began when he became a member of the Kreissau circle, which I am about to discuss. Albrecht von Kessel had the good luck to be in the Vatican on July 20, 1944; otherwise he would have met the same fate as his friends.

There is one more—among so many—whom I must mention: Otto Kiep, the former consul-general in New York, who was condemned to death in June 1944, and was executed a few months later, together with that courageous woman, Elisabeth von Thadden.

From about 1941 on, the Kreissau circle was concerned with establishing a program for future domestic and foreign policy. Its approach to these problems was essentially a socialistic one. Strictly speaking, it was no circle but a group, composed of men of relatively the same age who were bound by ties of friendship, but who represented the most diverse political views. These men tried to establish bases for a common socialistic policy. The fruit of their labors was preserved in memoranda which, when published, will testify to the number of progressive and truly European-minded men who were waiting for the hour of liberation.

Publication of their conclusions will prove something else. It will demonstrate how many principles which may be branded as idealistic were accepted as a matter of course by those who had passed through the purgatory of Nazi rule. Very few had any patience with a change of personnel or an amelioration of existing practices—which would mean, of course, simply an improved totalitarianism. The rejection of nationalism and imperialism was fairly general; so also was the desire for a federated Germany. The Socialists, on the basis of their collectivist doctrine, did not want to go so far in decentralization as the conservatives and liberals. The Socialists considered it essential that governmental direction of the economy and social policy be retained; the others desired a thorough relaxation of all controls.

Goerdeler, Leuschner, and Jakob Kaiser were not members of this Kreissau circle. At the risk of being condemned as too "old" and too "reactionary," the three forbore to consider premature experiments. Goerdeler in particular was given short shrift by the "youths"—an attitude which was to have a fateful effect upon the preparations for and the execution of the *Putsch* of July 20.

The name Kreissau circle derived from the meetings that were held on the Silesian country estate of Count Helmuth von Moltke, who was not only the host but the intellectual chief of the circle. Von Moltke had many personal and professional ties with the Anglo-Saxon countries. During the war he served as an administrative official in the foreign branch of the Abwehr and dealt with questions of international law. A clever, thoughtful, energetic man who was worthy of his great forbear, he was probably "the most vigorous militant among the socialistic conservatives," to quote Emil Henk's depiction of the "Tragedy of July 20." "But as a politician his fiery days were over," Henk continues. This lack of fire made it easier for Moltke to hold undeviatingly to the line he considered correct and to pursue with tranquil persistence his preparations for the period after the inevitable collapse. On the other hand, it prevented him from understanding fully the point of view of the "activists."

It is essential to note this. For von Moltke's great significance lay in his being the most prominent advocate of inaction—and one whose purity of motive could not be doubted. All his zeal and all his imagination were devoted, on principle, to what would come after the fall of the Nazis. Profoundly skeptical of any action on the part of the military, Moltke had in mind something like a "directed defeat."

Because of Moltke's personality and political weight, his leadership was trusted by many oppositionists who were not at all prone to fold their hands in their laps and who, in another situation, might have enlisted their minds and wills under the banner of those who favored "action" rather than "politics." The most vigorous advocate of this latter line was Goerdeler, who certainly could not be considered an unpolitical man. But in politics men can ill afford to let their opponents plunge ahead into disasters. Once the situation is out of hand, chaos devours even the best-laid plans of the men who are holding themselves in readiness to take over the inheritance.

General Ludwig Beck, in truth, stood above all the parties. Consequently, there were no dissenting voices at all when, in the winter of 1939, he was appointed head of the *fronde*. This nomination was the result of Oster's urging. It had become clear since the outbreak of the war that any attempt to overthrow the regime would be doomed from the outset unless the problem of the future head of the state were solved to the satisfaction of the army. The military and civil executive power could be conferred only on someone whom the soldiers would acknowledge as a leader. Beck was the only general with an unimpaired reputation, the only general who had voluntarily resigned. No one among the military men could surpass him in personal or soldierly capacity.

In the past year it had become a kind of mania within the Opposition to hunt for *the* general. Everyone beat the bushes, and wherever someone had a cousin who knew an officer on the staff of an army commander, word of this "connection" was passed on in whispers, to the accompaniment of mysterious and significant winks. Complete nonentities were puffed up into noble tyrannicides, and in every case infinite trouble ensued first to pierce the secrecy and discover what legendary general was being referred to and then to determine the extent of his resolution or the actual force of soldiers he commanded. This sort of unnecessary but mandatory detective work could

be done only by an informed military man like Beck. It was
above all necessary to reassure the few generals who were really in on the conspiracy for they were likely to be frightened off
when all sorts of well-meaning persons spoke to them about
their alleged or actual plans.

Carl Friedrich Goerdeler also cannot be assigned to any
one circle. He chose his numerous friends and collaborators
without regard to their group allegiances. The particular task
he had set himself was to unite the most variegated individual-
ities, temperaments, and theories under a common banner. Of
his indefatigability, his courage, his zeal, I have spoken frequently, but his chief merit was that he rationalized the Opposition. With a truly admirable one-sidedness he refused to see
the things that divided oppositionists; he saw only human
beings who were striving toward the same goal of eliminating
Hitler. He straightway tried to bring these people together.

Naturally he was keenly aware that the Opposition had to
have a program for government, and he had in fact masterfully
succeeded in uniting his grand coalition upon such a program.
This accomplishment was largely due to the wisdom with
which he limited his aims. He was convinced that everything
that did not have to be settled during the first days and weeks
after the establishment of a post-Hitler government could be
safely left to the discretion of the new order. Indeed, a new
government would not acquire significance and permanency
unless these problems could be discussed with full freedom.
What Goerdeler tried with all his might to avoid was the coup
within a coup—confronting the public with the accomplished
fact of definite reforms as soon as the overthrow of Hitler succeeded. No matter how justified such reforms might be, he felt
that they would violate the democratic character of the future
regime.

In this respect, then, Goerdeler did not engage in "politics," although he was overbrimming with ideas and proposals of his own. To him all conferences had but one item on the agenda. First the Nazis must be overthrown; then it would be time to think of governing. Consequently he endeavored to divert the thoughts of the men with whom he negotiated from the dispute about persons and programs and impress them instead with the need for action. His letters and memoranda referred incessantly to what was to be *done*. For the sake of action he traveled constantly. For the sake of action he occasionally took the risk of passing on his prognoses and information, in order to stimulate the hesitant.

He was often suspected of being too free with secrets, and undoubtedly the Goerdeler critics were often right. Nevertheless, he found himself, as time wore on, forced more and more into an unenviable, even a tragic role. It was not that people became tired of his "harassing," as they called it. Rather it was that the stragglers in the Opposition Movement balked at giving him the respect which was due him as an established leader. In the underground as anywhere else a man can outlive his usefulness. When the knell sounds, he can be pushed aside by the bold throng of his followers, not because he has become too old, but simply because he stands too high in the seniority list of active rebels.

The greatest tragedy for Goerdeler consisted in the fact that he, with his temperament, his energy, his eagerness, with his eternal invocation of action, was himself never in a position to act. He always had to wait for others; he always had to urge others; his was the painful task of challenging others to risk their lives on an act that he himself could not attempt. For how could he personally carry out a *Putsch*? For a civilian to prove to a general that there did exist a possibility for revolt, that it was merely a question of his having the courage to risk his own life, was an extremely embarrassing affair when one was disqualified from going ahead and providing a good example. There was no reason to assume that the sentinels of the three protective cordons around Hitler's headquarters or the SS guards outside—and inside—the Fuehrer's conference room would admit a civilian simply on his assurance that the briefcase in his hand contained matter of the greatest importance.

Consequently, Goerdeler had to wait and wait, until it was too late and he himself was no longer an actor, scarcely a coadjutor but dragged down by others into the maelstrom. After July 20, 1944, he fled like a hunted animal for a full month— and what "flight" means in such cases can be understood only by those who have experienced the terrible physical and mental strain of being pursued incessantly. Then he was arrested in West Prussia. Who will be the first to cast stones at him for what followed? For the technical experts in torture and drugs extracted far more information from him than this thoroughly decent man would ever have given out had he been in full possession of his senses. Resistance to interrogation from the first to the third degree is not primarily a matter of character. It is essentially a question of physical constitution.

If Goerdeler can be blamed for anything, it is at most the fact that he unquestionably spoke to more people and informed more people about the conspiracy than, afterward, proved needful. We frequently had bitter disputes about this matter. I had been thoroughly convinced by Oster's example and by Nebe's constant warnings and had made it a point of pride in underground work to make as few personal contacts as possible and not even to confide in those whose agreement with our principles was beyond doubt and whose friendship was gladdening and encouraging. Goerdeler felt that he himself had to be an exception to this general rule. He felt that, quite apart from all questions of conspiracy, he was so much the drummer and politician of the Movement that he had to obtain a person-

al impression of all the leading figures behind the rebellion—
leading in the broadest sense. Someone, he maintained, had to
have a comprehensive view of the whole situation.

In February 1945, Goerdeler died a pious and dignified
death. His fame will remain as the man who, throughout the
whole frightful time of Hitler's war, achieved the stature of the
most indefatigable and undaunted warrior for religion, justice,
and humanity.

I cannot conclude my remarks on the Opposition without considering a man to whom I was very close. I find myself constantly wondering whether, of all the diverse personalities that
I met in the course of those twelve years, he was not after all
the wisest. Certainly Wilhelm Canaris was one of the pro-
foundest and most perplexing personalities among the oppositionists. More significant than any sketch which I could offer
is that of General Lahousen, written after he was taken prisoner. His portrait of Canaris ought not to molder away in some
dusty archives. I quote it here:

> Any attempt to get to the bottom of Canaris's personality will
> probably always remain no more than an attempt. I am under-
> taking it here only because it is necessary to illuminate the back-
> ground of many events that would otherwise remain incompre-
> hensible.
>
> Many people will deny my ability to judge Canaris objective-
> ly. They are both right and wrong. For I was too close to Canaris
> to achieve that objectivity in judging his complicated personality
> which only distance from a person can assure. On the other
> hand, precisely because of my close relationship with him and
> because I was one of his confidants within the Opposition circle
> of the OKW, I had the opportunity to gain insights into his

complex mind which were inevitably withheld from many outsiders.

Canaris was the most difficult superior I have encountered in
my thirty-year career as a soldier. Contradictory in his instructions, given to whims, and not always just, always mysterious, he
had nevertheless developed intellectual and, above all, human
qualities which raised him far above the military rubber stamps
and marionettes that most of his colleagues and superiors were.
He never struck me, Austrian that I am, as the typical German
military man; rather he seemed a cosmopolitan in the uniform of
a German admiral.

As one who shared his secret plans I know that Canaris
played a double game; in the existing situation he could not help
doing that. Nevertheless, I can scarcely say where the limits of
that game lay. In general, in all that Canaris did or, as the case
might be, omitted to do, it was very difficult to define the limits
or to recognize a clear and undeviating line. The role he played
was conditioned, in this respect as in all others, by his peculiar
personality. He hated violence in itself. Therefore, he was
repelled by the war. And therefore, he hated Hitler and the Nazi
system. The weapons he used against that system were intellect,
influence, cunning, above all his "double game."

Canaris was not at all a technical expert in his work; rather he
was a great dilettante. The underground circle that he had gathered around himself was as colorful and heterogeneous as his
own personality. Men of all classes and professions, people
whose horizons were broad and narrow, idealists and political
adventurers, sober rationalists and imaginative mystics, conservative noblemen and Freemasons, theosophists, half-Jews or
Jews, German and non-German anti-fascists, men and
women—all of them united only in their underground resistance
to Hitler and his system. This circle was by no means directed by
secret orders. Rather, it was an intellectual association which

Canaris constantly influenced by slight or direct hints and which he guided by active intervention only in rare cases. Only a few initiates received concrete instructions, and even these were not always perfectly clear.

Canaris's urge to travel was literally a mania with him. Like Ahasuerus fleeing from himself and other men, he journeyed from town to town, everywhere spreading unrest and disorder in the Nazi system. Some of his intimates would then always have to put in order the things that Canaris had jumbled as might an overgrown child his toys. This they had to do in order not to endanger him and themselves. Their reward was rarely gratitude; it was usually an irritated reproach. Yet at many other times Canaris would take care of situations with exemplary clarity and without equivocation—with the same clarity and directness with which he (and to my mind he was the only one) sensed and predicted the actual course of this latest world-wide catastrophe.

His diary is impregnated with this fundamental understanding of the impending disaster. Those notes of his constitute, I think, an essential contemporary contribution to the history of this war's origins and are especially valuable as an expose of its character as an aggressive war. All the chief actors are to be found in this document, and the subsidiary figures as well. We meet the men who bore the main responsibility, the knowing and the unknowing, the guilty and the innocent and the mere henchmen, those who profited by and those who were robbed by the Nazi system. Only one character is absent: Canaris himself. He does cite his words, his opinions, and his actions; but ordinarily he presents only one half, perhaps one third, of himself. The rest remains hidden.

Canaris rarely estimated men by their accomplishments or their character. Sympathy and antipathy were the guiding factors in his view of men—these and a number of curious complexes deriving from his exaggerated love for animals. "Anyone who does not love dogs I judge out of hand to be an evil man," he once said.

I was one of his closest intimates. An intimate, but not a friend, as some ignorant people have maintained. Whether the conclusions that Canaris drew from his knowledge of affairs were correct or incorrect, I do not know. But that he did draw conclusions I do know, and he was willing to follow those conclusions to their ultimate consequences. Canaris was not the man to oppose boldly and openly something that seemed wrong or bad to him. Nor do I know whether such conduct would have produced any meaningful result in the situation that then existed. He fought with the weapons with which his Creator had endowed him: his extremely flexible intelligence, his lively imagination, and his gift for cunning. But he fought against Hitler!

I lived with this confused, iridescent personality in every conceivable situation. Never did I witness in Canaris a trace of crudity or brutality, neither in thought nor in action. On the contrary, I have witnessed only sudden revelations of his deep-seated humanity, and somehow I was always greatly affected by each such revelation. I shall never forget his complete psychological breakdown under the impression of smoking and devastated Belgrade, where the stench of unburied corpses still lingered. And at such moments Canaris was not dissimulating.

It was his awareness of this and similar acts of violence and brutality which hardened his resolve to do everything in his power to prevent a victory of the Nazi system. I do not know what other motives may have influenced Canaris or what other aims he may have had. But I am certain that a knowledge of good and evil based on purely human considerations was the chief mainspring of his actions.

From about 1942 on, the admiral was inwardly a completely broken and distrait man. The hopelessness of his struggle and a premonition of his personal fate had left their mark upon him outwardly as well. At the end Canaris probably stumbled and fell—over Canaris. But in a time of incredible horrors he always remained, in contrast to many persons around him, decent and thoroughly human.

Of the admiral's instrument, the Abwehr, one might choose to say a great deal or very little. A great deal if one wished to write about the secret history of the war. In such case it would be necessary to enter a field far broader than that of German military espionage and counter-espionage; a narrower span would falsify the picture. Perhaps it is still too early for that, but very little need be said beyond the statement that work in the Abwehr proceeded along quite normal and ordinary lines. A number of investigators of the victorious Powers are nowadays extremely astonished to learn how badly they overestimated this organization around which mercenary sensational journalists wove the most incredible legends. Actually, the Abwehr functioned well in small matters and very badly in large.

That, to be sure, must be accounted the merit of its chief. Now and then, among the heaped-up pebbles of daily reports from agents, a gold nugget gleamed, but there were always busy hands ready to bury the nugget at once in the useless pile of "reliable" news from "informed sources." Canaris would then demonstrate his remarkable talents, on the one hand, by praising the ambitious prospectors for their zeal and, on the other hand, by offering them his expert help: no, they must not dig there but here; what they had found was a piece of false gold, but they must be close; was not this other glittering fragment of glass in reality a precious gem? He was an artist in reducing a vital report by his intelligence service to such a trifle that it vanished amid the mass of false information; or else he slashed away at the material his agents brought him until in the end they gaped in confusion and wondered how they could possibly have stumbled on such a false trail. In every case he intuitively found the right course, and always, of course, he played his part of a keen and industrious chief of counter-intelligence. Everyone around him felt that he held firm opinions and definite intentions, and everyone reckoned that he would be better off not to get too much involved with this mysterious man.

Thus the Abwehr became his own personal instrument, upon whose keyboard he played with sovereign grace. He passionately hated not only Hitler and Himmler, but the entire Nazi system as a political phenomenon, but there cannot be any doubt that far more could have been achieved by full employment of the Abwehr. Canaris tolerated the seditious activities of the Oster circle by deliberately refusing to take cognizance of them. Except for a brief aberration of some twelve hours, he never wanted an assassination. He was particularly emphatic in his disapproval of any contact or collaboration with the enemy in the war. If I were to attempt to describe the nature of the man's activity—which sprang from a well-thought-out philosophy of life and a deep religious faith—I would say that his sole aim was to "prevent." Never did he want to play an active part in determining the fate of Germany and the world. To his mind, what could not be prevented was fated to happen as it did happen—even if it meant disaster for Germany and for himself personally.

"Passive leadership accompanied by the appearance of extremest activity"— that was the watchword he gave his associates to guide them in their official duties. He was everywhere and nowhere at once. Everywhere, in that he traveled to and fro, at home and abroad and to the front, always leaving a whirl of confusion behind him. Nowhere, in that, when the situation grew dangerous or the Fuehrer's headquarters was threatening to ask unpleasant questions, Canaris was never around. Even

Hitler employed the much-traveled admiral, whom he saw personally no more than once every two or three months, to carry out extremely important secret foreign missions.

The manner in which Canaris carried out these missions can be indicated by a single example. At the apex of the Nazi successes a plan for conquering Gibraltar was drawn up. Canaris was assigned the task of softening up Franco's foreign minister, Jordana. He flew to Spain, accompanied by General Lahousen, and even before the audience was held he dictated to his general a secret report on Jordana's flat refusal of any assistance by Spain. Afterward he was somewhat disquieted when the foreign minister expressed himself in far more compliant terms than those Canaris had put into his mouth.

Prevention! As a result of the Nuremberg Trials the skill with which Canaris prevented the murders of Generals Giraud and Weygand has become public knowledge. When Hitler censured him for letting these men escape, Canaris cleverly made use of the assassination of Heydrich to shift all the blame to the Black hangman. In the spring of 1943, when Oster heard of the scheme for kidnaping both the king of Italy and the pope, in order to prevent the fall of Mussolini, he made a brief telephone call to Canaris and hinted at what he had learned. The admiral at once emplaned from the Crimea to Berlin, and from there flew on to Venice to warn his Italian colleagues.

Similarly, many carefully planned acts of sabotage against the enemy were suddenly revealed as technically impracticable; Canaris saw to it that they failed for inexplicable reasons. On countless occasions assistance was given to Jews, Christians, or citizens of enemy countries who were threatened by death; such work was part of the regular "official" activity of the Abwehr. Canaris approved these instructions and concealed them from the Gestapo. This last was often the most difficult part of such enterprises. It is hard to say whether Canaris instituted or composed those courageous memoranda in which the diabolic intentions of the SS in occupied territories were revealed beforehand or their cruel practices proved afterward by documentary evidence. What is essential is that he was responsible whenever such "undesired" proofs were laid before Keitel, Brauchitsch, Halder, Raeder, or anyone else whose conscience he felt needed stirring.

One might imagine that only a particularly robust personality would be capable of such a dangerous double game as Canaris played for an entire decade. In reality, this small, frail, and somewhat timid man was a vibrating bundle of nerves. Extremely well read, oversensitive, "sicklied o'er with the pale cast of thought," Canaris was an "outsider" in every respect. In bearing and manner of work he was the most unmilitary of persons. To be sure, he could at times be harsh, so that the "little Greek" as he was called enjoyed the respect of everyone. (Although his family had been settled in Germany since the seventeenth century—his father was the manager of a Westphalian mine—Levantine origins were so marked that his nickname was virtually inevitable.)

Canaris had a natural bent for leading his opponents astray. He could recite the Nazi verses so convincingly that even the greatest skeptics temporarily no longer dared to question the genuineness of his claims. As one of the leading Gestapo officials would exclaim in angry candor to one of the few survivors of the July 20 *Putsch:* "That Canaris fooled everyone, Heydrich, Himmler, Keitel, Ribbentrop, and even the Fuehrer."

Canaris, however, would never go far enough. The fact that he did not remains, to my mind, the great weakness in his philosophy and his way of life. On the other hand, he was not of the passive school. He did things; he did a great deal; and he ventured something that was even more valuable than life: his honor as it would be judged by those who could not comprehend his attitude.

"What do they say about me abroad?" How often he asked me this question! I might almost say he put the question to me as a challenge, but with trembling voice, as if he expected my reply to be a verdict which I had neither the will nor the right to pronounce.

"Your game will soon have to come out in the open," I used to say to him at such earnest moments. I meant by that to persuade him to rebel openly; that was what so many expected of him precisely because he had stamped himself outwardly as a devout functionary of the Nazi system.

His game did indeed come out in the open, but in another and more tragic sense. By murdering him his executioners themselves freed him from the Nazi embrace. Death the reconciler intervened and clarified on a higher plane the many ambiguities which he would never have been able to resolve fully in life.

Fruitless Peace Feelers, Useless Warnings

ONCE THE WINTER MONTHS were past and the spring of 1940 smiled upon the land, the Opposition stirred again.

It is not by chance that the Ides of March and the Eighteenth Brumaire (November 9) are the classical days for crises in revolutionary epochs. When the sap is rising and new life throbs the spirit of enterprise mounts. Similarly, it flickers up one last time before the long winter sleep descends. I recall only one case in which plans for revolt took concrete form in the hot summer months. That was in July 1944. We know the result.

All the reflections in which we had engaged during November were revived that spring. No one knew what interpretation to put upon the *drôle de guerre*. Some thought it had been merely a necessary winter pause. Others claimed to know better; it had all been a matter of histrionics, they asserted. After a decent interval in which both parties had played "Let's pretend" with remarkable stagecraft, they would now sit down at the conference table and negotiate.

This spreading of peace rumors from time to time was a favorite trick of the Nazis. Such rumors encouraged the populace, which was very unenthusiastic about the war. On the other hand, they aroused considerable uneasiness among the Western Powers. Thus the Pied Piper of Hamelin attained his end. With skirling pipes of peace he led his people from one campaign to the next, while at the same time he aroused in his enemies such apprehension that their own coalition would break up that they stopped considering the possibility of a pact with the German *fronde*.

Among our circle of friends no one doubted that Hitler would venture an offensive in the West. We, therefore, had to hurry if we wanted to prove to the generals that a possibility for peace with honor still existed. Beck decided to continue along the lines of the conversations that Joseph Mueller had begun in the Vatican in the fall of 1939. Mueller enjoyed such confidence in Rome that the reliability of his information would not be questioned. Thus the doubts of the British would be allayed, and on the other hand, Halder and Brauchitsch could not question the sincerity of the British negotiator—which they could have done in any other case, for if the Pope were intervening personally, the two generals could no longer fall back upon such an evasion.

The German Opposition was not a government competent to offer a binding signature to treaties or agreements. It, therefore, redounds greatly to the honor of the Pope that he, for the sake of European peace, put aside all misgivings and volunteered his services as a mediator. The conversations covered a wide range; there were repeated questions and inquiries referred back to sources at home. The details are no longer important in the light of the five years of war that followed, but the result cannot be overstressed. Provided, of course, that the Nazi system was thoroughly and completely eliminated, an arrangement was still possible!

At Beck's instigation a detailed final report was prepared. Toward the end of March, General George Thomas handed this report to the chief of the general staff; but now, in the midst of war, Halder did not dare take the course which he [together with General Erwin von Witzleben] had been prepared to take in 1938—going over his chief's head if necessary. He made his decision contingent on Brauchitsch's approval and Brauchitsch refused to act. Not only that, but he indignantly threatened to have Thomas and Oster arrested.

Thus failed the last impressive attempt to prevent the extension of the war and to persuade the top leadership of the Wehrmacht to take action. Brauchitsch and Halder had their choice, and they made it. They chose Hitler—and world war.

This is the proper place to interlard a few words on the other peace negotiations that were conducted by the Opposition.

Throughout the war there was incessant talk abroad of alleged peace feelers by an Opposition resolved on revolt. Many travelers from Germany—only those who possessed "good connections" received visas, after all—hinted darkly about a legendary field marshal or an even more legendary group of conspirators. Most of these amateur diplomats hoped to elicit a favorable reaction to stimulate the forces of resistance at home in Germany. These advocates of a "Dutch wedding," who claimed to have the agreement of the one partner in order to win the consent of the other, were quite numerous in the innermost circles of the Opposition. They hoped to bring about a marriage of convenience—in this case a *Putsch* by the skeptical generals.

Unfortunately, their zeal did more harm than good. The enemy secret services were so swamped with reports from "reliable" sources that they no longer knew whom to believe. Indeed, the task of intelligence on the other side was complicated by the fact that some of these peace rumors were spread by agents of the *Sicherheitsdienst* [Heydrich's organization] or the Abwehr, in order to test the enemy's firmness, or by Gestapo spies who hoped to get on the trail of the Opposition. In order totally to confuse the situation, a good many of the oppositionists who spread such reports were of the type who at home either rejected any thought of revolt or declared stoutly that a *Putsch* would be premature. Since all of these conversations naturally awakened certain hopes on the other side, the disappointment abroad was all the greater afterward. In the end various people had cried wolf so many times, had announced revolts and named dates so often, that the very existence of an Opposition to Hitler was no longer believed.

In reality there were very few authorized peace feelers. Naturally Goerdeler, von Hassell, Count Moltke, and Trott zu Solz—to name only these few—had kept up their old ties with highly placed personages abroad and had endeavored to make new connections, partly in order to obtain information and partly to pass on what they themselves knew. Every chance had to be exploited to create understanding abroad for the difficulties the Opposition faced and to prevent all ties from being broken off. Beck, however, constantly warned against our going too far. He was absolutely against giving any definite assurance which would necessarily discredit the Opposition if no *Putsch* was forthcoming. Therefore, he narrowed his negotiations down to those few situations which seriously presented a chance for an uprising. There were only five such occasions during the war: in November 1939, in the spring of 1940, in the early part of 1943 after the disasters at Stalingrad and Tunis, at the end of 1943, and in July 1944.

Certainly there is no validity to the argument that the Opposition wanted to overthrow Hitler but that the *Putsch* was repeatedly hindered because statesmen abroad were not ready to come to an agreement. Up to January 1943, when the Casablanca formula of "unconditional surrender" was propounded, any such formulation was flatly incorrect and served only to further the lie that the Allies were prolonging the war. It may be that a few encouraging words from abroad would have helped the Germans to come to their senses, but even this is not absolutely certain, for during 1940, 1941, and 1942 the German diplomats in neutral capitals—the oppositionist diplomats as well, unfortunately—wrote continual messages home about the splendid chances for an arrangement with England. They merely served as a stimulant to Hitler and the Nazis, while at the same time our vacillating generals sighed with relief because now they could let the situation "mature" for another six months—by which they meant that they would wait for the British to "soften" or until they had attained by conquest a more favorable position for negotiation.

The conversations that Dietrich Bonhoeffer had with the Bishop of Chichester in Stockholm in May 1942, were intended to offset any false impression produced by the negotiations in the Vatican. The idea was to show that the Opposition involved other than purely Catholic circles. There was, however, no intention of breaking off the connections that had been established through the Vatican; Bonhoeffer's proposals were coordinated with those of Joseph Mueller. At that time we could not give the Allies any definite assurances of a *Putsch* because the three field marshals who were the prospective *Putsch* leaders had been eliminated. Mannstein wanted to conquer Sebastopol first;

Kluge was wavering as he always did; and Witzleben, who sincerely wanted to overthrow Hitler, was in Paris at the time—a commander who had no soldiers to command.

As is well known, the British government was not interested in the Bishop of Chichester's communications. After having overcome tremendous difficulties to arrange Bonhoeffer's trip, we were deeply disappointed by this inflexible refusal to consider negotiation. The zenith of Hitler's successes was past; his armies were rushing toward their first obvious disaster. Should it not have been time for the Allies to prepare for a psychological counter-offensive, in close collaboration with the German *fronde*? Such an offensive should certainly have begun after the shock of Stalingrad—and begun with a more generous gesture than the formula of "unconditional surrender."

Let us return, however, to Halder's and Brauchitsch's fateful refusal to act against Hitler. For most of the world, though not for German "insiders," one of the greatest revelations of the Nuremberg Trials was that our generals' guilt was not what it had been thought to be. In place of the charge of having planned aggressive war, the charge had to be that they let themselves be forced into it step by step, first into their intoxicating triumphs and then into their shameful defeats.

Such was the case with their Viking expedition to Norway. As in all the military adventures up to the end of 1941, the generals and admirals expected an outright failure. The success of this coup depended on too many reckless calculations; it seemed impossible that all the factors would divide out evenly. For example, some of the slow, heavy whaling vessels in whose holds entire regiments could be concealed required two weeks to make the crossing. It could scarcely be assumed that the extensive ship movements in the ports would escape the attention of British air reconnaissance or of the secret service. The experts declared that the British fleet would certainly be on hand to intercept the German transports sailing for Bergen, Trondheim, and Narvik. Today, knowing as we do what actually happened, it is hard to re-envision the dismay of the generals at learning early in 1940 of Hitler's plan for the Norwegian invasion. By that time the generals were inclined to acknowledge that their Fuehrer was politically infallible, but they continued to make fun of him as a "corporal" and were highly unwilling to yield the field of military strategy to him.

Consequently, a failure of the Norwegian expedition would undeniably constitute the "setback" that Halder had talked of so often. On the other hand, its success would do for Hitler's military prestige what the bloodless conquest of Prague had done for his political renown. The fate of Holland and Belgium hung upon the outcome of this northern campaign—as indeed the whole question of whether the war was to be extended.

For the first time during the war, the question arose in our circle of friends of transmitting military information. During the Polish war we had not needed to worry about this matter. The campaign was transparent, and indeed there was nothing that could be done about it. Now the situation was fundamentally different. The end of tyranny was within reach if—yes, if the other side knew what was to happen and what was at stake.

Some of us laughed aloud at the suggestion that Hitler's preparations could possibly be unknown to the British. Others refused to accept, personally, the role of destiny. If the British muffed this unique chance, they simply could not be helped, these friends maintained. Still others pointed out that British intervention based on our information would cost the lives of thousands of German sailors and soldiers. A minority in our circle took precisely the opposite view. Did we have the right to consider only the German casualties deriving from such an invasion?

No agreement was reached. In any event the actual number

of persons who were in a position to transmit warnings to the British was extremely small; and some of these did resolve to obey the commands of conscience and "betray" their fatherland. At that historic hour, however, the Norwegians had their quislings; the British contented themselves with laying a few mines—after the Nazi transport fleet had passed the danger zone.

There are still some worrisome souls among the Germans who will not admit that such warnings were issued, because they want to prevent the creation of a new "stab-in-the-back" legend. The answer for such people is that the legend of 1918 was based on an historical lie; that these warnings by German oppositionists, on the other hand, are historical facts. In the long run truth cannot be suppressed, and in this case it also ought not to be. It is important and necessary to demonstrate that during Hitler's war there were Germans who endeavored to turn the evil tide of events.

In any case, every one of these warnings was in vain. In 1940 Hitler was able to exploit his victories to the full. No one can possibly claim that the war was lost for the Germans because of such vain warnings. On the other hand, for those who seek more adequate explanations than that afforded by branding sixty million people guilty, is it not significant that the usurper was able to fascinate the entire world with the succession of his triumphs? There was no power inside Germany—but none outside Germany either—that was able to stop him. Not only the Germans, but the rest of the world as well, were hypnotized by the wizard's baleful eye, and it took some time before the spell was broken.

After the Norwegian triumph, of course, there were no longer any generals who would have dared to mutiny. The *fronde* made desperate, utterly desperate, attempts to do something, for its members had a premonition of the fate that would inevitably befall Germany and Europe if Hitler were permitted to attack in the West; but it was no longer possible to make any moral appeal to the generals and their answer to military arguments was always the same: "It's working."

But would it really "work"? First the bridges over the Meuse and the Rhine, as well as Fort Ebenemael near Liége, would have to be taken by a coup. If the tanks and their supporting infantry columns did not cross the bridges at the very beginning, the break-through into the fields of Flanders would be blocked and Hitler's surprise tactics would fail. Practically, this meant that the success or failure of the offensive would be decided in the first twenty-four hours. Hitler had devoted all his thought and imagination throughout the winter to this *Blitz* and to the notorious secret weapons—the gliders that were to land on the top of Fort Ebenemael, the parachute troops that were to secure those strategically important bridges far behind the front, and the sabotage troops in Dutch uniforms which were supposed to operate at dawn on the day of the offensive and prevent the destruction of the bridges.

Once again the question arose as to whether we ought not to reveal these secret weapons. There were some among us who thought it no longer necessary, since a courier plane bound for Cologne from Munich and carrying essential deployment plans, including instructions for the parachute troops, had made a forced landing in Mechlin, Belgium; but the Belgians had assumed that the forced landing was a refined deception. As if they and the Dutch had not received enough information to prove that the danger was by no means over and that extreme alertness was imperative!

It was tremendously important at that time to convince Hitler or at least the generals of the tenuousness of their hopes that the key strategic positions would fall into their hands intact. Actually, they would believe in this only if the Dutch blew up their bridges before the invasion. Unquestionably that was an expensive undertaking. Nevertheless, it did not seem too high a price for them to pay if thereby the Dutch prevented an invasion of their country. If that had been done, the *Blitz* would have been started somewhere else, presumably directly against the Maginot Line—for the plans called for an offensive through Holland only if those bridges could be taken. Such a shift would have involved extensive dislocation of troop deployments and a complete revision of the timetable, and it certainly seemed more than doubtful that the hesitant generals would then have gone ahead. A thrust against the unprotected flank followed by the alluring war of movement was one thing; the prospect of long battles of attrition such as had been fought during the First World War was quite another.

All the Opposition's messages to the Dutch to forestall Hitler fell on deaf ears. Never fear, they would be on the alert; that was the reply we received. They needed only to press a button in order to blow up a bridge. Moreover, they were fully aware of the recent theft of Dutch police uniforms—the matter had even been mentioned in the newspapers; and none of the many travelers who were passing constantly back and forth between Germany and Holland could have failed to notice that whole armies were on the move along the Rhine. Seldom had the German Opposition received such self-assured and reassuring statements as during those last few week before the storm broke.

At that time conscientious oppositionists took great risks in order to convey warnings to the threatened neutrals. I shall mention but one case, one that created a great stir inside the Abwehr. At a certain neutral town the Belgian Embassy was receiving constant warnings of the impending invasion. With astonishing naïveté, the Belgian ambassador telegraphed a long report to his government, the greater part of which consisted of his arguments for discounting these warnings. His information, he said, came from a high German military source, for which reason it was probably intended as a deceptive maneuver, for otherwise the informer must be a—traitor.

This telegram, like so many others, was decoded. There was a great scandal. The Abwehr set feverishly to work—trying to cover up. I did my best to get in on the investigation, so that I could guide it into proper channels. Some day, perhaps, I shall write a special account of all the indiscretions—each one endangering someone's life—which were uncovered in the course of this investigation. It seemed that certain statesmen and certain countries simply did not want to be helped.

On the evening of May 9 a last urgent warning was issued. For the duration of the war the infuriated Hitler was to keep after the Abwehr and the Gestapo with demands that they find out who the "traitor" or "traitors" had been.

The events were afterward reconstructed in minute detail. It appeared that an hour after the final order was issued, the Dutch military attaché at the embassy in Berlin, Lieutenant-Colonel Sas, had word that the invasion was to start at four in the morning. Evidently he passed his information on to the Dutch army leadership, for two hours later—over the regular telephone lines!—he received a call from the Dutch secret service chief in The Hague. The chief simply could not believe that Mrs. Sas would actually have to go to the hospital and that the "dental operation" was really going to be performed at four in the morning. He asked whether Sas had "consulted several doctors."

According to the sober stenographic record of the telephone-tapping department, the military attaché had brusquely replied that it was so, that all the doctors were agreed, and that the operation would undoubtedly take place early that morning, but that he could not understand how they could have the bad taste to trouble him over the telephone at such a moment as this.

Six hours later, Hitler's panzer armies rolled across the intact Dutch bridges, and the surprise assault upon Fort Eben-emael also went through without a hitch. The rest followed inevitably.

On June 14, Paris fell. Can we remember our feelings? The very thought was inconceivable. At first the Germans respond-ed timidly and with a touch of embarrassment to the news of the victory. They, too, could not really believe that Paris had been taken; or rather, they hardly dared admit—what was already inevitable—that now Hitler could no longer be stopped; that now there was no one to block the onrush of the Revolution; that now there were no longer any limits.

I shall never forget those days after the fall of Paris. There was no sign of rejoicing, no trace of jubilation. One would have thought that they, the totalitarians rather than the democrats, had received terrible hammer-blows. The propaganda ministry had to put forth great effort to shake out of their mental paral-ysis these *Herrenmenschen* who were overwhelmed by their own victory. But then, as if only this prompting had been needed, as if overnight invisible defenses had been torn down, the choked tumult of victory suddenly poured out over Germany with tremendous vehemence. Madly intoxicated, these chil-dren of fortune pounced upon their new treasures; they divid-ed up the goods and the lands of Europe. The doubters were put in stocks; the triumphant dictator was canonized; the Rev-olution went mad.

A few weeks later, Hitler held a session of his Reichstag. In the hall all the Nazi Party dignitaries crowded together. The jubilant wave of brown surged up to the platforms where, gray row upon gray row, each gray uniform splashed with the red of the coat-flap, the victorious generals sat and received decorations and honors from their "greatest general of all time." New generals of the army, new colonel-generals, twelve field marshals and a Reichmarshal—Goering's title, newly invented for the occasion. Twelve field marshals! It was enough to take one's breath away. Afterward the people tried to console themselves with a joke: "They're cheaper by the dozen."

What were they to console themselves for? Clearly, for the conclusion of a campaign which, as everyone felt, was only a beginning. For a victory would not be succeeded by peace, but by incessant new campaigns.

On the rare occasions thereafter that the field marshals were to be seen, they seemed to be clinging desperately to their marshal's staffs; for they themselves knew best what the people did not suspect: that they were no more than the chief technicians for a usurper intoxicated with his own power, for a tyrant who was ruthlessly killing *off* the flower of his own people in order to satisfy his insatiate zest for destruction.

Wasted Years

I AM FORCED TO SUMMARIZE briefly the interval between the offensive in the West and the dramatic events of July 20, 1944—not because there is too little, but because there is too much to say. The full story of the ebb and flow of events during that dramatic time, and especially the tale of the many missed opportunities, cannot be told until the other side has also revealed its secrets.

The fall of 1940 brought about a significant change for me personally. In the autumn of 1938, my furlough to private industry was rescinded. After considerable trouble I succeeded in obtaining a transfer to the Potsdam administration. Thus I remained within arm's reach of my friends in Berlin. It soon turned out that this was not enough. The obvious thing to do, it seemed, was to find a place for me in the Abwehr, but for this a clean bill of health from the Gestapo was necessary, and I could scarcely expect that. Without more ado, Oster filled out a printed induction form in my name, calling me up to service in the Abwehr. Naturally, this forged document did not offer a permanent solution, but we were counting on the régime's being overthrown within the next few months, and there was no other way to have me on the spot in Berlin. There was a considerable risk involved for me under the stringent military laws, and Canaris and Oster tried to lessen this risk by sending me off to Switzerland during quiet periods. This could be done without attracting attention, since the Abwehr had authority to issue its own passports which did not have to be checked by the Gestapo.

With the fall of Paris, our oppositionist hopes were smashed. We now had to reckon on a much longer term of Nazi rule. Moreover, we now more than ever needed some kind of base abroad. Canaris, therefore, took advantage of the fact that the victorious Wehrmacht was at this time riding high. He appointed me to fill a post in the consulate-general at Zurich which was at the disposal of his counter-intelligence service. It was only some time later that the Gestapo found out what had happened, and then, for "diplomatic" reasons, it was more difficult to have me recalled than it would have been had I been employed in the Wehrmacht headquarters.

This solution by no means legalized my position inside the Abwehr. I had refused to take any constructive part in the internal work of the Abwehr, but it was so organized that neither the admiral nor his chief of staff was empowered to make special assignments. Only the section heads of counter-espionage or information could cover up such an off-color affair. Thus it constantly cost us a tremendous amount of trouble to find new and urgent missions for me, investigations and approaches to persons of importance, and each of these missions had to be patently so delicate and complicated that my information could not be committed to paper, but had to be reported to the admiral or to Oster in person. Only by such pretense could my frequent trips back and forth between Berlin and Zurich be justified.

Even then the difficulties remained. The previous Abwehr chief in Berne had to be deposed and a new and more tolerant officer located who would already find me there busy with my special assignment. Unfortunately, the gallant colonel asked all sorts of indiscreet questions and finally requested my recall. Whereupon he was promptly relieved of his post. Since he was demanding not only my head, but that of his military superiors, Canaris and Oster, his own was just as much imperiled under military law unless he really could provide proof of treason. With these considerations urged upon him, he agreed to a decent compromise. It was not long before the colonel began to doubt his own reason and was relieved when he was summarily dismissed from the Abwehr and sent off to a psychiatric retreat.

We had even more trouble with his successor. This officer started out in a somewhat more promising manner than his predecessor; after half a year he began to spy upon me, and in another half-year he had prepared a very annoying—and more-over erroneous—indictment of high treason against me; but by this time it was the spring of 1943, when Oster's fall and the subsequent dismissal of Canaris in any case put an end to this ambiguous situation.

Severe Setbacks

THE YEAR 1943 was a year of disasters for the Opposition. Everything failed—first the projects for a *Putsch* and then several attempts at assassination. For there was more than one. That dauntless Lieutenant-Colonel Schrader and General Stieff, who joined the *fronde* toward the end of 1943, also made attempts. On one occasion Hitler called off a meeting; on another the explosives went off by spontaneous combustion. This latter incident produced a piquant situation. As Abwehr chief at the Fuehrer's headquarters, Schrader himself conducted the investigation of the explosion, and it cost him a great deal of trouble to lead it into false channels and finally drop it.

Toward the end of the year, Mierendorff was killed in an enemy air attack. With him was lost the strongest and most ardent personality among the Social Democrats. A few weeks later Count von Moltke was struck: the Gestapo arrested him early in 1944. Thus the Kreissau circle lost its leader. What that meant we were to learn during the days before July 20. Moltke's balance and moderation undoubtedly had prevented many careless and improvised actions.

The worst blow, however, was the destruction of the Oster circle, which took place in April 1943. As early as the winter of 1942 we had heard from Nebe that the Gestapo was preparing to strike; but Himmler still did not dare. An attack on the Abwehr would stir up too much dust.

Brigade Leader Schellenberg, however, was urging action. As chief of the political intelligence service he had kept an especially suspicious eye on the bustle surrounding Oster. In addition, Schellenberg was impelled by pure rivalry. For a long time he had aimed at becoming head of a unified political and military intelligence service, and unfortunately he was the cleverest of the department heads in the *Reichssicherheitshauptamt.** He saw through the camouflage of exclusively "military" intelligence work with which Oster's "special deputies" in Sweden,

---

* Through this "main security office" Himmler controlled the entire police forces of the Reich. The criminal police, which Nebe headed, was subordinate to the *Reichssicherheitshauptamt*. Helldorf's police forces, the uniformed *Ordnungs-polizei*, were directly subordinate to the ministry of the interior, which at this time was also headed by Himmler. *(The translators.)*

Spain, Switzerland, or the Vatican disguised their "seditious" conversations. Indeed, Schellenberg saw more closely than the Gestapists, whom we succeeded in persistently deceiving up to July 20, 1944.

It was very nerve-racking to hear Nebe's accounts of the pertinacity of this evil genius, and, as if everything were conspiring against us, Schellenberg secured a first-rate "pretext." A Bavarian industrialist, a member of the Abwehr in Munich, had wormed his way into the confidence of Doctor von Dohnanyi and had offered his services in political work. In a mutual exchange of opinions the industrialist had learned more than necessary. Arrested for smuggling foreign exchange, he had tried to use his knowledge to extort protection from Canaris. When Canaris indignantly refused, the man had testified to what he knew. Thus, the Gestapo, among other things, found out about Joseph Mueller's and Dietrich Bonhoeffer's negotiations. The report sounded so sensational that at first the Gestapo chiefs, Kaltenbrunner [Himmler's chief of security] and Mueller—Gestapo Mueller, as he was called—refused to believe it.

Naturally the gentlemen of the Prinz Albrechtstrasse knew very well that "something was wrong" with Oster, but even they could not imagine so much high treason all at once. At any rate, they deemed it too dangerous to call a spade a spade, for it was quite clear that in such a situation Canaris would have to defend himself by every conceivable means. If the denunciation were only half true, the Canaris-Oster group could only end on the gallows. Himmler, with his typical cowardice, therefore circled his victim for months. Telephone tapping, opening of letters, shadowing, were continuous, but we were now on our guard: the Black gangsters could not get the "final" proofs.

The agents of the *Sicherheitshauptamt* were very well aware that they would learn nothing by surprise raids on dwellings or by initial interrogations, and even in this relatively late year of 1943 they would not have been able to put over a coup that would last for longer than twenty-four hours. Then the machinery of military justice would have intervened, for the military alone could conduct investigations of the Abwehr. The SS would be robbed of its prey. With Sack running the investigation, he would have insured that there would have been a great to-do that came to nothing, and in such tempestuous times actions that misfired tended to boomerang against their initiators Himmler did not want to run that risk. Therefore, the SS leaders conferred for months before they at last found the proper "twist."

They uncovered a vast and scandalous story of fraud. Jews in danger had been aided by being smuggled into Switzerland as Abwehr "agents." In addition, considerable sums in foreign exchange had been paid out to them to compensate them for the loss of their German property. The technical basis for this had not been too far-fetched; "agents" could not, after all, be sent across the border without funds. The difficulty was that the Gestapo had not for a moment believed this tall tale, although Canaris personally argued the matter out with Kaltenbrunner. Of the fourteen Jews who had by this means escaped death, no more than two or three could possibly be considered to have the qualifications of espionage agents. So far as the others were concerned, the charitable motive was all too unmistakable. With their characteristic bravado, the Gestapists now asserted that these "agents" had been employed by the Abwehr in smuggling foreign exchange for the personal profit of members, and unfortunately they uncovered a number of personal missteps by a leading member of the Abwehr—who had no connection at all with the Oster circle or with the rescue of the Jews. With their usual adeptness at coloring the truth, however, the Gestapists stirred the two "cases" together into such an impenetrable mixture that any unsuspecting observer would have to agree that these wholly "unpolitical" and purely "criminal" charges must certainly be investigated by the appropriate authorities. At any rate, no uninitiated person would be inclined to stop such proceedings once they had been instituted.

People who are conducting a risky underground conspiracy can afford to become involved in rescue work only to a very limited extent, no matter how well camouflaged such work may be. Naturally there had been no trace of fraud in this matter. Every imaginable safeguard had been taken to make sure that the funds for the agents were deposited with some neutral institution, but fraud was not the issue. Even before the investigation began, the Gestapo knew what the outcome would be, as they cynically admitted a few days afterward. Unfortunately, they attained their end completely. They now had a safe and simple pretext for making initial arrests. Then, in the course of the interrogations—quite by chance, of course—they would shift from the criminal to the political problem.

The plan was diabolically clever, but it was still necessary to obtain the consent of Hitler and Keitel to the initiation of an indictment. Calculating cleverly, the men in black hid behind Goering. They knew that Goering wanted revenge for the discovery of the "Red conspiracy" in the air ministry. What was more obvious than to discover the existence of a "Christian conspiracy" in the OKW? They would prove collaboration with the Vatican and Geneva! Goering persuaded Hitler to appoint for the investigation of the Abwehr that tried-and-true grand inquisitor who had just handed down his ninety-fifth death sentence as "Special Commissioner with the Reich Military Tribunal." This man, Chief Provost Officer Roeder, a thoroughly vicious scoundrel, requested the Gestapo to assign a number of agents to him. Thus "legal" military proceedings were instituted. There was no connection with "politics," no connection with the Gestapo.

On April 5 the long-awaited blow was struck. One of the first to be arrested was Doctor von Dohnanyi. As bad luck would have it, there was an incident when he was arrested. When Roeder, accompanied by Canaris, appeared in Oster's office and requested his presence at the arrest of his subordinate, Oster refused to let them pass into Dohnanyi's room, which adjoined his. If Roeder wanted to arrest someone, he said, then let him arrest him, not his subordinate, for whose official activities he took the full responsibility. Humanly speaking, this was beautifully courageous; politically, it was unwise and, moreover, quite impossible, since the order for arrest referred, not to official activities, but allegedly to Dohnanyi's private affairs. Oster had to yield. All that remained of his gesture was an atmosphere of extreme irritation, which was discharged in the scene that followed.

The day before, Canaris had warned Dohnanyi and had made sure that his private safe was "in order." The admiral could, therefore, not be reproached for admitting Roeder to Dohnanyi's office without announcing him. Nevertheless, Dohnanyi was apparently caught by surprise. While Roeder was searching the safe, Dohnanyi excitedly whispered several times to Oster, who was standing by his desk: "Those papers, those papers!" Oster went through moments of mental torment. Should he ignore these pleas, or play the part of a correct superior and order his collaborator to be quiet? Or should he not try his best to take possession of the papers which lay on the desk? Dohnanyi would never have made so rash a suggestion unless the papers in question were matters of life and death. Oster chose the second course—and the Gestapo official who was assisting Roeder observed him.

A few hours later Oster was relieved of his post, and because of the bit of byplay that had accompanied their discovery, the "important papers" acquired even greater importance. One of them was a letter from Dietrich Bonhoeffer asking for the release of seven "indispensable" Protestant pastors from military service. Even before the "political" side of the investigation had begun, the Gestapo had in its hands the first evidence for the Christian conspiracy. One of the leading members of the *Bekenntnisskirche*,* Dietrich Bonhoeffer, whom the Gestapo had forbidden to speak or travel, was revealed as an agent of the Abwehr in Rome, Geneva, and Sweden. In addition, Oster was virtually convicted of releasing clergymen from military service under false pretenses. According to the latest "legal" practice, the punishment for such manipulation of the draft machinery was death.

There is not space to go into the details of what followed; I must restrict my account to the tragic circumstances of Oster's fall, for it is both significant and grotesque that the Gestapo needed this "pretext" in order to overthrow its most dangerous adversary.

As I look back on my experiences in the Third Reich, those two days when I was interrogated by Roeder, under constant threats of arrest, still seem to me the most exciting. It was with great hesitation that I obeyed his summons to testify, but my remaining away would have badly incriminated Oster. My feeling about the situation did not betray me. All was not yet lost. For a full day I listened, a doubting Thomas, to the questions and recriminations that Roeder put to me with the spiteful smile of one who knew more than he cared to say. On the afternoon of the second day, when I was called upon to take the

---

* An organization of ministers who upheld freedom of worship and maintained that religious allegiances took precedence over national allegiance. Literally, "Confessional Church." *(The translators.)*

oath, I suddenly refused to testify. To the utter amazement of Roeder, I asserted that Field Marshal Keitel had just forbidden me to testify on such "political" matters which concerned only "internal conditions in the service." The interrogation had to be broken off for an hour while they checked up on this assertion of mine, and that was the last I ever saw of Roeder.

I made good use of that hour by hurrying off to Chief Magistrate Sack. I shall never forget his invaluable help; he intervened at once and secured a twenty-four-hour postponement of the warrant for my arrest. In great haste I dictated a detailed complaint in which I demonstrated that the questions Roeder had put to me were directed against neither Dohnanyi, Oster, nor Canaris, but in reality against Field Marshal Keitel in his capacity as supreme chief of the Abwehr. I will not attempt to decide whether this argument was quite cogent. In any event it produced the effect I intended upon the chief of the OKW. Keitel intervened in his capacity as titular head of the Reich military tribunal. A few days later Roeder was promoted. He could not have gone higher or farther; he flew, quite literally, to Salonika as chief provost marshal of an air fleet. A new examining magistrate was appointed and the proceedings dragged on for more than a year.

However, I did not wait for this outcome. By taking a very devious route and by crossing the frontier at a small border station, I made my way back to Switzerland. I received a number of official or friendly invitations to return to Germany. When I did not respond to those overtures, I was asked to come to France. The chief of the Berne Abwehr had made an additional charge of high treason against me.

When Canaris heard of this, he tried for the last time to use his influence. In spite of my vigorous attempt to dissuade him from getting involved in a lost cause, he came to Berne. When I proved to him that Bureau F of the Abwehr had sent its spies into my apartment he immediately recalled the agent who was behind all this; but contradictory, as he always was, he demanded that I do something for him in return; he wanted me finally to renounce all activity.

My whole temperament and all my political views made it impossible for me to agree with the reasoning he outlined in our last conversation; and yet today, when I reflect on the disaster that befell Germany and Europe, I cannot refrain from thinking that a wise man correctly interpreted to me the signs of those chaotic times.

The New Dynamism

A FEW WEEKS LATER Canaris had been removed and the Abwehr broken up. The greater part of the organization, in particular the counter-espionage section, was incorporated into the Gestapo. Only the strictly military intelligence service retained a degree of independence—within the framework of Kaltenbrunner's *Sicherheitshauptamt*—until July 20, 1944.

Earlier precautions now bore fruit, for Colonel Hansen became head of this remnant of the Abwehr. Hansen used this rump Abwehr to steer a large number of friends through the perils of the Underground. During this period Doctor Struenck became, more and more, Hansen's political adviser. He repeatedly sent Struenck to Switzerland, so that even I was not completely cut off. At that time there were fresh sensations in the foreign press every few months when one diplomat or another deserted the Nazis. Hitler and Ribbentrop had no liking for this sort of thing, and Himmler, too, believed that unnecessary publicity should be avoided. For almost a year Hansen succeeded in convincing his new superiors that he was making the most strenuous efforts to get me back to Germany without a scandal.

Hansen went a step farther. In order to restore permanent contact with the Berlin *fronde,* he installed Eduard Waetjen as consul in the Zurich consulate-general. Waetjen, a confirmed antagonist of the Nazi system, had been in close touch with the Abwehr circle for years as well as with Count von Moltke and his friends. He had relatives in America and had often traveled to that country, so that we placed great hopes in his appointment. July 20, 1944, put an end to his "consular" activities, but in that short time we succeeded, after carefully conferring with Beck and Goerdeler, in transmitting a vitally important message to the Americans through Waetjen.

In March 1944, Beck concluded that we must once more determine whether there existed any possibility of an understanding between the Opposition and the Western Powers. In the meanwhile Germany's military situation had deteriorated to such an extent that there could no longer be the slightest doubt of an impending Allied military victory. It would certainly be ridiculous for any Germans again to speak of an army "unbeaten in the field." It therefore seemed all the more senseless for the war to be prolonged to the point of total destruction. Many of the leading generals began to realize that they must at last break with Hitler and his system. But the military disaster had not yet reached such proportions that they could decide to surrender unconditionally. Had not the time come now to pave the way psychologically for a cessation of the war by persuading the Allies to drop the rigid Casablanca formula, or at least to moderate it somewhat by a generous interpretation? Beck desired clarity: Did the Allies still want a constructive solution of the chaos in Germany—that is to say, a dissolution of the Nazi system by co-operation with the German *fronde?* Or were they themselves by now no longer able to relax the imperatives imposed by their alliances and by ideological and strategical considerations?

The best way to direct these questions to the political chiefs in the opposing camp appeared to be through Allen W. Dulles, who worked at the American embassy in Berne. Toward the end of 1942, Dulles had come to Switzerland as head of the Office of Strategic Services (OSS), and since then he had made his impress not only upon the American intelligence service, but upon all the other Allied intelligence services in Europe. In spite of our many efforts, it had hitherto proved impossible to maintain permanent political contact with the enemy. There had been only occasional meetings because the Allies restricted themselves largely to pure espionage. Naturally no serious conversations could be conducted on such a basis. The British above all stuck to the old-fashioned scheme in which the "enemy" was considered solely as an object of espionage. It was saddening to observe how this point of view hindered them from drawing any political advantage from the existence of a German Underground.

Dulles was the first intelligence officer who had the courage to extend his activities to the political aspects of the war. With his keen mind and his broad knowledge of European problems, with which he had been familiar since the First World War and the peace negotiations in Versailles, Dulles concluded that it was time to think intensively about the political end of the bloody struggle. Therefore, he tried to establish contact with all the Resistance groups in Europe. His bureau on the Herrengasse in Berne grew in time into a virtual center of the European Resistance. Not only Germans, but Austrians, Hungarians, Italians, Rumanians, and Finns, not to mention the citizens of occupied countries, met there. Everyone breathed easier; at last a man had been found with whom it was possible to discuss the contradictory complex of problems emerging from Hitler's war.

Dulles was assisted by Gero von Gaevernitz. A German-

American who had been living in Switzerland since the outbreak of the war and who was amazingly well informed on
German conditions, von Gaevernitz worked indefatigably to
make important contacts. This was not always the easiest thing
in the world; it required a great deal of understanding; even
more perseverance; and most of all—discretion. With the end
of the war approaching, everyone wanted to be in touch with
him. To make the proper choices, to shake off burdensome
curiosity-seekers, to outwit the Nazi spies who found this spot
a rich new hunting-ground, and at the same time to pursue
ardently all foci of opposition to the Nazis—these difficult
tasks must have given Gaevernitz and his chief quite an exciting time.

The Dulles bureau was particularly troubled by the flourishing guild of professional spies, the traders in espionage
materials, who would visit the agents of the Abwehr or the SD
in the morning, the secret service in the afternoon, and the
Dulles office on the Herrengasse in the evening, offering to
each their carefully prepared and sensational reports. The mysterious Dulles not only kept the German counter-espionage
agents busy; he proved a difficult customer for these professional spies because he was so tactless as to check up on their
information. A good many humorous memoirs could be written about the manner in which Dulles, by his character and his
multifarious activities, "Americanized" the peaceful idyll of the
secret services in Switzerland.

To a large extent Anglo-American policy was governed by the
fear that any unilateral conversations with the German Opposition might ultimately lead, through maladroitness, indiscretion, or deliberate intent, to an agreement between the Nazis
and the Bolshevists. From our conversations with Dulles,
Waetjen and I were more aware of this than were our friends

in Berlin. Consequently, we decided to lay our cards on the table.

We informed the Allied representative that the German *fronde* was now going to attempt assassination, and we gave him details about the generals and civilians who were ready to strike at the Nazis. We also discussed earnestly the demand, raised by so many Allied statesmen, that this time all Germany must be occupied by the Allied Powers. Whether or not this demand was politically correct, one thing seemed quite clear to us: if the invasion did not lead definitely to the military defeat of Germany by September 1944, the war would be protracted until the spring of 1945 and a wholly new situation would be created. We did not, of course, know when the invasion would take place, or even whether there was to be one at all, but we felt that whatever psychological value a conquest of Berlin in open battle would have, it could never outweigh the inevitable increasing devastation in Germany—and Europe!—which would follow from prolongation of the war.

This last peace feeler of ours had been authorized by Beck, and unquestionably Dulles transmitted it to his superiors and laid the proper stress upon it. Unfortunately, we received no positive reply. The terrible conflict had to run its course.

Goerdeler retained his hope that some political arrangement would be attainable after we had succeeded in overthrowing the Nazis. Beck held a more skeptical view; but he, too, though he recognized the necessity of asking for an armistice as soon as possible, never planned his first act as chief of state in the new German régime to be the sending of an emissary to Eisenhower's headquarters in order to negotiate immediate surrender.

It is quite possible that some persons in the group of younger military leaders—though not Hansen and not Stauffenberg, who looked toward a reconciliation with Russia—

might have harbored their own plans behind the backs of the political leaders of the *fronde*. This is quite likely in view of the general political confusion which was the chief characteristic of the preparations for the July *Putsch*.

These political problems bring me directly to the most important development of the year 1943. The fall of Oster and the destruction of his network was an event of far-reaching consequence for the entire Opposition. As always happened after such rude blows by the Gestapo, the psychological shock produced paralysis. A kind of conspiratorial vacuum was created until, toward the fall of the year, the gap was filled—and a new dynamism came into being.

Colonel in the General Staff Count Klaus von Stauffenberg, who now came so powerfully and commandingly to the fore and established a new cell of resistance in the OKW, was very different indeed from Oster. In the account of the events of July 20 there will be ample occasion to elaborate on the nature of this man and on his place in the history of the National Socialist Revolution. Here I shall speak less of him personally than of what I have called the new dynamism.

Up to this time the military men had made no claim to leadership inside the *fronde*. In his oppositional activity Beck felt and behaved as a civilian. Oster had renounced all political ambitions. Canaris refused to play any part in the activistic conspiracy. Thomas had withdrawn in disillusionment in 1942. Witzleben deliberately kept out of all non-military affairs. The recent convert, General Henning von Tresckow, submitted to Goerdeler's political leadership. Such purely military men as Otto von Stuelpnagel and Friedrich Olbricht were entirely colorless politically. In short, the oppositional officers had confined themselves to the technical functions which were naturally theirs—and indeed these functions were highly responsible and important. But Stauffenberg introduced a basic change into this situation. He and his "officers against Hitler" suddenly began to claim, if not the right to political leadership, at least the prerogative of sharing in the political decisions. A man of intractable will, contradictory in many things, Stauffenberg was clear and purposeful in one respect: he did not want Hitler to drag the fatally imperiled army down with him in his own destruction. A soldier to the core, the salvation of his fatherland was equivalent in Stauffenberg's mind to the salvation of the Wehrmacht.

Some authors have attempted to show that Stauffenberg went over to the Opposition primarily out of Christian motives. Unquestionably he was a deeply religious Christian, but these Christian elements in his make-up were not what motivated him to commit assassination; if that had been so, he would not have needed to wait until July 1944. Rather we might point out it was the religious qualms which inclined him to waver; up to the last moment he doubted whether he ought to commit assassination. Nor, as others have held, was Stauffenberg as a South German revolting against the domination of the Prussian type. The National Socialist leaders, and Hitler in particular, have abundantly proved that the South Germans who adopted Prussianism usually developed into super-Prussians. Stauffenberg was above all a passionate soldier who saw everything from the standpoint of his profession, and for this reason it took the military disaster to shock him into the Opposition.

In this he was by no means alone. He was representative of the military leaders of the Opposition of July 20. It is not at all by chance that a tightly knit group of officers, all firmly resolved to direct events, first coalesced in 1942, and grew in number and determination with each successive defeat. Generals von Tresckow, Olbricht, and Fellgiebel began it; in 1943 they were joined by Count Stauffenberg and Colonel Merz von Quirnheim; toward the end of that year by General Stieff and still later by Quartermaster-General Eduard Wagner and General Lindemann; finally Kluge and Colonel-General Hoeppner fell in line; and last of all came Field Marshal Rommel. These generals, either because of their strength of numbers, their key positions for a revolt, or because of the recognition that the fate of their class was at stake, began to feel an increasing sense of unity. It was they who on July 20, 1944, set the tone of the conspiracy and of its technical execution. Men like Beck, Witzleben, and Oster were crowded out more and more, when they were not actually lied to.

In addition to this structural change within the Opposition, there began, from the middle of 1943 on, another development that might even be considered more important. The powerful influence of military—and militaristic!—men probably could have been held within bounds after a successful *Putsch* by a united civilian oppositionist group. But the chance for such inter-civilian unity was destroyed when, under the impression produced by the Russian victories and the Anglo-American air bombings, significant sections of the military and civilian Opposition formed an ideological and political merger.

From 1943 on, there arose out of the chaos within Germany a kind of militant socialism which attempted to tame the National Socialist torrent and divert it into a new bed, once more in accord with the temper of the times. Could there any longer be an understanding with the West, this socialistic group demanded? The West refused to take cognizance of the Opposition; with its bombings it seemed to be trying to bring all Germans together in collective anguish. Was not a new agreement with the East the only possible recourse? A significant group of the "younger" men, whose politics ran diagonal-

ly from Left to Right, so that they can really be classed neither
as Left nor Right but rather as adherents of a peculiar new line,
theorized about the potentialities implicit in the wave of fraternization between the foreign forced laborers and the German
working masses. As it happened, no such wave of fraternization
between the foreign forced laborers and the working masses had
occurred.

As early as January 1943, Trott zu Solz, when visiting
Geneva, had made a statement to the effect that this social-
revolutionary turn toward the East on the part of the Opposition had already been completed. His remarks were intended
for the ears of the British. For my part, I always feared that
such commentary would simply intensify the determination of
the Allies to let this German crater burn itself out thoroughly.

There is no doubt, however, that Trott voiced what his
closest friends were thinking. The fiction of a social-revolu-
tionary fraternization between the German and the foreign
laboring masses lent a tremendous impetus to the already
thriving Stauffenberg circle. In April 1943, on the occasion of
Trott's last stay in Switzerland, I discussed these matters with
him. I was frankly shocked to find how radically this diplomat,
whose fundamental attitude had been a "Western" one, had
made his choice for the East—or rather, had completed psychologically his rejection of the West. For this deeply disillusioned man was no longer concerned with the desire for political equilibrium; he no longer felt any interest in what in normal times is called political rationality. Carried along by a new
and surging tide, he let himself be driven by a new, or, if you
will, the old revolutionary dynamism.

Throughout the history of the Nazi Revolution, Moscow
always exercised a remarkable subterranean influence. In 1932,
when the Communists by their tactics helped the Nazis to take
power; in 1939, when the Moscow Pact finally freed Hitler for

his war—in every case the decisive impetus, the solution, the salvation, came from the East. What in 1944 could have led the "dynamic" Opposition to believe that a pact with Bolshevism would lead to a result other than that the totalitarian Revolution—without Hitler, perhaps, but with General von Seydlitz's Moscow League of Officers—would take another gigantic leap forward and into the abyss?

It is only against this political background that two facts are comprehensible. After the unsuccessful ventures at the end of December 1943, Stauffenberg withdrew from all action for months. It is hardly credible that this long period presented no opportunity for an assassination. Convinced that the front in the East would remain stable, Stauffenberg and his circle wanted "to give Hitler a last chance." What they meant by that was the repulse of the Allied invasion of France, for until the summer they had all firmly believed that the invasion would either fail or come to a halt near the coast. Naturally it was not that they wanted Hitler to have this success to his credit. If the "plutocrats" were dealt a bloody defeat there, the chances for an agreement with Russia would be heightened.

Logically enough, the immediate circle around Stauffenberg sought an alliance with the extreme Left, the Communists. The initiator of these proposals was Administrative President Count Fritz von der Schulenberg. The son of a well-known general of the First World War, Schulenberg had toyed with Communistic ideas when he was a Korps student at Goettingen. From intellectual socialism he had later moved over to National Socialism. In the Opposition once more from 1938 on, it was he who converted Stauffenberg and who remained closest to him to the last. Schulenberg was unquestionably the most active officer in the circle and he vigorously opposed the candidacy of the "reactionary" Goerdeler for chancellor after the overthrow of Hitler. Instead of Goerdeler, Schulenberg nominated the former Social Democratic military expert in the Reichstag, Julius Leber.

From that time on, the Opposition was split wide open. For it was not a question of Goerdeler or Leber as individuals, but rather of two diametrically opposite political lines and ideological aims. This underground struggle for power characterized the first half of 1944, although the majority of the oppositionists knew scarcely anything about this conflict and continued to believe there was a unified leadership. Even Beck, Goerdeler, and Leuschner did not learn of the tragic consequences of this conspiracy within a conspiracy until it was too late. I shall cite the report of Emil Henk, the Social Democrat, about this incident:

> As so often, an unexpected event wrecked all the plans again. At the end of June members of the Kreissau circle had begun a series of conferences with the so-called CC (Central Committee of the Communist Party of Germany). . . .
>
> Beforehand, there had been lively disputes within the circle about this step.... For years the rule had been: "Collaboration with the Communists only after X day." ("X" day had always meant the day Hitler fell.) Reichwein and Leber urged that this rule now be abandoned, but no one else shared their view. Leuschner knew nothing of these events or designs. Had he known, he would have done everything in his power to prevent the meetings; afterward he protested bitterly about his having been kept in the dark. In any case, Leber and Reichwein went to the first conference with the leading Communists. . . .
>
> In the course of the discussion the Communists expressed the desire to be put in touch with the active military Opposition. Such a request was flabbergasting, for cross-contacts between groups were very rare in the underground and were only allowed after long acquaintance and the most careful check-ups on the

persons involved.... At a second conference, which Reichwein attended alone, all the participants were arrested. It turned out that one of the three men of the CC was a Gestapo spy!

This took place in the first week in July, 1944. A wave of arrests commenced and Leber too fell into the hands of the Gestapo.... Leber was well known to be a stalwart; he would preserve silence. But in this most important of hours, the secret was out and the Opposition could no longer afford to lose time. If they were to keep the initiative, the oppositionists would have to act before the agreed time. In addition, Stauffenberg knew both Leber and Reichwein very well and respected both men highly. He felt that the assassination would lose much validity unless these two men could be rescued. The most important members of the Opposition were therefore once more tremendously pressed for time, and thus compelled to improvise.

From then on, everything happened with a rush. Stauffenberg's justified fear that the Gestapo would soon uncover the entire conspiracy influenced all decisions. Nevertheless, it would be wrong to attribute the failure of July 20 to pressure of time or the necessity for improvisation. There was enough time for reflection and careful action. After all the previous preparations, two weeks should really have been sufficient. It was not time that was lacking, but inner clarity and resolution. It was the ideological and political conflict over the "true" meaning of the German Revolution, the question of whether it was to be carried on, "completed," or utterly swept away, that hampered the chief actors.

The dramatic course of the tragedy which was about to befall the Opposition was governed by ambivalent emotions and divided minds. Before the *Putsch* began, an inexorable text was writ large above that catastrophe: *too late*.

2

Too Late—
July 20, 1944

Prelude

I NEED MERELY GLANCE THROUGH my appointment calendar for the last weeks of June and the beginning of July 1944, to confirm once again the condition of nervous tension which was mine throughout that period. I traveled back and forth throughout Switzerland, stopping now in Berne, now in Geneva, now in Zurich, with a few scattered days in between for walking tours in the mountains. When would the thunder and lightning break? Would the generals let pass this very last chance to act?

The disaster on the Eastern Front could no longer be covered up. The Russians had ripped a great hole through the army group in the center, and their victorious armies were advancing without pause into this gap. Dozens of generals, cut off from their communications, were surrendering their troops virtually without a fight. It seemed evident that the military collapse was so drastic precisely because it was also a moral breakdown.

The situation in the West was no better. The [Allied] invasion was still in its first stages; the decisive break-through had not yet taken place. But the very fact of the success of the invasion could not be explained away. The Hitler-Rommel strategy had failed; the German army was unable to force the enemy into a wearing battle of position in Normandy. It was evident that the dikes would soon give, and then there would remain no more inane excuses for those vacillating generals who insisted that the *Putsch* must wait until the invasion was beaten back or at least contained so that, coupling it with the Bolshevist threat from the east, they would have a basis for negotiations with the Anglo-Americans.

July 9

I WAS VACATIONING in the mountains when I at last received a long-awaited telephone call. Struenck was back in Switzerland. It was exactly a month since I had sent him to Germany with my messages to Beck and Hansen. The fact that he returned at all was a good sign. If Hansen had taken my letter amiss, he would not have sent Struenck with an answer. The situation, of course, had deteriorated tremendously in the meantime. The message I had sent a month ago was even more timely now. I had written that an opportunity for negotiation with the Allies no longer existed and that there was no longer any sense in preliminary discussions; it was now time to act.

The urgency of Struenck's telephone call misled me into thinking that the critical moment had come at last. Instead, he barely took time to shake hands with me before he assailed me with warnings that I was in terrible danger and must go into hiding at once. A particularly embarrassing indiscretion had occurred and Schellenberg had made a great fuss about it. Nebe and Hansen had been questioned by Kaltenbrunner and by the Gestapo officer Mueller, whom we called Gestapo Mueller to distinguish him from our own Joseph Mueller. Then Himmler had ordered that I be brought back to Germany by hook or crook. Since they knew that I would not come voluntarily, they decided to call me to the colors so that I could

be defamed as an army deserter. Then they would try to kid-
nap me. Struenck reminded me of the cases of the two unfortunates in Madrid who had been dragged into the embassy and
shipped over the border inside a trunk, labeled as diplomatic
baggage.

Hansen's request that I should be suddenly taken ill
seemed to me quite reasonable. Hitherto he had skillfully covered up my refusal to return, but if I did not obey an induction
order, Colonel Hansen would undoubtedly be held responsible. We were prepared, and had a physician ready to certify
that I was undergoing an operation for appendicitis or that I
had just broken a leg.

"Aren't they ready yet?" I asked, cutting short this inter-
minable discussion of personal affairs. There were really more
important matters to talk about.

"Yes and no," Struenck replied precisely. "The assassination is supposed to take place any day now, but you know how
often we have been strung along with promises. Even Hansen
is doubtful that Stauffenberg will actually do it."

"Does he at least want to?" I asked.

"He is said to want to," Struenck replied in the same non-
committal manner. "But part of the Stauffenberg group has
religious scruples."

Struenck was weary and resigned. I could see that after so
many failures he did not want to encourage premature hopes
either in himself or in me. But since he had brought with him
concrete requests from Beck, Goerdeler, and Hansen, I quickly realized that the affair had progressed beyond the stage of
mere theorizing. Their doubts no longer revolved around the
question of the validity of assassination. What concerned them
now was the fear that someone might lose his nerve, or that it
would prove impossible to get at Hitler, or that the Gestapo
would strike at them a few minutes beforehand.

Waetjen, who joined us, shared my impression. He and I sat up late at night talking and assuring each other again and again that this time it really looked like business. Too bad I could not go to Berlin, but our comrades in Berlin had expressly forbidden that.

July 10

OVERNIGHT I DECIDED that it would be absolute madness for me to stay away from Berlin. For years I had hoped for the great event—and now that the assassination was about to come off, was I to watch it from afar in Zurich? Every fiber of my being revolted against this paltry safety. I made up my mind to go after all. Himmler was no longer counting on my coming to Germany voluntarily. Consequently, I should be able to manage the critical crossing of the frontier. In Berlin I could disappear at once.

Before I set out, there were a number of technical preparations that had to be completed quickly. I thought it wise to prepare myself for a rather lengthy stay this time, and for possible complications.

First I hurried off to the consulate-general. There my appearance aroused considerable surprise. The consul was even more surprised when I explained to him the purpose of my visit. But I assured him that in this case there was no need to fear Berlin's disapprobation. After all, I said, Himmler would certainly not object to my returning to Germany.

The consul saw the light; he gave me the visa.

Then I carried out a few errands, put my papers in order, and in the afternoon Waetjen and I took care of a number of technical problems that Hansen had committed to us. I left behind with Waetjen a lengthy memorandum for Dulles, which was to be given to him after my departure. I considered myself duty-bound to give Dulles a sketch of the European and

German situation to which my friends and I looked forward if the *Putsch* succeeded.

July 11

IN BERNE, Waetjen and Struenck rode to the embassy. Struenck was traveling as a courier; he too had to give Bureau F a specious explanation of the purposes of his journey, so that no one's suspicions would be aroused.

Meanwhile, I went to the federal building to call on the chief of the Swiss police department, Doctor Rothmund, who for months had handled with encouraging benevolence Struenck's requests for visitor visas. He was understanding and helpful this time, too, when I asked him to make out a return visa for me without going through the formality of inquiry at the German embassy.

Then I rejoined Struenck and Waetjen. Apparently Struenck's frequent reappearances in Switzerland at such short intervals had excited no suspicion at all.

It is hard to escape a mood of depression when one is setting out on an adventure whose end may be bad indeed. During the hour's ride between Berne and the border at Basle we could not manage to cheer up. It was as if we felt a need to suffer a little in advance before we took the short step from the peaceful idyll of Switzerland into the uncertainties of Naziland.

The passport formalities were completed without any trouble at all. Struenck, bearing his courier's visa, was treated with proper respect. Since I was in his company and was able to show a diplomatic passport, it did not occur to the officials to look into their list of wanted men. If they did not get the idea later on and telephone ahead of me, I should be able to sleep peacefully all the way to Berlin. From the platform I saw a German railroad train for the first time in a whole year. It was shocking to see how neglected the cars looked. They were covered with grime; there was not a trace of paint left; the windows were smashed.

Frau Struenck was waiting for us in Weil. I found her as lively as ever, although she was startled and frightened by my unexpected appearance on the train.

With the aid of a little coffee concentrate and a few of those wrapperless Swiss cigars, I convinced the conductor that he must arrange a sleeper compartment for me. Two sips of cherry brandy were enough to persuade him that he need not make me surrender my passport. Why give extra work to the Gestapo agents that accompanied every train? With a sigh of relief we shut ourselves up in Struenck's compartment and celebrated our reunion. High above us in the darkness the enemy bombers were probably hurtling along with their load of death and destruction.

In Karlsruhe I saw how much the sum of destruction had mounted during the past few months. Soon these twisted iron girders protruding out of ruins, these wrecked railroad stations and the vista of more ruin would become familiar sights again. But the first impression was tremendously powerful. It was necessary to return to Germany from afar to see how inexorably the whole land was progressing toward utter annihilation. Soon, I felt, Germany would be a single burnt-out crater, on the model of these thousands of smaller craters that lined the railroad track.

July 12

THE STRUENKS were going to be met in Berlin. I myself did not think it safe to arrive there by this train. Therefore, I left the train at Potsdam, rushed through the underground passage to the commuters' platform and had the good luck to catch a train that was just leaving.

At Wannsee I changed trains. The route passed through

the neighborhood where I had lived. Sorrowfully, I looked down the smashed street on which lay our bombed-out house. It was not until a full year later that I was to look about in that blackened hole in the ground. There, scattered, soaked by rain, partly torn, or in pieces, lay a few things that were really more valuable to me than all that the bombs and the pillagers had taken away: a few family photographs, the last mementoes of people and of times that will never come again.

In Zehlendorf, I got out and walked the few hundred yards to Count Helldorf's home. Once this street had been a splendid boulevard lined with mansions. Now ruins gaped on either side. It was with difficulty that I found the house, which had recently received a direct hit. The police chief was now living in a hotel in the city; a few servants were still using the concrete shelter of his former home. This was rather upsetting. My plan had been to ask Helldorf to put me up. The Gestapo certainly would not have been likely to look for me in the home of the Berlin chief of police.

None of the coin telephones were in working order. Through a patrolman I telephoned the Count over the official police wires. Foolishly, Helldorf did not recognize my voice, and since I did not want to give my name there was a good deal of fussing back and forth until he finally caught on to the identity of his caller. Then he said I ought to come to see him at once. When I asked in a roundabout manner whether his office was the most suitable place for us to meet, he replied, with that cheek that was always so charming in him, that at the moment I could be safe with him from unwelcome bombings.

He was not able to send a car for me. Not even the Berlin chief of police had that much gasoline at his disposal any more. I had to take the subway, which was just as well because it gave me the opportunity to gather some impression of Berlin and the Berlin populace. Because of the continual night attacks, all the people were overtired—they fell asleep standing up. Accustomed to the normal, rested look on faces in Switzerland, I saw what human havoc had been wrought upon these people. And yet the shift from total war to total destruction had just started.

Alexanderplatz was a ghastly scene of wreckage. But the bombs seemed often to have spared the strongholds of the tyrants. In the midst of this smoke-blackened and razed area rose the remains of the police headquarters; what was left of the building still sufficed to shelter the most important offices.

In Helldorf's anteroom I found familiar faces. These police officers who had grown old in the service were former patrolmen who had been transferred to office work when they were nearing the end of their period of service. They were fine men, honest, devoted to duty, very decent. How were they to defend themselves when, one morning, they were informed of an order by which they had been transferred into the SS? Or what could they do upon being suddenly ordered to serve in the "fighting police troops"? "Combating guerrillas" was the ostensible function of this force; in reality it was assigned to murder Jews or patriots. What course remained open to them? Could they desert to the Russians, who were not especially benevolent toward members of Himmler's SS? Could they openly refuse to obey orders, which in the most favorable case meant concentration camp? Could they attempt to vanish amid the internal confusion of Germany, which meant that they might be picked up by Himmler's henchmen at any time and that their families would suffer as hostages? In condemning the horrors wrought by Himmler's police we ought not to forget the fate of these unfortunate men who, as a consequence of pursuing a decent profession, had voluntarily been enmeshed by the Nazi machinery and were now being ground between the millstones of the Revolution.

Helldorf was not at all surprised to see me. Had I guessed, he asked, that the assassination planned for yesterday would be called off? At the last moment Goering and Himmler had not appeared, and Stauffenberg had been unwilling to take responsibility for the assassination unless there was a good chance of killing Goering and Himmler as well. This was the first I had heard that "the day" had been yesterday.

Then Helldorf gave me the details. Basically it was the old plan. After the assault, General Olbricht would call Helldorf to the OKW headquarters and declare the Berlin police subject to the orders of the Wehrmacht. Helldorf would then use this as a pretext for calling his police officers together and paralyzing the police apparatus for the next few critical hours. The regular police would resume their functions—under military supervision—only after the panzer troops had surrounded all the crucial buildings. Nebe was informed about the entire plan and had made the necessary preparations for handling the criminal police.

Helldorf reported all this to me in the most casual of tones, as if he were discussing the next air-raid drill. I noticed at once, however, that he seemed to be not sure of himself. His lackadaisical tone worried me. Sure enough, he finally got around to saying that I must not deceive myself; the old crew was no longer around and he didn't really have confidence in the young men.

I asked whom he meant.

"The whole clique," he replied.

"Olbricht? Beck?"

No, he trusted both those men fully. But he was never able to see them; Stauffenberg barred everyone. And although Stauffenberg's emissary, Schulenberg, kept assuring him that everything was prepared perfectly, Helldorf could not shake off his hunch that something was amiss.

Count Fritz von Schulenberg had for a long time been assistant police chief under Helldorf. Helldorf complained that Schulenberg always gave the same answers; it was impossible to find out anything from him. Now, he had the impression that Schulenberg was not so much concealing something from him as lacking the necessary clarity on all points. Up to the present moment not a single directive on police measures had been laid before him.

Helldorf said that he had not "been able to get in touch with Stauffenberg at all. Stauffenberg had behaved like a sphinx, and had not even admitted openly that he intended to set off the bomb. Helldorf felt that so much wariness was a bit insulting, especially in view of the role that had been assigned to him as Berlin police chief. I had better talk with Nebe, he suggested. Nebe was even more pessimistic than he and had repeatedly proposed withdrawing entirely from the whole affair.

Helldorf said all this without a trace of malice or excitability. Involuntarily I wondered whether he was already so dulled by the past that he could no longer summon up the inner strength to participate energetically. But perhaps his calm and impassive manner at this critical juncture was rather the product of his curious temperament, of that remarkable compound of reckless *Landsknecht* and nonchalant aristocrat that I had so often observed in him. Once things began to happen he would surely be on the spot.

Helldorf stretched his gasoline to take me to Struenck's in his car. From Alexanderplatz to Heerstrasse is a considerable distance. Now and then I asked him to make a detour down some of the worst-devastated streets. Had anyone told me that the bombs would be raining down on these ruins for eight months more, that the bombings would be followed by days of street-fighting, and that at the end of it all three million human beings would creep out of the rubble and try to pursue their usual occupations, I think I should have laughed at the grotesqueness of such a thought.

Helldorf told me some astonishing things about the persistence of normality. Almost as soon as the "all clear" was sounded, the clean-up squads set to work, and within a few hours the trains were running again. Long interruptions were rare. Mail was still delivered on the minute. As yet there had been no trouble about the distribution of food. In short, the gears were clashing, but the war machinery, both its technical and human aspects, continued to run.

I asked Helldorf about morale. He said that everyone was longing for the war to end; that no one would fight for the Nazis on the barricades; the general sense of weariness was overwhelming. Nevertheless, there were no signs of revolt. The terror of the bombings forged men together. In rescue work there was no time for men to ask one another who was for and who against the Nazis. In the general hopelessness people clung to the single fanatical will they could see, and unfortunately Goebbels was the personification of that will. It was disgusting to see it, Helldorf continued, but whenever that spiteful dwarf appeared, people still thronged to see him and felt beatified to receive an autograph or a handshake from him.

Helldorf was not trying to annoy me. He was firmly convinced that the *Putsch* was both essential and possible. He warned me, however, against the error of imagining that the masses would act on their own account. They would, he said, certainly never do anything at all without a signal from above. How often I had argued this point with German and foreign friends in the past years! The matter came up whenever they confided to me their "reliable information" about impending mass action—strikes or local uprisings. For the most part they insisted that I could not understand such matters because I was not sufficiently Left and had no contact with working-class circles.

One of the most remarkable phenomena of the war years, moreover, was the creation not only of a collective frenzy of jubilation, but a collective sense of misery as well. In calculating the inner strength of a government based on terror, one must take into account the tremendous efforts that frightened men will put forth, not out of enthusiasm, desire for victory, or blind submission, but quite simply out of hopelessness and despair.

The Struencks's new home was on a small side street in the West End. Schacht owned a villa there. When he was banished to the country, he had rented it out, keeping only two rooms in the cellar for storing his furniture. After the Struencks were bombed out, Schacht had placed these cellar rooms at their disposal. I had never known how comfortably a cellar could be arranged. It seemed to be sealed against the outside world, and concealed from it as well. These cellar walls were, at any rate, microphone-proof.

Hansen had sent word that he intended to come to see me toward evening. Nebe would not be free to see me until the next day.

After lunch I wanted to go to see Beck at once. Aside from other considerations, I wanted to shield myself against Hansen's taking my disobedience in bad part. After all, the Abwehr was a military organization. He was my chief, and he had expressly ordered me not to come to Berlin. I didn't want him to take it into his head to give me orders "officially." I thought I would block that possibility by meeting him from the first on the plane of rebellion; there we had a different scale of rank.

The ride out to Lichterfelde was time-consuming under the existing conditions. It was nearly four o'clock when I arrived at the Goethestrasse. All the houses around had been destroyed; Beck's little place alone had been spared by the bombs.

The doorbell, of course, did not work. I had to pound energetically on the door before the housekeeper came. She looked suspiciously at me and said that Beck was not at home. I told her to say that Herr Doctor Lange was calling, and followed her. This alias was not particularly ingenious, since my friends generally referred to me as "*der Lange*."* Nevertheless, I said it with so credible a ring that it was weeks before the Gestapo found out who Doctor Lange really was.

The general looked up in amazement from his desk. He was as glad to see me as I was to see him. "Well, at last!" he exclaimed. He said he had been expecting me for days. Stauffenberg had frequently assured him that I would be there in time.

Beck was having his Wednesday at home that day; it was the only opportunity he had to meet Popitz and Hassell without attracting attention. Nothing would be happening before Saturday, he told me; therefore, we arranged to meet again on the following afternoon, when he would have more time. For all his customary caution, Beck was optimistic this time, but he warned me that we must not expect too much afterward. In the East the situation was very bad; the center army group no longer existed. If they had the presence of mind, the Russians could advance far across the Vistula. In the West the front was being held for the time being, but Kluge had already sent word

* *Lange* means "tall," and is also a common name in German.

that there might be a break-through within a fortnight; in Rommel's opinion within at most three weeks. For the first time Kluge of his own accord was demanding action.

Beck asked me to get in touch with Stauffenberg as quickly as possible. Stauffenberg had helped him tremendously during the past few months, he said. He had borne the entire burden of practical preparations. After the elimination of Oster, his had been the only wholehearted work to be carried on in the OKW.

By six o'clock I was back at the Struencks's. There I met Walter Cramer, our loyal and energetic comrade who had never compromised since 1933. General manager of one of the largest Leipzig textile firms, he had for years been assisting Goerdeler wherever he could. He had hidden many important documents in the files of his factory, had made many a trip abroad for Goerdeler, and had been helpful to me too in many ways.

A year ago the Gestapo had deprived Cramer of his passport, so that he was no longer able to travel abroad. He was constantly watched. Now he was going to visit his daughter in Vienna for a few days. He was never to get there; the Gestapo picked him up on the way. As I bade good-bye to this white-haired man, I tried to register emphatic optimism. But it was in vain. From the way he shook hands with me I suspected that he thought this would be a last parting.

It seems to me that for years Cramer had lived with a premonition of how frightfully they would torture him to death. Did he also guess, this cultivated businessman spoiled by luxury, who had reached an age when he was certainly no longer any too strong—did he also guess how he would rise above himself during his suffering? Did he suspect that some day the few survivors of the prison near the Lehrter railroad station would mention his name with admiration whenever they recalled those days of horror?

Goerdeler came. We had agreed to surprise him. When "Doctor Blank" telephoned to ask whether he could call about his insurance policy, Struenck had given him no hint that a visitor would be present. From the cellar window we heard and saw him walk toward the building with his energetic, elastic step. The Struencks received him in the kitchen. Then he appeared suddenly at the door. He reeled back thinking for a moment that his eyes, adapted to the bright sunlight outside, were deceiving him in this dimly lit cellar. I heard him murmur a long-drawn-out "Gisevius!" Had not the years of struggle brought us so close together, I think this welcome alone would have been enough to make me vow fidelity to him for the rest of my life.

Frau Struenck had made coffee. For Goerdeler, rushing as he did from conference to conference, a cup or two of good coffee was wonderfully refreshing. At first we talked about purely family affairs. This was one of the pleasantest aspects of our small group. For a long time now we had not confined ourselves to the political plane alone. We had come to cherish one another on a human basis and to share each other's domestic joys and sorrows.

I quickly noticed that, although Goerdeler held himself erect as ever, he had grown weary and older. There was a melancholy droop around the corners of his mouth. Even the indomitable Goerdeler no longer radiated his old optimism; somehow he too was at the end of his rope. I could not forbear speaking to him about it.

"Yes," he said, with an expressive, resigned gesture, "this past year has really not been easy. The way the generals have managed it, we will have to drink the cup to the dregs."

"But now?"

He replied with a shrug. A year ago he would have poured out a torrent of hopes and plans. "Apparently it is going to be done at last, but ..." Again he shrugged wearily.

I asked how he got along with Stauffenberg. To my amazement he replied that he had seen Stauffenberg no more than two or three times. All other negotiations had been conducted through Beck. "But Beck thinks a good deal of him, and he certainly is a very courageous and energetic man," Goerdeler added evasively.

"But how have you got along with him?" I insisted.

Goerdeler tilted his head back and stared at the ceiling—a frequent gesture with him. "Well, you know," he replied, "if he were not young and I were not much older, I would not be able to stand the way he cuts me off short. But as it is ..."

And then he broke out and confessed all the disappointment and worries that had been consuming him for the past few months. Until recently, he recounted, the division of labor had been strictly adhered to. The military men were to deal with the technical strategy of the *Putsch;* the civilians were supposed to take care of everything connected with politics, for they consciously wanted to avoid the faintest semblance of a military *Putsch.* A real overthrow of the Nazis was conceivable only if the entire civilian Resistance Front, from Right to Left, collaborated. The military officers had completely discredited themselves on the moral plane. Beck was one of the frankest advocates of this position; that was precisely why he had entrusted Goerdeler with all the political preparations.

Stauffenberg, however, would not adhere to this agreement. Goerdeler reported that since their first meeting Stauffenberg had insisted on taking over the political as well as the technical direction. The young colonel could not and would not deny his origins in authoritarian National Socialism. What he had in mind was the salvation of Germany by military men who could break with corruption and maladministration, who would provide an orderly military government and would inspire the people to make one last great effort. Reduced to a formula, he wanted the nation to remain soldierly and become socialistic. Only in this way, he thought, could Germany escape the deadly peril from East and West and fight her way through to a tolerable peace.

Goerdeler, too, did not count on immediate capitulation. Yet he thought the enemy would be inclined to end the war, once a fundamental change in the German regime had taken place. But the views of Goerdeler and Stauffenberg differed fundamentally. Goerdeler's deepest and sincerest convictions led him to desire a democracy. Therefore, he was working for a grand coalition of all non-totalitarians, which meant all the forces of Resistance from the Social Democrats to the conservatives. Stauffenberg wanted a military dictatorship of "true National Socialists." Now that the Nazi leadership had failed and Hitler had been exposed as the bungling strategist he was, the soldiers were to spring into the breach and save the lost cause. Stauffenberg wanted to retain all the totalitarian, militaristic, and socialistic elements of National Socialism.

No wonder Stauffenberg avoided Goerdeler and even took an open stand against him. Not without bitterness Goerdeler told me that the colonel had tried to persuade even Leuschner and Jakob Kaiser to oppose him, Goerdeler, for chancellor. Both men had refused. Then Stauffenberg had found a new candidate in the former Social Democratic Reichstag deputy, Leber. Presumably a man of the Left and former specialist for his Party fraction on military affairs, a secret love for the object of his constant criticism had led Leber into the circle around young Colonel Stauffenberg. Leber had instructed Stauffenberg to base himself primarily on the forces of the militant

Left, and to make sure beforehand that he had the Communists on his side.

Goerdeler had no objection if the Communists honestly wanted to take their place in the front ranks of the forces for defense and reconstruction. But he did refuse to endanger our project by needless preliminary conferences. After all the indiscretions that had taken place in the past, Goerdeler had this time preserved absolute silence. Aside from Leuschner, Letterhaus, and Kaiser, not even the candidates for ministries had been informed.

And now the thing that had always been feared had happened at last. Stauffenberg had continued his political conferences. The day before yesterday his intermediaries, Leber and Professor Reichwein, together with three leading Communists, had been arrested, just as they were on the point of arranging a meeting between Stauffenberg and the Communists. Goerdeler did not yet know that one of the three Communists had been a Gestapo spy, but he was outraged. What would happen if one of those men made any revelations and put the Gestapo on the track of Stauffenberg?

"Take my word for it, what I said to Stauffenberg as I left him after our first meeting is true as ever. 'I want to warn you against playing the part of a political military man,' I said, 'or you'll end as Schleicher did.'"*

Goerdeler did not believe that the Western Powers would adhere to their demand for unconditional surrender. If the army succeeded in halting the Russians, he felt sure that the British at least would reconsider. It would deny the whole meaning of their fight against Hitler's attempt to achieve hege-

* General Kurt von Schleicher, war minister under the Weimar Republic and chancellor for eight weeks before he was succeeded by Hitler, was one of the first victims of the blood purge of June 30, 1934. (The translators.)

mony over Europe if they permitted the vast Russian Empire to overrun Europe.

I disagreed with Goerdeler about this. The war had already gone too far, I felt; the Allies also could not turn back. On the other hand, I thought that the question of which Power occupied Germany, and in what manner, was of vital importance. Despite the agreements made at Teheran and Yalta concerning the zones of occupation, there was the possibility that the Anglo-Saxons would be the first to reach the line running through Koenigsberg, Prague, Vienna, and Budapest.

Goerdeler felt that my view was far too pessimistic.

We talked about personalities. The list of ministers was by and large the old one. Besides Goerdeler as chancellor, Leuschner (Social Democrat) was to be vice-chancellor. The ministry of economics was assigned to Lejeune-Jung (Conservative); of culture, Bolz (Center); finance, Losser (National-Liberal); labor, Letterhaus. On the insistence of Stauffenberg, Leber would receive the ministry of the interior and Olbricht the war ministry.

The foreign ministry was in dispute. So far Hassell had been the only candidate. But Goerdeler now asked me to influence Beck in favor of Count von der Schulenberg, the former ambassador to Moscow. Schulenberg had hazarded the hope that he might be able to reach an agreement with Stalin. At any rate, he could not be considered anti-Russian. During the past year, he had got in touch with Kluge, while the latter was still on the Eastern Front. He proposed that Kluge smuggle him through the Russian lines as a secret negotiator. Kluge was willing—but when the ambassador asked the concrete question whether, if any agreement were forthcoming, he would be able to give Stalin his word of honor that Hitler would be overthrown, the field marshal had backed down—as usual.

Goerdeler wanted me to be his assistant secretary in the

chancellery. Temporarily, he thought, I could administer the police force also, or rather the "Reich Commissariat for Purgation and Restoration of Public Order,"* as we now wanted to call it. Since that office had been intended for me since 1938, I asked him to settle this question with Beck, who had requested me for his chief assistant.

Goerdeler unfortunately had to leave for Frankfurt-am-Main, where he had an urgent appointment. Living in Leipzig as he did, it was not practicable for him to remain in Berlin all the time—especially since every journey now had to be approved by some public authority. For a long time it had been necessary for him to disguise his political conferences as business affairs. We finally parted at the Potsdamerplatz station.

Since I was in the center of the city, I walked the few steps over to the Hotel Excelsior, where Helldorf lived. As I was passing, I glanced at the Prinz Albrechtstrasse. The Gestapo building was still standing, although the bombs had created much havoc in the whole vicinity.

Helldorf said he had met Olbricht and had arranged for Nebe to go to the Bendlerstrasse at eleven o'clock tomorrow so that Olbricht could show him the plans for the police preparations. Since Helldorf's own car was not in, he telephoned around the neighborhood for half an hour, but could find no car that could be placed at the disposal of police headquarters. Here was another instance of the mounting shortages. Only the Gestapo officials still received their old allotment of gasoline. All the other police authorities were restricted to a fraction of their needs.

I rode back by subway. The Struencks were already beginning to worry about me. They informed me that Olbricht and

* *Reichskommissariat zur Saeuberung und Wiederherstellung der oeffentlichen Ordnung. Saeuberung* implies both "purge" in the political sense and "purification" in the moral sense. *(The translators.)*

Stauffenberg were planning to come to see me later. Naturally I felt very curious about this meeting with Stauffenberg. Since he had appeared in Berlin after I had fled, I knew him only by hearsay. The descriptions given by various people were so contradictory that I had been unable to obtain any clear conception of him.

It was past midnight before we heard loud footsteps resounding through the cellar. Hansen could easily find the way in the darkness; he felt quite at home at the Struencks's place. Then there was a knock, and the powerful frames of the two colonels appeared in the doorway. Stauffenberg was, if anything, even bigger than Hansen. At least his broad, vigorous body gave that impression. He held out his left hand; his right arm had been terribly wounded. There was a black patch over his eye, too, and in the course of the conversation he frequently lifted this patch to dab the eye with a wad of cotton.

The appearance of the man was not inspiring. It was easy to divine the psychology of so energetic and talented an officer who suddenly found himself crippled. I sensed at once that this unfortunate man must renounce the hope of attracting masses of people to his cause. His effectiveness must henceforth be confined to small groups. It was as if a pitiless destiny had deliberately planned to thrust him into the role of a conspirator.

With a brief greeting, Stauffenberg dropped into one of the wooden chairs. He pulled open the jacket of his uniform and demanded rather than asked Frau Struenck, who was somewhat taken aback, to prepare a cup of coffee. It had been a hot day for him, he sighed, and with his hand he wiped the perspiration from his forehead, brushing it back into his tangle of hair.

I don't know whether Stauffenberg had always showed his ruder side. But now, consciously or unconsciously, he was trying to overcompensate for the inferiority feelings engendered by his mutilation. As he sat there with his arms dangling limply and his legs in their heavy top-boots sprawled out in front of him, I marveled at the vast difference between this Stauffenberg and the disciple of Stefan George whom I had imagined. I tried to see the connection between this unquestionably forceful but rather boorish person and the verses of the aristocratic poet.

Stauffenberg's voice made an interesting contrast to his massive build. There was a hoarse softness about that voice; a voice such as the "Iron Chancellor" must have had. I would never have taken this young colonel for the model of the traditional officer, nor for a credible representative of that younger generation which had already been inwardly alienated from the Nazis. Undoubtedly this Stauffenberg was a swashbuckler who knew what he wanted; but he struck me as rather typical of the "new" class of general staff officers: the kind of man best suited to Hitler's purposes—or to purposes of assassination.

Frau Struenck left us to prepare the coffee and to chat with Hansen's chauffeur, whom we did not want to hear our conversation.

Hansen exclaimed cordially, "I knew you would come." It required a certain generosity of spirit on his part to accept tacitly my breach of military formalities. In this respect he was pleasingly different from most of his colleagues, who enjoyed giving orders to civilians.

Stauffenberg took over the conversation almost at once. In curiously circumlocutory phrases he said to me that I probably knew how grave the situation was. As chief of staff to the commander of the home army he wanted me to "inform" him about phases of the situation with which he was not acquainted. I came from Switzerland where all sorts of information was available. Would I give him my impressions?

Goerdeler need not have tipped me off beforehand. Here

was the true "political military man." Here was a professional soldier who was being drawn willy-nilly into the complex problems of a revolutionary era and was making his first groping steps in politics. He made the mistake common to a fundamentally unpolitical person when he essays being diplomatic; he considered complicated and even tortuous speaking to be a kind of higher diplomacy.

I willingly expounded my view of the radical shift that had taken place in the past few months. Since the invasion, I said, there could no longer be any turning back for the Anglo-Saxons. It was quite possible to argue about the specific meaning of "unconditional surrender" but to my mind we could no longer avoid total occupation with all the consequences implicit in that. The only matter for discussion was whether the final act would be brought about from within or without, and whether the army—now at least—would muster up its courage for internal action.

While I talked, Stauffenberg had stared at the floor, a meaningful smile on his face. I did not know whether he was trying to express disapproval or whether he intended to confide a special secret to me.

"Isn't it altogether too late for the West?" he interjected. With that he launched into an endless divagation in which he attempted to show that I was a hopeless "Westerner."

The long and short of it was: What could I hope to gain by coming to an agreement with the Western Powers, whether before or after the collapse? Didn't I know that the central army group had ceased to count for anything? Within a few weeks Stalin would be standing before Berlin. The decision in the East had already been reached; therefore, all political activity had to be directed toward the East.

Hansen cast a significant look at me. In the first place, I had said not a word that might indicate I was in favor of a one-sided "Western" policy. I had spoken only of "unconditional surrender" and of the fact that it was already "too late"—and that these factors must influence all our thoughts on foreign policy. In the second place, Stauffenberg, of course, knew about the numerous messages that Beck and Goerdeler had sent to Switzerland requesting that if possible we come to a preliminary accord with the Anglo-Americans. Why this sudden polemic against the West?

If, however, Stauffenberg had formulated his opinion with any clarity there would have been a basis for discussion. But the above summary is only an approximation of what he said, for he contradicted himself in the same breath; after each statement he added that he did not want me to misunderstand him, that he had not really decided the matter in his own mind, and was for this reason simply taking the role of an *advocatus diaboli*. From the vehemence with which he developed his ideas, I clearly perceived that he had long since made his choice, but that he was not yet sure how he could justify his change of heart to Beck or Goerdeler.

Finally I lost patience and told him that I should now like to hear his real opinion. It was no use, however, for Stauffenberg did not say outright that an arrangement with the Russians was possible. Instead he pictured the situation on the Eastern Front as being so black that any reasonable man would give up all hope. We began disputing whether the Russians really would conquer Berlin within a few weeks. Stauffenberg backed his assertion with a technical knowledge that I, of course, could not counter. He took my one halfway-cogent argument—that up to now all military prognoses had proved false—as a personal insult. Actually I was referring to the field marshals and not to him. I was prudent enough not to remind him of how positive he had been at the beginning of the year that the situation on the Eastern Front was stable and that the invasion of Europe by the Western Powers would be a reckless and at best a time-consuming enterprise.

The more involved the conversation became, the more I tried to approach the man from the human side. After all, we were comrades who were working toward the same goal. For all the differences of opinion among us, I wanted him to feel that we applauded his courage. "How do you know whether I will set off the bomb at all?" he suddenly burst out, after we had spent some time talking over the technical details of the assassination. I retorted, "Why else have you come here?" And the subject was dropped.

That evening I certainly had the impression that before me was a man who would go the limit. But in the light of what followed, I must, in retrospect, ask myself whether this mysterious posturing, this bent for dialectic, this talking around the subject and playing the devil's advocate—whether this behavior did not have its origin in a basic lack of clarity, if not confusion. Stauffenberg was motivated by the impulsive passions of the disillusioned military man whose eyes had been opened by the defeat of German arms. And now, with an exaggerated sense of his mission, he thought he had to be everything at once: soldier, politician, tyrannicide, savior of his fatherland. Political life during revolutions is fantastically equivocal. On the one hand stood this soldierly revolutionary who in the final analysis was fighting for the continuation of Nazi-militaristic "legality;" on the other hand stood the anti-revolutionary civilians militantly striving to achieve something new.

Stauffenberg insisted that the problem of purging was to be attacked with extreme caution. Naturally he had no objection to administering just punishment to the Nazi and Gestapo murderers, but he would not tolerate a verdict of guilty being passed against the top generals for "political" reasons; that is, he would not condemn Brauchitsch and Halder for their well-known cowardice or the field marshals for their characterless attitude toward Hitler's invasions.

I objected that only a broad, self-inflicted purge on our part could convince the Allies that a fundamental change and not a merely tactical shift was taking place. Stauffenberg would not agree. How could he hope to save the reputation of the army for the future if once it were revealed with what recklessness and smallness of mind the army leaders had allowed our nation to plunge into the calamity of war?

I was somewhat taken aback by the candor with which Stauffenberg announced that my book, with its description of the Fritsch crisis and its attacks on the generals, would have to be banned. By this time it was already growing light. We had to break up. Perhaps our nerves were overstrained. At any rate, we quarreled almost at the last moment.

I asked Stauffenberg to give my regards to Olbricht and to tell him that I would be ready to see him any time he wished. Stauffenberg became terribly agitated. I knew the Gestapo was after me, he told me hotly; I must not let myself be seen or everything would be endangered. I had, of course, not the slightest intention of being rash, and I therefore assured him that aside from Beck, Goerdeler, Nebe, and Helldorf, I did not expect to talk to anyone.

"Not even Oster!" he retorted in a tone of command. His manner was so sharp, so peremptory, that I could not help replying with equal sharpness that if Oster should show up in Berlin, I would see him the moment he arrived.

Oster had been banished to the country. Naturally I was not so mad as to send him a telegram informing him of my arrival or of our plan but I was infuriated by this exclusion of a man who had laid the foundation for all the work which Stauffenberg was now doing. In a flash I saw how this bit of byplay really illuminated the whole psychological situation. Oster was

the officer who had fought most clear-headedly, most resolutely, most indomitably against the Brown tyranny—and had
fought it longest. There was a vast gulf between his mentality
and that of Stauffenberg, who had shifted to the rebel side only
after Stalingrad. These two army men were representatives of
two different worlds.

Hansen warned that they had better go now, but I wished
I knew what he had been thinking all evening. During the conversation he had turned frequently to look searchingly at Stauffenberg, then at me; then for a while he had stared in embarrassment at the floor. Was he merely being courteous to Struenck,
as our host, or was he reluctant to show me openly that he was
displeased with me?

Now, just as they were leaving, I saw that he wanted to
speak to me. As soon as he felt sure his comrade was not
observing him, he turned back and gripped my arms with both
his hands. I could feel his fingers digging into my flesh. Agi-
tatedly, he whispered to me: "We absolutely must talk. I'll
come tomorrow morning to see you."

This still did not tell me what he really thought, but before
I could ask, he gave me a long, meaningful look and spoke two
sentences which I shall always remember as the final word on
the history of July 20. I shall never forget the tone of voice in
which he spoke, the gestures that accompanied his words.

"It all strikes me as so playful," he said. "It... can't... be...
done... this... way."

July 13

THERE WAS NOT MUCH TIME LEFT for sleeping; first we had
to air out the smoke-filled cellar. Early in the morning there
was a radio signal. I knew nothing about the newly invented
radar, which gave the position of approaching bombers, and
therefore I did not understand the haste with which the Stru-

encks packed their belongings, for the sirens had not yet begun howling. We put our belongings into the adjoining bunker and waited outside in the garden to see what would happen.

This was the first daylight attack I was experiencing. A year ago the nonchalance with which those great flights of bombers flew across all of Germany to Berlin would have been inconceivable. Now no one thought anything of it, or of the fact that fighter planes no longer rose to combat them and that the flak was pretty ineffectual. People accepted the inevitable apathetically and sighed with relief if the attack proved mild. A "mild" attack meant, of course, that the quota of bombs rained down on some other quarter of the vast area of Berlin.

It was all over in an hour. Although the attack had been directed against the center of the city, I noticed on my way to Alexanderplatz that normal business activity continued in spite of fires and blockaded streets. When I asked the police officers in Helldorf's waiting room what had happened, they had to dig out their reports before they could give me a list of the larger fires and the more serious bomb damage. "Nothing special," I was told. They were so dulled to destruction that they took notice of it only when a serious traffic obstruction was created or when a government building was hit. To one who had come from an oasis of peace, this equanimity, or rather this lack of ability to react, was altogether uncanny. How could people who no longer had any emotions left be willing and able to break with the hard-won habits of daily life in order to participate in a rebellion or even in a riot?

Helldorf was not at all surprised by my impressions. He had not volunteered his opinion forcibly the day before, he said, because he had not wanted to influence my initial impression. But he simply could not arrive at any precise and unambiguous relationship with Stauffenberg. As he had told me, it was the same with Schulenberg. Before 1933, Schulenberg had been one of those intellectual Socialists who gathered around Otto Strasser and the East Prussian *Gauleiter,* Erich Koch. The difference between Stauffenberg, Helldorf, and Schulenberg— all three of them counts—was that Helldorf had come to the Nazi Movement as a primitive, I might almost say an unpolitical revolutionary. The other two had been attracted primarily by a political ideology. Therefore, it was possible for Helldorf to throw everything overboard at once: Hitler, the Party, the entire system. Stauffenberg, Schulenberg, and their clique wanted to drop no more ballast than was absolutely necessary; then they would paint the ship of state a military gray and set it afloat again.

Nebe came. We greeted each other warmly. As if we were right in the middle of one of our old discussions, he poured forth his usual plaint against the generals. "Take my word for it, they'll never get anything done. Everything will go wrong this time too."

I soon found what the excitement was about. According to prearrangement Nebe had gone to the Bendlerstrasse at eleven o'clock. This in itself took some courage on his part. When he got to Olbricht's waiting room, an adjutant at once took him in hand and, as befitted an SS general, led him directly to his superior, who politely inquired what he wanted.

Nebe did not know Olbricht by sight. Fortunately, he noticed that the officer to whom he was speaking wore three stars. So far as Nebe knew, Olbricht was not yet a colonel-general. Therefore, Nebe was cautious and said he had come at Helldorf's request in regard to certain police officers whom Helldorf wished released from military duty. The officer replied that he had better discuss such questions of detail with General Olbricht. He had been led in to see—Colonel-General Friedrich Fromm!

This, of course, was just the sort of thing that would happen to the cautious Nebe. Olbricht had merely laughed about the incident and had then introduced Nebe to one of his junior officers, who was to show him the plans for the police action. Nebe was put out by this as well. "Those generals are always ready to call in help, but they themselves like to keep away from dangerous conferences," he growled.

What had made him absolutely furious was the fact that the maps of the city which he was shown had seemed very familiar to him. Incredible as it sounds, they were our own maps from the time of Stalingrad. Nebe himself had made notes on them. The only hitch was that in the meantime a vast number of the buildings indicated on the maps had been converted into heaps of rubble, and many other dislocations had occurred.

Helldorf came in excitedly. The acting *Gauleiter* of Berlin had just paid him a visit and had poured out his heart about the terrible reactionary generals. But at least, he had said, the *Grossdeutschland* battalion of guards had been entrusted to a sensible commander who was a National Socialist of unquestionable loyalty: Major Roemer. Stauffenberg was counting upon this same Major Roemer to conduct the action during the first—and therefore the most important—few hours, until the panzer troops moved up. This was too much for Helldorf. He asked me to arrange an audience with Beck for him. I was more than willing. To my mind, the assistance of the police force would be the decisive factor in the *Putsch*. It seemed to me that Stauffenberg was staking everything on the opposite card. He was relying completely on his bomb and on the military forces.

Helldorf drove me back to the Struencks's. Hansen was already waiting there. He was overtired, for he had had to take Stauffenberg home. On the way they had quarreled furiously. They had continued their argument in the car—much too long and much too loudly, so that the chauffeur would be able to testify to a great deal. Hansen and especially the Struencks were to pay dearly for that indiscretion.

During lunch Hansen told me all that was troubling him. He still admired Stauffenberg for his superb talents as a military man, for his noble manner, his gift for organization, his culture. On many evenings Stauffenberg had recited Stefan George's poems for hours at a time. His deep religious feeling also marked him as many notches above the average of his colleagues; but it was impossible to discuss politics with him.

Nowadays Stauffenberg no longer seemed to be the same man, Hansen said. Of late he had been secretive, subject to whims, tyrannical, and noticeably nervous. Was all this solely a result of the tremendous psychic pressure upon him since he had resolved upon the assassination? Hansen did not think so. Formerly he had been a man without nerves. The great change in him had come with his terrible wound.

Hansen said that it was possible to talk with Stauffenberg alone, but that he felt himself an alien in the "debating club" that Stauffenberg had recently gathered around himself. Hansen was a talented, uncomplicated professional officer. It was quite natural that he would not know how to handle this curious mixture of "putschist" and theoretician. Everything was too vague and misty, he felt; there was a lack of inner discipline. What with all the profound debates on the moral justification of assassination and on the salvation that would come from socialism or from the East, it became impossible to discuss with Stauffenberg and his circle the technical details of a *Putsch*. At once they became evasive. Somehow, they took it all too lightly.

Hansen mentioned again what he had said the night before and tried to explain to me what he meant by "playful." He did not deny the firmness of Stauffenberg's resolution. What was missing was a basic conception of the gravity of the undertaking. He informed me that Stauffenberg had been playing hide-and-seek with me. A few weeks before he had counted upon playing off the West against the East; now he was imagining a joint victorious march of the German and Red armies against the plutocracies. It was an open question whether the recent military disaster had not accelerated this radical reorientation.

I had to hurry off, in order not to keep Beck waiting. In Lichterfelde I made a slight detour in order to examine Beck's house from all sides for possible lurking watchers. The immediate vicinity of the Goethestrasse had been so shattered by bombs that it would have been difficult for spies to find any inconspicuous post.

When I mentioned this to Beck, he smiled slyly. The watch had been given up last November, he informed me. A bomb had struck the house adjoining his. He had spent the night helping to extinguish the fire, and in the early hours of the morning he had invited his neighbor in for a glass of brandy. The neighbor had drunk his health and congratulated him—for the corner room of the ruined building had been requisitioned by the Gestapo so that they could watch and photograph his visitors.

As he had so often done before, Beck had drawn up extensive notes in preparation for our conference. He could not give up this habit, although he must have known how dearly he would have to pay for such scribblings if the Gestapo should make a sudden raid. But he was and remained the model of a chief of the general staff. He never said a word too much or too little, and he was fond of thinking in writing. Because of this habit, he did not hurdle any of the more obvious steps. Although there was really scarcely any need for us to discuss the matter, he led off with the question of whether we should undertake an assassination and why at the present moment it was morally, politically, and militarily imperative.

For Beck also the prime factor was the situation in the East. Once more I heard a description of the disaster that had befallen the army group of the center. The situation of the northern army group was even more perilous, he said. There a new Stalingrad was in the making. Hitler had refused to withdraw the two hundred and fifty thousand men—and his obstinacy appeared all the more grotesque because these armies were urgently needed on the border of East Prussia. According to Beck's information, it would prove impossible, in the long run, to continue supplying those troops by sea or by air. And there were not enough forces available to relieve them by an offensive. If the Russians were cunning, they would draw a powerful ring around the troops in the north and then avoid further battles there while advancing across the Vistula. This latest absurdity of Hitler's amateur strategy had evoked a revolt in the general staff. Zeitzler, the chief, had suffered a nervous breakdown and was at the moment hospitalized. This abandonment of an entire army group had had the effect of preparing many of the generals at headquarters for an uprising against Hitler.

In the West the [Allied] invasion had succeeded. A number of unforeseen pieces of good luck had helped the Anglo-Americans. In spite of the ban on furloughs, Rommel had secretly flown home for a birthday celebration. By the time he reached the front again, hours had passed. More precious hours were lost because Keitel had not dared to wake Hitler, a late sleeper, too early; and Hitler had undertaken sole command of the mobile defense corps.

Kluge, who had just succeeded Rundstedt, sent word by special courier that Hitler had deceived him as to the true situation. He had been given false figures on the forces at his disposal. No wonder he urged a speedy revolt. Falkenhausen, after his dismissal from the post of military commander in Belgium, had remained in Brussels to await events and to work for us at Kluge's headquarters.

Beck traced anew the course of events which I had been able to follow only somewhat vaguely from Zurich. After the failure of the previous December, the idea of an assassination had been postponed for months. Even the Stauffenberg circle had been willing to give Hitler a last chance to beat back the invasion and then initiate peace negotiations.

Now, Beck believed, it was too late. He stressed his conviction that Germany was beaten; total occupation could not be prevented, he said, and the fate of the army was sealed. Under the conditions of the present collapse, only a German Badoglio could resolve the situation, and he, Beck, was probably the one general who was still respected both abroad and by the troops at home. For that reason he was willing to take over the thankless task and help see to it that the inevitable bitter pill was swallowed with a certain amount of dignity and respect.

Naturally Beck asked me whether I thought any chance still existed for an agreement with the Western Powers. He found it unfortunate that we were unable at least to discuss the matter with them. In contrast to Goerdeler, I believed that we should have difficulty in persuading the Allies to recognize at all a Reich government capable of functioning. In his circumspect manner Beck summed it up: he could not exclude this pessimistic possibility, but we must try to get whatever we could out of Goerdeler's optimism and zest.

We now turned to a discussion of the technique of the *Putsch.* Not much had changed. The opportunity for Stauffenberg to commit the assassination would come at a conference in Hitler's headquarters. It was still an open question where Hitler would be at the time—whether in East Prussia, at

Berghof, or in Munich. Olbricht had arranged matters so that a number of important orders would have to be reported orally to Hitler. This would be done during the usual morning conference, which was ordinarily attended by a variable number of high officers. There was the chance that some innocent person might also be killed.

No matter where the bomb exploded, the headquarters' communications center would be blown up immediately afterward. The communications chief, General Fellgiebel, was in charge of this. This would insure that the headquarters would be cut off from the outside world for several hours, so that the initial action could not be thwarted by counter-orders.

As soon as the code word *Walkuere* [Valkyrie] was given, the troops stationed around Berlin would start moving. For the first three hours, however, only the guards regiment would be at our disposal, because giving the alarm, issuing live munitions, and getting the troops going would be time-consuming. These three "stagnant" hours represented the real danger to us. During that period the Gestapo could get set to strike back. Therefore, it was especially important for us, with Helldorf's cooperation, to paralyze the Berlin police. According to our information, no significant number of Waffen-SS troops were stationed in the Reich capital.

The attempt would be made to draw Colonel-General Fromm over to our side, since this would greatly facilitate the progress of the *Putsch*. Olbricht thought it quite likely that Fromm would accede to a *fait accompli*. If he did not, Colonel-General Hoeppner would replace him. Before I had the slightest chance to protest, Beck assured me that his opinion of Hoeppner had not altered in any way. He still considered him an intolerable opportunist. After all the disappointments we had had with Hoeppner in the past years, Beck did not intend to let him hold any office for more than three days. But Stauffenberg and Olbricht felt that they needed Hoeppner as a counterpoise to Guderian.

Hoeppner had been with us in the conspiracy of 1938. He had also been one of the revolting panzer generals in November 1939. But in the spring of 1940, when the soil of Flanders was no longer a muddy swamp and decorations, laurels, and military glory could be won so easily there, Hoeppner was unable to resist the allure. He did not even object to the Russian campaign. Occasionally, however, under the influence of alcohol, he had boasted to his intimates of the plans he had harbored back in 1938.

Fate caught up with Hoeppner before Moscow. The greatest general of the ages was dissatisfied with him. A simple telegram was sent and the colonel-general found himself out of the army and on his way home. Back in Berlin, Hoeppner spent a few days protesting. He insisted that his legal position be clarified. Had he been degraded to the rank of an ordinary cavalryman? Had he been completely expelled from the army? Who was going to pay his pension? And how big was the pension?

The jurists in the OKW racked their brains. Our immortally generous Fuehrer found the solution. Hoeppner was and remained expelled from the Wehrmacht, but he was compensated by continuing to draw his pay; he was also permitted to retain occupancy in his official mansion.

Witzleben would take general command of all the armed forces and direct command of the army as well. Witzleben was waiting near Zossen, where the major part of army headquarters was stationed. Quartermaster-General Wagner, who was at last co-operating unreservedly, was making the fullest preparations at Zossen. The *Luftwaffe* had been so terribly shattered that we no longer needed to fear it. Doenitz's cruisers were at the bottom of the sea, and he could hardly hasten to the aid of his Fuehrer in Berlin with submarines and destroyers.

Since Beck would become head of the state, he would thereby be the supreme commander of the Wehrmacht. He had no intention, however, of interfering with Witzleben's and especially with Olbricht's and Stauffenberg's work. He did not want to create confusion and obliterate responsibilities á la Hitler by interference from above in questions of detail.

He had an excellent plan for preserving the civilian character of the coup d'état. Just as the troops were subordinate to him as chief of state, so he would also place the police directly under his authority during the early period. Thus, during the emergency, he would be able to co-ordinate the Wehrmacht and police. In order to facilitate this co-ordination, he would insist that I remain as his immediate assistant with the title of "Reich Minister to the Chief of State." This provided me with an opening for discussing the events of the night before. I described the long conversation with Stauffenberg and let Beck know how worried I was. He thought these political digressions on the part of a young colonel should not be taken too seriously. During the past half-year he had come to respect Stauffenberg highly, he said, as the sole activist among the soldiers. He, too, had noticed Stauffenberg's temporary uncertainty and nervousness, but considering the tremendous risk he was about to take, that was hardly surprising. We should let him be, thought Beck; we had no right to try to change his plans beforehand. Once the assassination succeeded, he, Beck, would possess the necessary power of command. Then he would know how to handle the situation, and he did not doubt Stauffenberg's loyalty; he felt sure the colonel would consent wholeheartedly to his decisions. This sounded clear and reassuring. Nevertheless, Beck said he would talk to Stauffenberg about the stupidity of Nebe's being led into Fromm's office and about the outmoded maps of the city. And he would also have to look into Helldorf's warning against Major Roemer.

I hastened back to the Struencks's, to find Nebe waiting for me. The past year had left its traces on Nebe; it had tried his nerves more than all the other war years. He described the present attitude of the Nazi leaders in the face of the mounting disasters. Himmler was wavering between his slavish submissiveness toward Hitler and his natural shrewdness which warned him that evil days were coming. Nebe was sure that Himmler knew nothing of our preparations. He was counting on the general fear of the Russians and on the formula of unconditional surrender, which played right into his hands. Because he correctly judged the majority of the generals, he considered the domestic situation at the moment less tense than it had been many times in the past, when the powerful pressure from outside was lacking.

Goering had lost all standing, Nebe said. The failure of the Luftwaffe during the invasion had been the final mark against him. For this reason we need no longer worry about his attitude during the *putsch*. On the other hand, Nebe pointed out that a fundamental change had taken place in the popular attitude toward Himmler. Much as he was feared as a hangman, he was also looked to as the only man amid all the confusion who still had power behind him. The people were in terror of the twelve million foreign workers who were virtually overrunning Germany. They also feared grave disruptions in supplies to the cities should an uprising take place. Scarcely anyone could conceive of a change in the system without the participation of Himmler. For this reason Nebe proposed that we drop our old plan of attributing the assassination to Himmler. For by now anyone who undertook to kill Hitler would be so popular that we should merely be contributing to Himmler's prestige. However, the chief consideration was the first reaction among the troops, and for them Himmler was the hated Gestapist.

The administrative apparatus was already extensively disorganized, Nebe informed me, so that resistance from the provincial satraps was improbable. He nevertheless was thoroughly pessimistic. "You'll see, nothing will come of it again," he said gloomily. At the very least, he thought, he himself would be killed in the course of the *Putsch*. The assassination was to take place between twelve noon and two. Every afternoon around two o'clock the department heads of the *Sicherheitshauptamt*—Mueller, Schellenberg, Ohlendorf, and Nebe—had lunch with their chief, Kaltenbrunner, in the Prinz Albrechtstrasse building. Usually this was a welcome opportunity for Nebe to keep his ears open. But on the *Putsch* day—just two days away now—he would prefer, he said, to stay away. However, that would be too dangerous; if something went wrong, they might draw conclusions about the reasons for his absence.

I consoled him with the assurance that by two o'clock it would all be over and the guards regiment would have rolled up to the Prinz Albrechtstrasse. Nebe shook his head. The news would undoubtedly burst in on them during their lunch, he averred. And he pictured the scene: how annoying it would be for him to be shot down at the last moment, and in the company of such high-ranking SS gangsters as these.

July 14

A QUIET DAY. This was just as well, for on the morrow we should have need of steady nerves. I saw Beck briefly. He had talked with Stauffenberg, who had refused to take any heed of Helldorf's warning against Major Roemer. In any event, they had a gallant stand-in for every commander. Each of these men, at the slightest sign of refusal to obey orders, would shoot down the uncooperative officer and take over the command himself.

Stauffenberg had also denied Nebe's statement that the maps of Berlin were outmoded. Schulenberg had examined them carefully, he said. Perhaps Nebe had been shown the wrong maps by mistake. Beck had let the matter drop. It was already too late for argument or reproof, he said. We could only hope that everything would turn out well. Stauffenberg, he said, had been extremely nervous. Tomorrow was the great trial. They had even decided to give the signal, *Walkuere* [Valkyrie] at eleven o'clock—before the crucial Hitler conference—in order to shorten the three "stagnant" hours.

Saturday, July 15

GOERDELER ARRIVED at the Struencks' promptly at eleven o'clock, and we went by subway to Beck's home in Lichterfelde. For the first time in many years the reticent Beck emerged from his shell to greet us with unwonted cordiality. "How good that you're here. This waiting alone is unendurable."

For a while we talked half-heartedly. In order to divert our minds from thoughts of what must now be happening at Hitler's headquarters, Beck took out a pad of notes and asked me about a large number of persons. He had made a long list of prospects for subordinate posts. To me it seemed highly objectionable to be endangering needlessly people who would not count at all until two or three days "afterward." In making plans for uprisings, rebels should concern themselves only with ministers, under-secretaries, and the governing heads of provinces. The names of such persons could easily be memorized. Any other lists of names were, to my mind, idle speculation and—in case of failure—virtually warrants for arrest. We were soon to have bloody proof of this thesis.

Waiting became more and more of a torment. At two o'clock lunch began at the Fuehrer's headquarters. The bomb was supposed to explode between twelve and one. What had happened? Had it been called off again? Then, certainly, we ought to have heard by now. I don't know how often each of us looked at his watch. Our mood became more and more depressed. We fumbled about for something to say to each other, but our minds were not on our conversation.

All afternoon we waited, talking intermittently. By six o'clock we could no longer stand it. By then it was virtually impossible that any news from the Bendlerstrasse would be good news. We decided we might just as well not permit the Gestapo to catch all three of us at once. Heavy-heartedly, we took our leave of Beck. In order not to attract attention, I went first. Goerdeler would meet me at the nearby public telephone. Meanwhile, I would try to get in touch with Helldorf.

Remarkably enough, the public telephone in front of the post office was still in working order, and I succeeded in getting Helldorf. Without waiting for me to ask a camouflaged question, he said, with provoking cheekiness, "You know, of course, that the celebration did not take place?" When I said I had not known, he decided it would be better not to continue the conversation over the telephone. He would drop in at the Struencks's in the evening.

At any rate, the Gestapo apparently had not yet been called in. For a moment Goerdeler and I considered whether we ought not to run back to Beck's and tell him. But a bus was just coming along and we automatically boarded it. We assumed that Beck would soon find out. Had we known that he would have to wait until midnight, we unquestionably would have turned back in order to relieve him of his suspense, now doubly hard to bear because he was alone.

Helldorf arrived at the Struencks's soon after we had finished a morose supper. At one o'clock he had driven over to the Bendlerstrasse, as had been agreed. There he met Olbricht and

Hoeppner and the Stauffenberg group, all assembled in the adjutants's room. They did not have to wait long for the pre-arranged telephone call from the Fuehrer's headquarters. Everyone stood around the telephone as Lieutenant von Haeften answered the call. Stauffenberg was at the other end of the line. The lieutenant replied apparently to a question from Stauffenberg; in a clear, unhesitant voice von Haeften gave his instructions. Then he hung up and informed the others that Stauffenberg had stated in a disguised fashion that Goering and Himmler were not present and had asked whether he should go ahead anyway. Haeften had at once said yes on his own authority. Although Helldorf approved of this decision, he thought Olbricht and Hoeppner were quite right in their indignation at the way the answer had been given over their heads.

A quarter of an hour later, Stauffenberg called again. When he had returned to the meeting, everyone had been on the point of leaving and Hitler had just rushed away. As Helldorf described it, Olbricht had appeared visibly relieved. At once he had locked the papers relating to the *Putsch* in his safe and had good-humoredly remarked that at least they could enjoy a quiet weekend. This bit of humor may have been a natural reaction to the tremendous nervous tension. Nevertheless, it was somehow symptomatic.

Helldorf insisted that if we had witnessed the scene we would undoubtedly have concurred with his opinion—that next time as well the affair would not come off properly. He could not, he said, rationalize his feeling, but a revolt could not be successfully carried out if it were to be undertaken in such an easy-going manner.

Had Providence once more saved Hitler by impelling him to leave the meeting in time? It can be taken that way, for after receiving an affirmative answer, Stauffenberg had gone back to set off his bomb. There was something inexplicable about this, however. Why had Stauffenberg felt any need to get confirmation by telephone? Last Wednesday the action had been called off because Goering and Himmler were unexpectedly missing. There could be no surprise about it this time. Either they were present or not present, and presumably Stauffenberg had decided on his course of action in either case. We did not know what decision he and his friends had framed for these eventualities, but they must have decided something. Why, then, had it been necessary for Stauffenberg to make a telephone call which would inevitably be answered as the lieutenant had in fact impulsively answered it? This dangerous as well as superfluous telephone call indicated that Stauffenberg had somewhat lost his head. Consequently, the melancholy conclusion was forced on us that Hitler had been saved not so much by a beneficent Providence as by Stauffenberg's psychological inhibitions. It seemed highly unlikely that he would succeed a third time where he had funked twice before.

Perhaps this failure today was a sign from above that we had to look for other ways and means. I suggested once more the "Western" solution, which we had repeatedly discussed in Switzerland. By that I meant that we would abandon the attempt at assassination and a *Putsch* in Berlin in favor of a unilateral action in the West. If Kluge and Rommel had crossed their psychological Rubicon, then let them refuse to obey Hitler and make an offer for a separate armistice to Eisenhower. Practically this would mean that the front in the West would be broken and the Anglo-American troops would pour across the Siegfried Line into Germany, meeting very little or no resistance. At the very least they would reach Berlin before the Russians. That, to be sure, had implications even deeper than "unconditional surrender." We should have to reckon with open civil war, and the legend of the stab in the back would once more create trouble. But how much destruction we could save this way!

But would Kluge cooperate? And how could we get to see him? Struenck reassured us on that point. Hansen had informed him several days ago that his official plane was prepared to take off for Kluge's headquarters at a moment's notice. Hansen had even taken the precaution of manufacturing an urgent pretext for visiting the general. These preparations, Struenck told me, were chiefly for my benefit, in case it proved necessary for me to disappear in a hurry.

We would confront Kluge with a simple alternative; if he wasn't going to act, he would have to arrest us at once. We also intended to inform him that we were quite ready to provide the Gestapo with all the information it required about his and Rommel's constructive proposals in the past.

Admittedly, this would be an act of desperation. But was there any other way to accomplish anything with those generals? They themselves had long since thrown overboard every ounce of old-fashioned chivalry.

The sirens howled. Helldorf rushed out to his car. He wanted to get to his shelter office in the center of the city before the bombs fell. Afterward we sat up together for a long time. Goerdeler wanted to leave early in the morning for Leipzig, in order to bid good-bye to his family. Whatever came, it was clear that this time the die was cast. Fate would permit no more evasions; we had advanced too far. The *fronde* could not go on forever fleeing from its own decisions.

At such times Goerdeler liked to discuss everything anew. Just as his whole mind had for years revolved around one central point, so his conversation turned endlessly in a circle.

At last weariness overwhelmed us. The Struencks fixed a

small room for the two of us. Around two in the morning we collapsed into bed. For a while we talked in whispers. Goerdeler urged me to see Beck early in the morning and win him over to our side—that is, persuade him to accept the "Western" solution.

After but two or three hours' sleep the alarm clock clanged. Goerdeler wanted to take the seven-o'clock train. To make sure of getting a place on it, he had to be on the platform at least an hour beforehand.

I heard him rise heavily. Half asleep, I shook hands with him. "Well, then, till Tuesday."

How gracious is Fate, in kindly concealing it from us when we are seeing our friends for the last time on this earth. Had I known what was to come, I would have sprung to my feet; I would not have released his hand until our eyes had met and contrived to express all the unspoken feelings, all the comradeship that cannot be put into words. As it was, I watched sleepily in the uncertain light of dawn while a dear and unforgettable friend walked softly out of the door and vanished—forever.

July 16

IN THE AFTERNOON I went to see Beck. The marks of his long vigil of the day before were still upon him. Waiting alone for six hours after we left must have tried him sorely. He informed me that Stauffenberg was coming to see him that evening, to explain personally what had taken place. I told him about the decision Goerdeler and I had come to—that we now favored an immediate adoption of the "Western" solution. He did not reject the suggestion outright. But he would not take a position on the question until he had heard Stauffenberg's report.

July 17

THE ENEMY BOMBERS took care that we did not sleep too late in the morning. Helldorf had telephoned. Between two air-raid alarms I made my way to Alexanderplatz.

Over Sunday, it appeared, the police chief had had an attack of nerves. He wanted to know whether Beck agreed to the "Western" solution. His disappointment was marked when I told him that Beck had not yet decided. While I was there, Kaltenbrunner telephoned. Helldorf let me listen in on another receiver. I was not yet acquainted with that famous Gestapist and was therefore interested in hearing his voice. To my surprise, it was not an unpleasant voice at all, much calmer and more distinct than the run of Nazi ranters. Of course, Kaltenbrunner imitated the typical Hitlerian accent; all the Party leaders who were able to reproduce the South German dialect did that.

The subject of the telephone conversation was a complaint of Helldorf's which to my knowledge he had already lodged the last time I saw him, a year before. Helldorf was police chief of Berlin and was also a *Polizeifuehrer*, which gave him an even higher rank. Nevertheless, on the basis of a reorganization within the ministry of interior, control over the local *Ordnungspolizei* and the *Staatspolizei* was taken from him. The net result was that Helldorf was left in command merely of the detective force and parts of the traffic police force. But since the ordinary mortal could never find his way through this snarl of interlocking responsibilities, Helldorf was generally thought to command the real police power in Berlin. He had decided that he would no longer put up with this situation. Twice he had offered his resignation. Once he had gone to the front to escape the intolerable situation of being held responsible while possessing so little power. At last he had appealed to Goebbels in the latter's capacity of Berlin *Gauleiter* and Reich defense

commissioner. That had worked. The ambitious little
Goebbels was extremely jealous of his rights, and even Black
Heinrich was unwilling to risk a brush with so accomplished a
slanderer.

Himmler had, therefore, ordered a reconciliation with
Helldorf, and Kaltenbrunner was now asking him to come to a
conference in the Prinz Albrechtstrasse on Friday. The whole
manner of his invitation, the fact that on the one hand he was
in no hurry and that on the other he was soft-soaping Helldorf,
indicated that he harbored no suspicions. That, at least, was a
consolation.

Helldorf wanted to meet Hansen. It is hard to imagine
how difficult it was to bring together men who were, after all,
pulling on the same rope. Each one was jealous of his "connections." The many mutual refusals to meet were always, of
course, justified on grounds of camouflage—in the end we
should be so occupied in covering our tracks that we would forget what we were planning to do.

I telephoned Frau Struenck to ask whether I might bring
along a guest. She was used to such troubles, and without asking any questions simply said yes. When we reached the cellar,
I could not refrain from laughing. In addition to Hansen
another unexpected guest was there—Doctor Hans Koch, an
old friend and comrade. It was quite an achievement for Frau
Struenck to have found provisions for one permanent guest and
three unannounced visitors who were not backward at table.

Hansen was indignant about the kind of "polities" the
Stauffenberg clique was practicing. Alongside of Goerdeler's
cabinet, which he detested, Stauffenberg wanted to install military administrators with full powers of control, who would
"establish order" during the first weeks. Nine months later, I
found proof of this interpretation of Hansen's. One of the few
survivors of the intimate group around Stauffenberg published

an account which employed almost Hansen's exact words about this *Putsch* within a *Putsch.* "In case the uprising should succeed, military administrators were to be appointed at once for the various Reich ministries...."

Hansen shared Helldorf's conclusion about the scene in the Bendlerstrasse that morning. Neither could say why he felt it so clearly, but both men believed that the affair would turn out badly. Both broke out that I had not put the matter of the "Western" solution strongly enough to Beck, and said that I must insist on it. Hansen expressly offered to put his plane at my disposal. He could guarantee my safe delivery to Kluge's headquarters.

Through the cellar window we saw a pair of high black boots trudge by. Struenck rushed out. In a moment he returned, red-faced. Nebe was outside, he said, and extremely excited. He would not come in and said that he had to speak to me privately. I went outside, and Nebe drew me into the darkest part of the cellar proper. Breathlessly he informed me that at lunch that afternoon the Gestapo chiefs had decided to issue an order for the arrest of Goerdeler.

The situation was not quite so bad as it sounded. It seemed that a certain retired colonel who had talked too carelessly had been arrested and had confessed under torture that Goerdeler had repeatedly been mentioned as a candidate to succeed Hitler. The colonel, a stouthearted old soldier who had been living on pension for a long time, was well known for his loquacity. We had always avoided him for that very reason, so that he could not have betrayed any real plans for revolt. He was merely a kind and decent old gossip—just the type the Gestapo men made a habit of picking up. They never seemed to catch any of the real plotters.

Nebe assured me that neither Kaltenbrunner nor Mueller had mentioned or hinted at Beck or any of the rest of us. This was some good luck amid bad; at least we knew that the Gestapists were as yet unaware of our conspiracy; but Goerdeler would have to remain under cover.

With difficulty I persuaded Nebe to come in. He was always like that; he had to be reassured repeatedly and coaxed out of the initial shock. Everyone was disturbed by his news. Helldorf, hard-boiled as he was, remarked that the Gestapo was beginning to make things hot for us. It would only be a question of days, he said, before the Gestapo drew their circles tighter and tighter and finally closed in on our cellar. As he sketched these circles on the table with professional calm and showed their ever-narrowing radii, we began to feel distinctly ill at ease. We would have to hurry.

Hansen lent me his car so that I could report to Beck. Sooner or later, I thought, the frequent appearance of a man so conspicuously tall as myself must attract attention, even in a quiet by-street like the Goethestrasse. Involuntarily, an order for the arrest of a comrade produces a peculiar psychosis: I suddenly decided that I had been extremely unwise these past few days with my reckless bustling around town as far as Alexanderplatz.

First, I listened to Beck's news. I didn't want to inhibit him by telling him my bad news at once. Even so, his description of his meeting with Stauffenberg was by no means encouraging. Stauffenberg blamed his friend and contemporary, General Stieff. This talented officer was one of Hitler's youngest generals, who had behind him a brilliant career in the general staff. For the past six months he had been one of the main activists in Stauffenberg's group. For months the bomb had been locked in his safe, awaiting its great hour. According to Stauffenberg's description, Stieff had suddenly lost his nerve on Saturday. While Stauffenberg was telephoning the Bendlerstrasse, Stieff had taken the briefcase with its deadly contents and carried it out of the room. That was all very well. But this account did not answer our pressing question of why it had been necessary for Stauffenberg to make that telephone call. Stauffenberg had again reassured Beck about Major Roemer, but Beck nevertheless intended to talk to Olbricht about the man.

The preliminary alarm on Saturday had had the effect we feared. Both Fromm and Keitel had heard about the measure and made further inquiries. Olbricht had assured both of them that he had issued the watchword *'Walkuere'* [Valkyrie] as a mere drill measure. But obviously such a "drill" could not be repeated twice within five days. Next time the unfortunate period of three "stagnant" hours would have to remain unabridged.

From the way Beck spoke, it was clear that he was still counting on the assassination, while my thoughts were occupied completely with the "Western" solution. I informed him of Hansen's offer to supply us with a plane and suggested that we start for Kluge's headquarters directly after Goerdeler arrived in the morning.

Beck reacted strongly to this suggestion. We must leave to him the final decision on the question of assassination or capitulation of the Western armies. Stauffenberg had given him his word of honor yesterday that this coming Thursday he would explode his bomb, come what may. In sheer loyalty to Stauffenberg, he had to let the colonel have this last chance.

I asked him whether, after all that had happened, he could still really believe that the assassination would succeed. His reply was disconcerting. He told me that he considered it highly questionable that the *Putsch* would be successful. Still, if Stauffenberg did set off his bomb, we could in all probability count on Hitler's liquidation, and this positive factor outweighed all other possible mishaps. An unsuccessful *Putsch* with a dead Hitler would be better than a partially successful uprising in which that master of the black arts would be alive to lead the other side in a civil war.

Beck explained this decision with such gravity that I could not help realizing how much inner struggle it had cost him. If we gave the signal for a civil war, it would be said that in our country's darkest hour we had stayed the hand of the tyrannicide.

Emotionally, I disagreed; rationally, I had to admit that Beck was right. There was no help for it; we would have to summon up the nervous strength to wait for Thursday, July 20. Afterward we were free. If nothing happened, Beck pledged himself to try the "Western" solution. "But mind you," he said to me, "Kluge will not take the hurdle either. At the last moment he'll back down."

I told Beck about the order for the arrest of Goerdeler, but also reassured him that the rest of us were at the moment not implicated. We agreed that Goerdeler must hide out at once, but be accessible within a few hours. Beck provided me with a messenger to send to Goerdeler: Captain Kaiser, an old schoolfellow of Beck's.

July 18

I SAW BECK AGAIN, and this time told him what I thought the trouble was. He must, I said, take over the leadership of the action—especially the military leadership. His fair-minded and retiring attitude—that he would not take the position of chief of state until the assassination succeeded—was not sufficient. Military men expected clear-cut commands.

Beck listened patiently to my argument. What else was there for him to do, he asked, but to sit here on his sofa and wait until the time came? "I am to be chief of state," he said; "I am to become the military supreme commander; everyone assures me of his confidence in me, and in the final analysis the responsibility is already mine. Yet I am still a civilian; I cannot issue a single order and must be grateful if my advice is taken."

Was he right? My whole feeling about the matter ran counter to his. His theory was that a good general must refrain—unlike the amateur Hitler—from losing himself in details or interfering with the technical execution of orders to subordinates. This might be all very well in the auditorium of a military academy, but uprisings could not be conducted according to the textbooks. They shattered the normal canons of subordination and command; they required arbitrary decisions, boldness, courage; they needed leaders rather than thinkers.

Beck took my arm. With an imploring gesture he continued: "You must know what a bundle of nerves Stauffenberg is. He has already threatened twice not to set off the bomb…"

There we had it! What good were the most intelligent commands if the initiation of the *Putsch* depended on the free will, or rather the unpredictable character, of one man who was resolved, precisely because of his own tremendous stake, to gamble everything on his own card?

At the Struencks's the telephone had been ringing all morning. They had taken care not to answer it. They had a fairly good idea who would be telephoning so persistently. When it rang again during lunch, we sent the maid to answer it. Of course it was "Doctor Blank."

Struenck went to the telephone and manifested his inflexibility when Blank announced that he was coming to pay a visit. Absolutely not; the insurance policy was already "in the works"; there was nothing more to discuss. There was no need for Doctor Blank to worry about it any longer; with all these air alarms it would be best for him to stay close to the safety of his shelter.

Goerdeler did not give up easily. He still wanted to propose a vital change in the policy; there were certain additional points that had to be discussed. Above all, he wanted to speak with the other business partner. Struenck had to give in and hand the telephone to me. Although I declared once more that the project had been thoroughly discussed, that it was a waste of energy to argue the matter out over the telephone, and that I was in any case bound by a decision of the directors, Blank insisted on the proposals he had made Saturday night. He absolutely must speak to me about that, he said.

I have always felt that fear brings on dangers. On the other hand, it would be wrong to behave with exaggerated carelessness. Our friend ought to have been happy that he had received warning in time and that he had a safe hiding-place for the next few days. Any more discussion could only lead to trouble. Therefore, I put an end to the useless argument with unmistakable firmness. For compelling reasons the directors could not alter their decision, I said. We must bow to their attitude. In any case, Doctor Blank could count on receiving additional information in the immediate future.

July 19

I SAW BECK briefly in the morning. There was nothing more to discuss. We could only hope that tomorrow the torment of waiting would be over. Since the Saturday experience had indicated the need for caution, Beck suggested that I stay with Helldorf while waiting for the signal and then accompany him to the Bendlerstrasse. We shook hands for the last time before the fateful day. He gave me a meaningful look and said: "I shall have two revolvers in my pocket...."

In the evening Helldorf and Nebe dropped in. We wanted

to talk over once more all the police measures that would have to be taken. It was clear that they would do their part. Helldorf realized that his long term of office under the Nazis had compromised him too thoroughly. Within a few days after the *Putsch* he would have to resign. I respected his acumen and assured him that we would know how to acknowledge the manner in which he had cooperated with us for so many years.

After we had again discussed for the thousandth time all the personalities and immediate orders to be issued, our conversation turned toward the general course of the action. We resolved not to agitate ourselves any more. At this point there was nothing we could change; everything would have to proceed along its predestined course.

I protested vigorously when Nebe expressed pessimism about the explosive effect of Stauffenberg's bomb. It was true, of course, that since the mass bombing attacks had been launched, every layman could cite the most astonishing peculiarities about bombs. There were stories of bomb-hits that had knocked down whole blocks of houses and left plaster casts in the very center of the explosion without so much as a chip. Helldorf described vividly how a thin curtain had protected all the objects in his study from the air pressure when a bomb burst directly in front of his home.

But what was the use of such speculation? It could only bring bad luck, I felt. Nebe and Helldorf both laughed when I brusquely cut short their musings about what guardian devil might shield Hitler on the morrow.

July 20, 1944

I AWOKE TO THE KEEN CONSCIOUSNESS of the importance of this day.

The bombers did not appear. If they were decent, they

would show up between twelve and two. Then the military action could begin while the Gestapo men were huddling in their air-raid shelters.

Even this early in the morning the heat was unbearable. The Struencks accompanied me to the railroad station. A certain solemnity in their manner made me recollect how much was at stake.

Around eleven o'clock I reached Helldorf's office. The police chief sighed with relief when I appeared. Soon Count Bismarck joined us. For the most part we mused dully or complained to one another about the heat.

Shortly after twelve the sergeant on duty reported that a major was outside with a message from General Olbricht. Helldorf and I were electrified. The major entered, a small man, ghastly pale, obviously nervous. To judge by his face he could not have been older than thirty. In one hand he clutched a black briefcase as if it contained a treasure in diamonds. His other hand he raised stiffly in the Nazi greeting; then he appeared to realize that he might at least omit the "Heil Hitler." With a suspicious glance at Count Bismarck and me, he asked Helldorf whether he might speak to him privately.

Helldorf could not refrain from smiling. He inspected this messenger of the fates who seemed overwhelmed by his historic role and said jovially, "Come, now, let's have it."

The young major did not dare talk. Helldorf had to assure him that we knew all about it and that he need not fear to speak openly.

Now, we thought, we would hear the great news. Instead, a very different bomb burst. The major stated that he was a member of the staff of the district command. General Olbricht had given him the city maps with the marked buildings which were to be occupied today. He was instructed to discuss the rest with Helldorf.

The map of the city that the young major unfolded with trembling hands seemed strangely familiar to me. Sure enough, it was the one we had used at the time of Stalingrad, the one Olbricht had recently had his adjutant show to Nebe, and which, we had afterward been assured, must have been brought out by mistake. A little study soon corroborated Nebe's statement that it had not even been corrected for recent bombings or evacuations.

The major wanted to know what help could be expected from the police. Helldorf replied that it had been agreed that the police would be completely restrained during the first few hours and would not begin to act until after the lightning occupation of all important buildings by the Wehrmacht had been completed.

Olbricht's emissary could not understand this. Would he at least have at his disposal Nebe's detectives to undertake the necessary arrests? He was informed that these men, too, could be used only after the occupation of the government buildings. The officer objected. The soldiers were merely supposed to surround the building; Nebe's detectives were to take care of everything else.

With exemplary calm Helldorf corrected these misapprehensions. But correction did not help much at this critical hour. Therefore, I asked whether it would not be possible for the police to go ahead and do what apparently was expected of them. Helldorf said he could not let his men act until the Wehrmacht had actually completed the seizure of power. He suggested that the major would do best to follow out the scheme outlined in Olbricht's plans and to surround all the buildings indicated on the map in their proper order. Undoubtedly headquarters would then issue the commands for further action.

I rather think the major left not much wiser than when he

had come. As he took his leave with exemplary military precision, I indulged in some private reflections on the scene. In the machinery of a total war that conscripted fifteen-year-old children, such young majors might have their place, but whether they were of the stuff of which uprisings were made, the next few hours would prove.

"A likely prospect"—that was Helldorf's succinct commentary on this little intermezzo.

The clock was already approaching one. Our wait would soon be over; for whether it was the oppressive heat and humidity or our enforced inactivity, time dragged unconscionably.

As I stood looking out of Helldorf's window down upon the wreckage of Alexanderplatz, upon the weary, gaunt people who moved slowly amid the ruins, I realized fully what was at stake now, perhaps this very second. Were death and destruction to continue to rain from the sky? Would there be no end to the blood-letting on both sides in East and West? Or was the explosion of a bomb at this moment ushering in a change in the course of history?

Enough of these thoughts. We had better wait without thinking. It would be time soon enough.

From one o'clock on, Helldorf had kept urging me every five minutes to telephone Nebe. Perhaps he would have heard something. I had already arranged with Nebe, however, that he would call the moment he heard anything at all. If I made an unnecessary call, he would take alarm. That was how he always reacted.

As the hands of the clock moved around toward two, the suspense became unbearable. Was it possible that Nebe, with his excessive caution, would leave his office without telephoning beforehand? At five minutes to two, I made up my mind

and called him on the phone. He pretended to be in exception-
ally good humor. When I asked whether we could not see him
for a few minutes, he said he was unfortunately too busy at the
moment. Something strange had happened in East Prussia and
he had to give instructions to two detectives who were to leave
with Kaltenbrunner in half an hour and fly to the Fuehrer's
headquarters in order to conduct the initial investigation.

Had the bomb already exploded? That seemed to be the
import of Nebe's message. But the communications center was
to have been blown up at the same time. Had some message,
nevertheless, leaked through? Why was Kaltenbrunner already
going into action? Were our men trying to lure him into a trap
in East Prussia? I could make nothing of Nebe's words or of his
tone of voice.

Naturally, I could not ask questions. Therefore I urged
Nebe to come. I absolutely had to see him at once, I said. At
first he would not consent. But when I insisted, "Where are
you?" he asked.

"Right near you," I replied. "In the restaurant—you know,
the one where we recently met with that mutual acquaintance
of ours."

Nebe said he would come right over.

Helldorf and Bismarck were as mystified as I was. For if
the assassination had taken place, Wehrmacht headquarters
would undoubtedly know about it, whether it had succeeded or
failed. And it seemed utterly out of the question that Olbricht
would let us wait unnecessarily for even a minute.

At two o'clock Helldorf was scheduled for a meeting with
the chief of his detective force. At three o'clock there was a
conference at his office with the staff of the Party district. He
had to pretend to have some official business today, and if the
Berlin Party leaders were "by chance" all gathered together in

his office, so much the better. We should not have to conduct a search in order to arrest them.

Helldorf asked Bismarck and me to wait in an adjoining room while he conferred with the chief of his detectives. As soon as Nebe came, he said, he would interrupt the conference for a moment and come in. But Nebe did not come. It was nearly three when Helldorf returned to the room where we were waiting in an agony of suspense. He was more nervous than annoyed. "We've had a bad break," he said. "My switch-board reported that Nebe was calling. Naturally, I thought he was waiting outside and sent word to him that the chief of the detective force was with me at the moment and that he should join you in my waiting room in the meanwhile. The sergeant delivered this message. Now I've just found out that Nebe called from outside. He was waiting in the Hotel Excelsior."

Such an idiotic misunderstanding could occur only on a day like this! Because I had mentioned a restaurant, Nebe had thought I meant Helldorf's hotel, which was also near his office. When he did not find us there and telephoned, he had apparently taken the message that the chief of the detective force was there as a concealed warning not to come to police headquarters.

I tried to reach Nebe at his office, but by then he was at lunch in the Prinz Albrechtstrasse.

At four o'clock Helldorf at last rushed excitedly into our room "It's starting!" he exclaimed. Olbricht had just tele-phoned him to hold himself in readiness; there would be an important message within half an hour.

This time, at least, we did not have to wait the full half-hour. Before four-thirty Helldorf reappeared. "Gentlemen, we're off!" he exclaimed triumphantly. "Olbricht has just given me an official order to report at the Bendlerstrasse: he says the Fuehrer is dead, a state of siege has been proclaimed, and he has urgent orders to deliver to me in the name of Colonel-General Fromm."

Helldorf said this with a completely credible imitation of surprise. His energetic manner bore witness to his full appreciation of the significance of this moment. Obviously he was already imagining the scene in which he would persuade his police officers that they must remain inactive for the time being.

During our ride in Helldorf's limousine, I involuntarily imagined that every pedestrian past whom we flitted must be able to sense the vibrations of our nerves. But the people of Berlin slouched along in the sultry heat, weary and dull to all that went on outside their immediate and pathetic concerns. We were sobered and disappointed when even the Bendlerstrasse presented a deserted appearance. Not the slightest change had taken place, even at the entrance to the OKW.

It seemed perfectly natural to me that the guards admitted Helldorf in his uniform of a police general. But I was slightly disquieted by the fact that they did not even check up on me, a civilian.

Only that part of Wehrmacht headquarters which had always contained the offices of Fromm and Olbricht was still standing. We rushed up the stairs and were led into Olbricht's waiting room directly, without being announced beforehand; but those few steps from the outer door to the office were enough for us to absorb the atmosphere of this headquarters of the *Putsch*. Not only Olbricht's but Stauffenberg's office was located here. Here—not far from Fromm's rooms—the crucial orders were being written, the secret telephone calls received. We felt at once: now we were "inside."

The general was standing quite a distance behind his desk as we entered. He came toward us, and we met somewhere in the middle of the big room. Even as we were crossing the room, however, I saw something that for the moment made me doubt my eyes. Those two officers standing at one side of the desk were—Stauffenberg and Lieutenant von Haeften who had accompanied and assisted him today. How could they possibly be here? They could not have been shot from East Prussia in a rocket. If they had come by plane, the assassination must have taken place hours ago. How did this fit in with Nebe's hint over the telephone? Were we limping along three and a half irretrievable hours behind the Gestapo? These and a thousand other thoughts were quickly swept aside by the overwhelming perception: Now you are about to shake the hand that struck down the tyrant.

Stauffenberg's appearance was impressive. Tall and slender, he stood breathless and bathed in perspiration. Somehow the massiveness of the man had been reduced; he seemed more spiritualized, lighter. There was a smile of victory on his face; he radiated the triumph of a test successfully completed.

Beck came toward us. We greeted one another with a silent, deeply felt clasp of the hands. What could be said at such a moment?

Olbricht was the first to speak. As if he had learned a text by heart, he informed Helldorf in the tone of a military command that the Fuehrer had been the victim of assassination that afternoon. The Wehrmacht had taken over the direction of the government; a state of siege was being proclaimed. The Berlin police were hereby subordinated directly to the *Oberkommando der Wehrmacht* and he, Helldorf, was to carry out at once the necessary measures.

Olbricht's voice quivered with excitement. Nevertheless, I had the feeling that there was nothing original about this. It did not sound like a proclamation of a great change; rather, it seemed like pure declamation, a histrionic accomplishment. The very theatricality of it restored me to reality. Of course—

the battle was not yet won, the Gestapo nest not yet cleaned out....

Helldorf played along. He made a brief military bow and started to leave in order to convoke the meeting of his officers, but before he was out of the door, Beck's quiet, firm voice reached out to him. The former chief of the general staff spoke more loudly than usual: "One moment, Olbricht. In all loyalty we must inform the chief of police that according to certain reports from headquarters Hitler may not be dead. We must now decide clearly how..."

Olbricht did not let him finish. Excitedly he exclaimed, "Keitel is lying! Keitel is lying!..."

Stauffenberg laughed triumphantly. Haeften did not join him.

Beck raised his hand in dissent. "No, no, no..."

But Olbricht obviously wanted the discussion to wait until Helldorf was gone. Again he interrupted and repeated, "Keitel is lying! Keitel is lying!"

Helldorf, Bismarck, and I looked at one another in utter consternation. All at once the fiction was being torn to shreds. Suddenly we were confronted with the brutal reality of the *Putsch*.

Beck would not be put off. "Olbricht, it doesn't matter whether Keitel is lying. What is important is that Helldorf must know what the other side has asserted about the failure of the assassination, and we must also be prepared for a similar announcement over the radio. What will we say then?"

Olbricht referred to Stauffenberg's conclusive report. Stauffenberg stated in confirmation that the bomb had exploded and that there had been a darting flame such as was produced by the bursting of a fifteen-centimeter shell. No one could have come out of the explosion alive, he said. At the very least, Hitler must have been critically wounded.

In growing agitation Olbricht insisted that he knew what a liar Keitel was.

Beck had no intention of casting any doubt upon Stauffenberg's report. Nor did he assume that Hitler would speak on the radio within the next few hours—although he did mention this as a possibility.

"Olbricht," he said, "a clear watchword must be issued. What will Helldorf say, what will you tell the other officers, if Keitel, Himmler, and Goebbels declare that Hitler is alive?"

Beck continued. He made a brief, explicit summary of the situation. He asked the others to keep their solidarity with him. "For me this man is dead. That is the basis of my further activity. Indisputable proof that Hitler—and not his double—is still alive cannot possibly come from headquarters for hours. By then the action in Berlin must be completed."

No one contradicted him. Helldorf hurried away to return to his office.

Colonel-General Hoeppner came into the room to fetch his suitcase which he had left with Olbricht. Two years ago Hoeppner had been deprived of the right to wear a uniform; now he wanted to dress up for his part.

Olbricht declared that it was high time to confront Colonel-General Fromm with an ultimatum. He wanted to do this before Fromm was alarmed by telephone calls of inquiry. The orders for the imposition of a state of siege were being sent out over the teletype in Fromm's name. Stauffenberg went with Olbricht to see Fromm. Then I impolitely suggested to Bismarck, the administrative president of Potsdam, that there must be urgent business awaiting him at the government building in Potsdam. Bismarck left.

Now Beck and I were alone. I asked him bluntly how it was that Stauffenberg was back so soon? Why had they waited so long? Beck responded to my questions with a typical gesture:

he shook his head repeatedly and struck his forehead with the palm of his hand. He was obviously none too optimistic. Then he took my arm reassuringly. "Don't ask too many questions," he said. "You can see how excited they all are. We can no longer change anything—we can only hope that all will go well ..." He still assumed that something had gone wrong at headquarters, so that the word of the assassination had not come through in time and Stauffenberg had brought it when he returned. It is sad that in the few hours of life that were left to him he was not spared the tragic knowledge that they had deliberately deceived him.

Around twelve o'clock Stauffenberg had arrived at headquarters in Rastenburg to participate in the conference with the Fuehrer. This usually took place in an underground shelter, and the explosive force of the bomb had been calculated for such a concrete-walled room. But on this day Hitler—was it the heat or one of his intuitive whims—had ordered a change of meeting-place just before the session. The conference took place in a wooden barracks.

Stauffenberg delivered his report. The briefcase with its deadly contents stood right under the table over which Hitler was leaning to study the maps. The mechanism of the bomb could be started by a slight pressure of his foot. Toward one o'clock the opportunity seemed favorable. Stauffenberg had himself called out of the room allegedly to answer a telephone call, and as he left he activated the detonating mechanism. He and Haeften were scarcely a hundred yards away when they observed the dart of flame from the explosion. There was a thunderous noise and a number of persons were hurled through the air and out of the barracks; the thin walls had permitted the air pressure to escape. Unquestionably the explosion had not been as effective as it would have been inside the concrete walls of the shelter.

The two men were satisfied, however, by what they had seen and sprang into their waiting car. In the panic they succeeded in making their way unhindered to the airport; but while their plane was hurtling toward Berlin, something totally unexpected took place at Wehrmacht headquarters in the Bendlerstrasse. A few minutes after the explosion General Fellgiebel telephoned Olbricht, as agreed, and gave the cue. But the blowing-up of the communications center, which had also been planned, did not take place.

Colonel-General Fromm was receiving a military report when, shortly after two o'clock, Olbricht stormed into his office. He said he had something of such vital importance to communicate that he must speak to Fromm privately. Fromm interrupted the report. Olbricht curtly informed his chief that Hitler had just been the victim of an assassination. How did he know? He had been informed by General Fellgiebel, who had just telephoned personally from headquarters. Olbricht proposed that under the circumstances Fromm should issue to the various deputy headquarters in charge of the reserve forces the code word for internal disorders: *Walkuere* [Valkyrie]. Thereby the state power would temporarily pass into the hands of the Wehrmacht.

Fromm was astonished, but not quite convinced. Under the circumstances he did the natural thing: he telephoned the Fuehrer's headquarters to check up. *And the Rastenburg communications center had not been blown up.* Olbricht, feeling perfectly sure of himself, listened in on another telephone. To his shocked surprise, the Fuehrer's headquarters responded to the call. Worse yet, Keitel answered the telephone. And still worse,

Keitel denied that anything had happened to Hitler. The text of the telephone call has been preserved. It ran as follows:

> *Fromm:* "What in the world is going on at headquarters? Here in Berlin the wildest rumors are afloat."
> *Keitel:* "What is supposed to be going on? Everything is all right."
> *Fromm:* "I have just received a report that the Fuehrer was killed by assassination."
> *Keitel:* "Nonsense. There was an attempted assassination, but fortunately it failed. The Fuehrer is alive and received only superficial injuries. Where, by the way, is the chief of your staff, Colonel Stauffenberg?"
> *Fromm:* "Stauffenberg is not here yet."

Not one word of indignation about the assassination. Not even an obvious inquiry as to what had taken place and whether anyone else was killed. Not a word about what either intended to do. Fromm wanted only to listen, Keitel to cover up. As soon as Fromm hung up, two generals sighed with relief. Thank God, it had turned out well once more. Well? Certainly—they need not make a decision.

Fromm informed Olbricht that in view of this situation there seemed to be no occasion to issue the code word for internal disorder. Obviously confused by the telephone call, Olbricht returned to his office to confer with the Stauffenberg group. Colonel-General Hoeppner was also present. But good counsel was scarce—at least here.

At the time if they had at least called Beck or sent for Helldorf, Nebe, and myself, we undoubtedly would have declared unanimously that the only course was to go ahead with the *Putsch.* But not even Beck was informed, let alone us "civilians." The leaderless and therefore mindless Stauffenberg group agreed with Olbricht's decision that in the face of so complicated a situation it would be best to wait until Stauffenberg's return, and meanwhile to do nothing at all.

We can imagine Stauffenberg's horrified dismay when he arrived at the Rangsdorf airport around four o'clock and heard that nothing had happened yet. In an understandable outburst of indignation, he ordered the *Putsch* to begin at once.

But as I have said, neither Beck nor I yet knew anything about all this. For this reason we were ignorant of the background of the scene that now took place with Fromm.

Olbricht and Stauffenberg informed the commander-in-chief of the home army that Hitler was indeed dead and that Stauffenberg could personally confirm his decease. The text of this scene is taken from the war crime indictment against Fromm:

> *Fromm:* "It is impossible; Keitel assured me that it was not so."
>
> *Stauffenberg:* "Field Marshal Keitel is lying as usual. I myself saw Hitler being carried out dead."
>
> *Olbricht:* "In view of this situation we have issued the code word for internal unrest to the commanding generals."
>
> *Fromm* (springing to his feet and pounding his fist on the desk): "That is sheer disobedience! What do you mean by 'we'? Who gave the order?"
>
> *Olbricht:* "My chief of staff, Colonel Merz von Quirnheim."
>
> *Fromm:* "Send Colonel Merz in here at once."
>
> Merz von Quirnheim enters. He admits to having issued the code word to the commanding generals without Fromm's permission.
>
> *Fromm:* "You are under arrest. We shall see about further action."
>
> Colonel Stauffenberg stands and declares icily: "General

Fromm, I myself detonated the bomb during the conference in Hitler's headquarters. There was an explosion like that of a fifteen-centimeter shell. No one who was in that room can still be living."

Fromm: "Count Stauffenberg, the assassination failed. You must shoot yourself at once."

Stauffenberg: "I shall do nothing of the kind."

Olbricht: "General Fromm, the moment for action has come. If we do not strike now, our country will be ruined forever."

Fromm: "Does that mean that you, too, are taking part in this coup d'état, Olbricht?"

Olbricht: "Yes, sir. But I am not a member of the group that will take over the government of Germany."

Fromm: "I hereby declare all three of you arrested."

Olbricht: "You cannot arrest us. You do not realize who holds the power. We arrest you!"

Somehow, the whole truth about the *Putsch* was expressed by this interview. "What do you mean by 'We'?" The question was quite justified. And the answer was not: "I." Had Merz, on Stauffenberg's orders, presented Olbricht with a *fait accompli,* just as they were now trying to do with Fromm?

In any case, there ensued an angry scuffle—though it did not come to much more than indignant words and a violent waving of hands. All four were equally relieved when Fromm, amid empty protests, permitted them to intern him in the adjoining room.

Olbricht and Stauffenberg returned to the office in which Beck and I were pacing back and forth. Both were exhausted as they informed us of the "skirmish" they had just been through. Stauffenberg had no time to go into lengthy reflections on Fromm's behavior. Activity halted whenever he did not stand behind it with his organizational talent and impulsiveness. He left us quickly, and looked in only now and then to say a word or to search for something in Olbricht's safe.

Beck and I remained alone—the only civilians among all these uniformed men. It was rather depressing to sit and feel wholly deserted, while all around us history was being made. As if we were schoolboys who had misbehaved, we were being punished by having to sit passively for three hours. We talked to one another in whispers, as if the Gestapo were still listening.

Beck was prompted to call out: "By the way, Olbricht, what measures have been taken to assure our safety in this building?"

Without rising from his desk, Olbricht replied that the doors had been shut and the guards had received orders to admit no one. Unfortunately, there were no more than the usual guards available. As Beck knew, the troops were just starting out.

Beck asked in his quiet, firm fashion: "Olbricht, what instructions have the guards been given? Whose orders do they obey?"

"Mine."

"What will the guards do if the Gestapo should suddenly appear?"

Olbricht shrugged. Nevertheless, he left his desk and approached us.

"Olbricht, will the guards shoot?"

"*Dinna ken...* (I don't know)"

Olbricht was the last person to be impolite, nor was he inclined to bluff his way out of rotten situations. For that reason it was easy to sense the insincerity and uncertainty in his reply.

For a moment Beck was silent. Then he repeated, quietly,

calmly, but with great emphasis: "Olbricht, will those soldiers stand to the death for you?"

"*Dinna ken...*"

With amazing equanimity, but with the same friendly urgency, Beck said: "Olbricht, when Fritsch was here it would have been different."

Olbricht flushed and shrugged in embarrassment.

"Olbricht, the soldiers would have stood to the death for Fritsch..."

I asked Beck whether he ought not to do something. He tried to quench my impatience. "Go easy, easy, easy." A general must keep his nerve, he said again. Now it was up to Hoeppner, Olbricht, Stauffenberg, and Witzleben to do their part. He did not intend to confuse them by unnecessary interference.

I admired his self-discipline. His behavior was perfectly reasonable—but emotionally I objected violently to it. I told him about our experience with the young major who had brought us the outmoded maps at noon.

"A number of things seem to be going wrong today," he remarked dryly.

Olbricht returned, accompanied by Hoeppner. Colonel-General Fromm had asked him for permission to go home. He offered his word of honor to remain quiet and undertake no action against us. Olbricht and Hoeppner recommended that he be allowed to go. Beck was obviously impressed by their recommendation. He disliked Fromm intensely, but if Hoeppner and Olbricht were willing to take the responsibility...

I intervened hotly. The best Fromm deserved was to be shot, I said angrily.

Just at this moment Stauffenberg joined us. Olbricht pointed out that Fromm had always been fair. If he gave his word of honor he would keep it.

"What does a word of honor mean?" I retorted. I reminded them that Stauffenberg himself had broken his word of
honor; a few months ago he had given Fromm his word of
honor not to take any action against Hitler. Consequently,
Fromm in his turn would not feel obliged to keep his. In fact,
having not decided for us, he must necessarily act against us.

I had not had the slightest intention of insulting Stauffenberg, but he took my parallel as a personal affront. He started
to explain—as if I needed explanation—what patriotic
motives had led him to feel that his word of honor was no
longer binding.

Beck ordered that Fromm be kept in custody.

Since we were all together and all slightly irritated, I
thought this was as good an opportunity as any to say all at
once what had to be said. Therefore, I suggested that we ought
to discuss what police measures were to be taken. At least an
hour had passed since Helldorf had left us. It was time he and
Nebe received further instructions. In my excitement I may
have asked too many questions or too precise ones. I wanted to
know what buildings were being surrounded, what was being
done about the radio, above all whether, among the immediate
tasks allocated to the *Grossdeutschland* battalion of guards, the
storming of the Gestapo building and the shooting of
Goebbels had been included.

I did not notice how angry Stauffenberg was becoming
until Beck plucked soothingly at the colonel's arm and with
great friendliness asked the three of us to leave him alone with
Stauffenberg for a moment; he wished to confer privately with
the colonel.

Olbricht and Hoeppner went off into Fromm's rooms,
which were one flight up. I stayed in Olbricht's waiting room.
My wait was interrupted by the exchange of a few words with
Count Fritz Schulenberg and Count Yorck. Then I saw Stauf-

fenberg hurry past the door. I went in to see Beck again. But I had no opportunity to talk to him, for as I entered, Olbricht rushed into the room, somewhat out of breath because he had been called down from upstairs, and somewhat at a loss because Keitel wanted to talk with him on the telephone. Olbricht wanted Beck to advise him whether or not to accept the call.

Beck thought there was little point to answering Keitel; I vehemently insisted there was. Perhaps it was a chance to worm out of him some information about Hitler. Such a conversation could do no harm, at any rate. Olbricht decided to take the call. There was a business of switching and cross-switching before the connection was transferred from Fromm's waiting room to Olbricht's office. By the time this was over, Keitel had abandoned the attempt and hung up.

Olbricht had to rush away again. Hoeppner had just run into a furious dispute with the acting military district commander of Berlin who was unwilling to cooperate. This prompted Beck to ask me where Witzleben was. So far as I knew, he was on the way to Zossen. He had received the code word while on an estate near Luebben and was now going to Zossen to take command there. Beck was dissatisfied with this. As commander of all three divisions of the Wehrmacht [army, navy, and air force], Witzleben ought to be in Berlin, he said.

By this time Olbricht was back, seething with indignation. Beck must come up to Hoeppner's office at once, he said. General Kortzfleisch was insisting that Hitler was not dead, and for this reason he refused to declare a state of siege in Berlin. He had come to talk to Fromm. Instead, Hoeppner had received him, but Kortzfleisch still wanted to see Fromm. Perhaps it would help if Beck talked to him. In any event, Olbricht had a stand-in ready to take the place of Kortzfleisch as commander in Berlin.

"You see," Beck remarked to me as he was going out. "I was right. Witzleben ought to be here."

I sat down on the sofa in the waiting room again. From minute to minute the bustle appeared to increase. Adjutants came and went. The telephones rang continually. Suddenly thumping footsteps sounded in the corridor. The door flew open and an SS *Standartenfuehrer* [equivalent to a colonel] of the typical butcher type appeared in the doorway. A more vivid, more typical SS hangman could scarcely be imagined. This creature clicked his heels with a report like a pistol-shot, raised his hand in the "German" greeting and growled loudly, "Heil Hitler."

For a second the thought flashed through my mind: Have they come already? But the hangman merely asked politely whether he might speak to Colonel von Stauffenberg. "On orders of the chief of the Reich security office," he added self-importantly.

The two men greeted each other curtly and formally. Then Stauffenberg invited his strange guest into his office. I had heard the man boom out his name. He was *Standartenfuehrer* Pfiffrather, one of the worst of the Gestapo crew who was now in charge of the counterespionage organization, the Abwehr, which had been placed under the Gestapo after it was withdrawn from Canaris. I was amazed at the boldness of the man at venturing into the lions' den. Evidently the Reich security office—that is, the Gestapo—was still groping in the dark. Otherwise they would not have sent one of their prominent men to the Bendlerstrasse.

After a while Stauffenberg returned. Pfiffrather had wanted to question him about his obvious hurry to fly back from the Fuehrer's headquarters. Stauffenberg's reply had been to lock the fellow up.

For a moment I was speechless. Then I said: "Stauffenberg, why didn't you shoot that murderer at once?"

His turn would come, the colonel remarked, and started off.

"Stauffenberg, how can you leave this man here to watch everything that's going on? Just imagine if he should make a break later on."

Now it was Stauffenberg's turn to be speechless. By the angry glow in his eyes I realized how many doubts he must have read into this advice of mine that such burdensome witnesses ought to be summarily put out of the way.

"Stauffenberg, we cannot wait passively for these full three hours. We must do something. If you don't want to shoot that fellow, let us form an officers' troop and drive over to the Prinz Albrechtstrasse. We must eliminate Mueller and Goebbels."

Stauffenberg would listen to proposals for action. The troops hadn't arrived yet, as I well knew, he said. Nevertheless, he had himself thought of an officers' troop. He would talk to Colonel Jaeger. Jaeger was a well-known daredevil whom we had long considered the natural leader for such shock-troop actions. How fortunate that he was here!

Beck returned. I had never yet seen him so angry. He described the scene that had taken place in Hoeppner's room. General Kortzfleisch had refused to cooperate on the grounds of his oath to Hitler. Beck repeated his indignant reply to me: "How dare you talk of oaths? Hitler has broken his oath to the constitution and his vows to the people a hundred times over. How dare you refer to your oath of loyalty to such a perjurer!"

Argument, however, had accomplished nothing. Kortzfleisch was now providing company for Fromm and Pfiffrather.

I was called to the telephone. Who knew I was here?

Helldorf's adjutant was waiting at the street entrance. He

asked me to come down; the guards would not let him in. I hurried downstairs. Helldorf wanted to know what was going on. I told the adjutant that the action was beginning and that Helldorf would have to be patient, since unfortunately I knew no more than he. The adjutant was none too satisfied with the meager information. His chief was beginning to grow impatient, he said. Couldn't I return with him to Helldorf; undoubtedly Helldorf would want to discuss things with me.

This suggestion seemed sensible. I had nothing to do upstairs in any event and could easily be back within three-quarters of an hour. I left word with Olbricht's adjutant and departed.

It was around six o'clock when I entered Helldorf's office. Nebe was with him. Both men were drinking coffee.

It was not easy for me to perform the mental shift from the turbulence of the Bendlerstrasse to this compound of peaceful idyll and challenging skepticism. Instead of asking any questions, Helldorf contented himself with a long-drawn-out, "What now?" Nebe gave me a look that seemed to say: "My poor friend, I myself don't think you're crazy, of course, but you can't deny that you've just come from an insane asylum."

I, too, of course, was not satisfied with all that was taking place at Wehrmacht headquarters. But for the present the tank troops were just moving up; they could not arrive before half-past seven. I pointed out—with perhaps a touch of hypocritical equanimity—that we were still passing through that period of three "stagnant" hours in which, as we had always known, nothing special could happen.

Helldorf refused to concede this. That might be true of Wehrmacht headquarters, but it was not true for him at police headquarters. In the two hours that had passed since Olbricht's instructions to him, nothing, absolutely nothing, had happened. According to plan, he had frozen his entire police apparatus; but not a single representative of the military had come to see him. Helldorf pointed out that General von Haase should long since have sent for him or come to see him or sent a liaison officer to him.

Moreover, where was Major Roemer's battalion of guards, who did not need three hours to reach Berlin and who were supposed to take care of the most essential immediate tasks? I could not make any rebuttal to this challenge, but I tried to explain it as a result of the confusion in the military district command.

I asked Nebe about conditions in the Prinz Albrecht-strasse. So far as he knew, up to half-past five the Gestapo knew nothing at all about the beginning of the *Putsch* and was not even certain that Stauffenberg had set off the bomb. A few minutes ago Helldorf had spoken with Group Leader Mueller. Mueller had brashly told him that there seemed to be a military *Putsch* in progress; there were troops around the Wilhelm-strasse and the Prinz Albrechtstrasse, but the Fuehrer was on the alert and a statement would be issued over the radio. SS reinforcements were on the march from outside Berlin.

As I re-entered the Wehrmacht building on the Bendlerstrasse I encountered Olbricht on the stairs. "Beck wants to see you," he said to me, "but there can't be such a hurry about it. Come to my office for a minute. I want to discuss something with you privately."

He informed me that while I was gone the radio statement about the failure of the assassination had been issued. No details were given and not a word had been said about the probable assassin. But, the general said, he no longer had the slightest doubt that Hitler was still alive. Colonel von Hayessen had also telephoned to confirm the fact. Hitler was having tea with Mussolini in the Fuehrer's pavilion; the Italian dictator had chosen just this day to pay an unexpected visit.

I waited eagerly to hear what Olbricht wanted to discuss with me. He had certainly not invited me in simply to give me information. Finally it came out. "My dear Gisevius—just for the sake of discussion I wanted to hear your opinion..." Pause. "But of course..." Another pause. "Of course—we can't call it off and deny it at this point, can we?"

Somehow, the manner in which Olbricht asked me this question drained all anger out of me. "No," I said, "you're quite right; we can't really call it off or deny it any more." Hadn't Beck wanted to see me? I excused myself.

I went upstairs to Fromm's spacious office. Beck caught sight of me and rushed toward me. According to a number of telephone calls, Hitler was about to speak on the radio. Was I prepared to make a radio statement for our side? I was amazed. Up to this moment the program had called for General Lindemann to read the first statement. If it seemed inadvisable to have a general initiate matters, then certainly the proper candidates were Goerdeler or Beck. But Beck would not hear of it. The situation had been fundamentally changed, he said, by the report that Hitler was still alive. Goerdeler was not here. He himself must stay around.

An evil premonition told me that perhaps this radio address would be all that the public would ever hear about the events of this day. I should be foolish to miss this opportunity to leave at least one visiting card.

I asked where the original proclamation was. General Lindemann, it seemed, had the only copy in his keeping—and Lindemann was nowhere to be found. He had been there earlier in the afternoon, but had not been seen for hours. I made my private conjectures about this mysterious disappearance and sat down in a corner of Fromm's office to write out a few sentences. Actually, I did not want to make any sort of outline. If I did eventually speak, it would be too good an opportunity to extemporize. Such a speech had to evolve out of the inspiration of the moment; it ought to sound like a rallying cry, not like a newspaper editorial.

Fromm's office was separated only by a sliding door from that of his chief of staff, Stauffenberg. There was a constant bustling back and forth between these two rooms. One moment the telephone on Fromm's desk would ring, then one of the two telephones on Stauffenberg's desk. Each time Stauffenberg rushed back and forth the twenty steps from the one telephone to the other. Everyone was asking for him—understandably. For the generals in the provinces scarcely knew Hoeppner, and the switchboard operators had been instructed to say that Fromm was not in.

Everyone listened to every conversation. Sooner or later there would have to be important messages from the provinces, and we could really do with a little good news. At our end of the wire Stauffenberg incessantly repeated the same refrain: "Keitel is lying… Don't believe Keitel… Hitler is dead… Yes, he is definitely dead… Yes, here the action is in full swing…"

The questions he was being asked could easily be imagined. What was interesting was the variety of tones in which Stauffenberg responded. One moment his voice was firm and commanding, the next friendly and persuasive, the next imploring. "You must hold firm… See to it that your chief doesn't weaken… Hayessen, I'm depending on you… Please, don't disappoint me… We must hold firm… We must hold firm…" Stauffenberg was the only one in control of the situation, the only one who knew what he wanted.

Beck, too, was impressed by Stauffenberg's conduct. In reality, however, our thoughts were on something else entirely: on the feeling we had, baseless, perhaps, but persistent, that the other officers were not holding firm. Hoeppner in particular depressed us by his obvious misery. Beck sat beside me watching the agitated bustle and repeating what he had said so often during these past few days. "A good general must be able to wait." All that he could do was to inquire about the progress of the *Putsch* in Zossen. Where was Witzleben? I stopped asking this question, because the mere mention of it so upset Beck. The latest news was that Witzleben had left Zossen and was on his way to Berlin.

General Wagner, whom Beck had telephoned twice and who was responsible for the cooperation of the headquarters at Zossen, would no longer answer the telephone.

Now and then Stauffenberg stopped for a moment in our corner. According to the Count, everything was proceeding splendidly. The tanks were on the way. They would reach the center of the city by half-past seven at the latest. Then the main action could begin, blow upon blow. This sounded reassuring because the hands of the clock were rapidly approaching half-past seven. As yet we had received no disturbing reports about Gestapo or Waffen-SS activity. We seemed to have the head start. Nevertheless, I could not shake off the tormenting feeling that we ought not wait so long.

When I had a chance to talk privately to Stauffenberg for a moment, I said urgently: "Stauffenberg, too little is happening. Goebbels and Mueller are still alive." I offered to accompany any group of officers that he would form into a shock troop. After the failure of the blow against Hitler, it would be a good idea to choose some other victims; with Goebbels and Mueller dead, the other side would be temporarily paralyzed and our side would be encouraged.

At first Stauffenberg would not agree. As soon as the tanks arrived, the program of arrests would begin. The most important buildings would be surrounded by a cordon; no one would escape. I pointed out that the question was not one of escape, but of psychological benefit. Apparently I convinced him by stressing this psychological aspect of the matter. He ran off to look for Colonel Jaeger; Jaeger would form a shock troop of officers, he said.

Had he not been seeking Jaeger an hour ago?

Beck came over to me to ask whether my radio address was ready. He might have seen that I had been writing nothing; most of the time I had been talking either with him or others; but how could I convince my formal-minded friend who was so fond of the written word that in certain situations it was necessary to depend on extemporaneous speech? He, when he saw that he could not persuade me to write out a draft of my speech, insisted that at least we must discuss it point by point. In clear, cogent sentences, he explained what he thought should be said. The basic idea was of the simplest: that it did not matter at all whether Hitler was dead or still living. A "leader" whose immediate entourage included those who opposed him to the extent of attempting assassination must be considered morally dead. From this starting-point all the rest fell naturally into line, no matter what radio statements emanated from Goebbels.

A sensation. Paris was telephoning. Up to now none of the commands from the front or from the occupied territories had reported. Beck hurried to the telephone to talk personally with Stuelpnagel. It was a refreshing conversation; we who were listening felt for once that the general on the other end was not trying to dodge the issue. Stuelpnagel reported that he had taken all the appropriate measures. The responsible SS leaders were under arrest. The troops were responding to his orders without demur. What about Kluge? Stuelpnagel advised Beck to talk with him directly.

Stuelpnagel succeeded in switching the call to the Western headquarters, which was situated near Paris. We all stood tensely around Beck as he spoke to Kluge in comradely, persuasive, firm tones. He described the measures that had been taken in Berlin, called upon the marshal not to vacillate at a time that was, psychologically, so critical.

I felt that Beck was not pressing him toward an unequivocal answer. I therefore whispered to him: "Make it clear to Kluge that he can no longer back down." He nodded agreement and handed the second receiver to me.

"Kluge, I now ask you clearly: Do you approve of this action of ours and do you place yourself under my orders?"

Kluge stammered a few phrases that were apparently the outburst of a tormented soul. It was impossible to make anything of them; yes was no and no was yes.

"Kluge, in order to remove the slightest doubt, I want to remind you of our last conversations and agreements. I ask again: Do you place yourself unconditionally under my orders?"

Kluge remembered all the conversations, but the failure of the assassination had created an unexpected situation, he said. He would have to confer with his staff. He would call back in half an hour.

"Kluge!" Beck exclaimed to me as he hung up. "There you have him!"

Colonel-General Fromm contrived to divert us from our gloomy thoughts. He sent one of the officers who was guarding him to inform us that he was hungry; wouldn't we permit him to go home? His offer of his word of honor still stood. In the present state of affairs, everyone agreed that Fromm must not be released, but one after the other, Beck, Olbricht, Hoeppner, and Stauffenberg, asserted that they wanted to treat him in a perfectly honorable fashion. They would have a bottle of wine and sandwiches sent in to him from the officers' canteen.

The guards telephoned up to us that Witzleben had arrived at last. He entered, holding his cap in one hand and waving his marshal's staff with the other in a casual reply to the greetings of the other officers, who were standing at attention. His face was beet-red. I did not need to hear his first words to know what he was thinking.

Stauffenberg went up to the marshal and saluted. "A fine mess, this," Witzleben growled at him.

Then he caught sight of Beck, toward whom the field marshal always—and this was a credit to him—observed our rebel scale of ranks. "Reporting for duty, sir," he said.

But even this was spoken in a surly tone. I was the only one he bothered to shake hands with. Then he took Beck's arm, crossed the wide room to Fromm's desk, and an excited debate began. After a few minutes Beck signaled to Stauffenberg, who was standing with our group like a drenched poodle, to join them. A few minutes later Stauffenberg fetched Ulrich Schwerin, who of late had been the intermediary between Witzleben and the Stauffenberg group.

Although we were standing too far away to make out a word, it was evident that Witzleben was sharply reproaching the two officers. Beck seemed to be trying to intervene in their favor. Witzleben would not listen and continued to address Stauffenberg excitedly.

I sat down again in my favorite corner, and here I was soon joined by Doctor Sack, who stood more or less in the middle between us, the civilians, and the military men. Sack was annoyed because he had been called openly on the telephone and asked to come, although the *Putsch* had not yet succeeded and there was nothing for him to do. He would soon pay on the gallows for the haste with which he had been invited to stand around in the Bendlerstrasse.

The conference at Fromm's desk lasted at least half an hour. Once, as I looked in through the sliding doors, I heard Olbricht and Hoeppner quarreling loudly. Hoeppner's voice sounded tearful, Olbricht's angry. Our eyes met—and Olbricht called me in. Certain snatches of conversation remain in our memories for the rest of our lives.

"Ask Gisevius."

"No, no, if it's such a risk, one oughtn't to take the gamble."

"There's a risk in every coup d'état."

"Yes, but one must have a ninety percent probability that the *Putsch* will turn out well."

"Nonsense, you'll never have a ninety percent probability. Fifty-one percent is enough."

"No, fifty-one percent is too little. Let's say eighty at least."

"Eighty? How do you expect to get eighty?"

"There you are, not even eighty! Then you can't go ahead and try a *Putsch*..."

Olbricht asked me my opinion. I looked at them in utter amazement.

Colonel Merz von Quirnheim came in to say that Helldorf had telephoned; he wanted "the gentleman who was with him before" to come at once. He had something very important to communicate. Merz said that Helldorf had sounded extremely excited. I could well imagine what he wanted and I had not the slightest desire to listen to his complaints and reproaches. The outcome of the conference between Beck and Witzleben was far more important. Neither Olbricht nor Hoeppner would hear of my declining to answer. Both urged me that it was tremendously important to find out what Helldorf's news was. Certainly nothing would happen in the next half-hour.

I thought, however, that the great decision was closer than that, and since I was sure that Helldorf merely wanted to complain, I insisted that I could not leave now. Schulenberg came over and also began urging that I go. This made me all the more obstinate. I opened the sliding door wide enough for Beck to see me signal, so that he could indicate whether or not he wanted me to come in, but he waved me away. Evidently he wanted no additional witnesses to the heated debate.

Olbricht had spied this bit of byplay. Now he insisted that I go.

By chance, Count Stauffenberg left the group in the other room for a moment. He came to get something from his desk. As he was on the way back, however, Olbricht blocked his way and told him that Helldorf had an important message for me, but that I insisted on staying to be ready to work with Beck and Witzleben.

Stauffenberg confirmed Olbricht's assertion that I would not be needed in the next half-hour. I objected that I had had trouble getting into the building a while ago and that by now I certainly could not pass through the street blockades.

Stauffenberg ran back to his desk and handed me a pass. It was printed on heavy brown linen paper and signed by Stauffenberg personally. As I took this piece of paper from him, I reflected that at least something had been well prepared. This document really looked impressive.

There seemed to be no choice for me; they even provided me with an ordnance officer who was to rustle up an automobile—no small undertaking—and see me through the street cordons.

Downstairs I had to wait a full quarter of an hour. The lieutenant ran from place to place, trying to find a car. Finally he drove up with a small private car. I was just about to get in when I saw Olbricht's face at the window above. "Are you still there?" he called out to me, and asked me to come up for a moment; he had something important to tell me. I raced up the stairs two at a time. Olbricht saved me the trouble of climbing the whole way. With radiant face he called down to me: "I just wanted to tell you that we've just had good news. The guards regiment is marching up to protect us. Tell Helldorf about it, please." Olbricht's joy was unmistakable. We waved to one another again as I started down the stairs.

As we drove up to the first intersection, a troop of heavily armed soldiers came marching toward us. I could not refrain from waving gladly to them. How much more hopeful the atmosphere in the Bendlerstrasse would soon be, now that these men had arrived!

At the Brandenburg Gate we encountered our first disillusionment. A heavily armed double guard stopped us. These two warriors, with their self-important expressions, their steel helmets, submachine guns, and harsh voices, were almost sufficient to remind us that a *Putsch* was in progress. I took out my handsome pass. But, incredibly enough, we were not permitted to drive through the Brandenburg Gate. We had to take the roundabout route by way of the Canal.

As I glanced into side streets on the way, two things struck me. Down one street I saw several blocks of buildings surrounded. Every twenty yards I glimpsed one of those awe-inspiring warriors holding a submachine gun. But a few streets farther on, I saw another such troop of soldiers forming ranks and marching away from the scene.

What was going on?

At Alexanderplatz I did not drive directly up to Helldorf's entrance. I left the car some distance away and slipped into the building from the rear. My precautions were not justified. Not a single Gestapo man was watching the police headquarters. Helldorf's "freeze" order was being carried out to perfection. I was greatly disappointed, however, not to find the Count in his office. He was in his air-raid shelter office on Karlsplatz.

A complicated business of telephoning ensued, because I did not want to compromise Helldorf by giving my name, and the men in the office were unwilling to connect me even with his adjutant unless I said who I was. At last I persuaded them to let me talk to the adjutant, who agreed to come for me.

I returned to the lieutenant, who was waiting below. The matter of those troops who seemed to be withdrawing was worrying me. I might be mistaken, but it would be better to inform Olbricht of my observations. And while beating about in unexplored territory, it is well not to carry any incriminating documents. Therefore, I divested myself of my note pad, which contained the notes for my undelivered radio address. I instructed the lieutenant to keep it for me until I returned. He then drove off and I waited in the deserted Alexanderplatz.

At last Helldorf's adjutant came and drove me quickly to the shelter. There was a misunderstanding and I had to wait for a while; the officers on duty informed me that the Count was having an important conference with an SS general. I fidgeted for ten minutes until the SS general turned out to be Nebe.

I was still unsuspecting when I entered the room. The glances of both men told me at once: it was all over. Helldorf manifested a calm about it all that was possible only for a person who had been a passionate gambler all his life. For with all respect for the fact that he ended his life on the gallows, I cannot falsify the drama of that moment by attributing to him the serenity of a devoted idealist who feels that his life and death are dependent upon the will of a higher power.

Nebe's eyes were mournful, profoundly melancholy, I scarcely want to say reproachful. There was, of course, an element of sorrowful reproach in his eyes; but at the same time there was a touch of compensatory satisfaction that he had been right after all.

Helldorf was sensible enough not to torment me with suspense. His account was derived from the fragmentary information that he and Nebe had been able to piece together. It seemed that the *Grossdeutschland* guards battalion had been alarmed and the commander, Major Roemer, had been ordered to arrest Goebbels. Goebbels promptly telephoned the Fuehrer's headquarters and Hitler personally talked to Roemer and conferred upon him full powers to crush the *Putsch*. At this very moment Roemer was marching to the Bendlerstrasse to arrest the "putschists." Himmler was reported to be en route to Berlin by plane.

When Helldorf told me this, he assumed treachery on the part of Major Roemer, against whom he had warned us so many times. We did not know that the major had at first been ready to carry out the order given to him simply because it was an order.

But an insane chance would have it that, the night before, a Nazi morale officer had delivered a lecture to the guards regiment and on this very afternoon had been invited by Roemer to have a drink with him before leaving. When word of the imposition of the state of siege arrived, this Nazi propagandist happened to be with Roemer. The lieutenant, in civilian life an official of the propaganda ministry, pleaded with Roemer to wait a few minutes until he checked up with Goebbels personally to make sure that Hitler was dead. Why act prematurely, he demanded, when there was a direct telephone wire to the Fuehrer's headquarters?

If... if only the order had not come over the teletype; if only one of the many generals standing idle around the Bendlerstrasse had appeared in person to give the order to this thirty-year-old major who at the moment was the most important troop commander in Germany....

As it was, Roemer yielded. He agreed to a half-hour delay. Goebbels summoned the major at once. Roemer hesitated; Goebbels was not his superior officer. But finally skepticism won out. Where was the Fuehrer?

For once Goebbels refrained from loquacity. He handed the telephone to Roemer—and on the other end of the wire was Hitler himself.

"Do you recognize me, Major Roemer? Do you recognize my voice?"

"Jawohl mein Fuehrer."

Thousands of majors had never exchanged a word with Hitler. But as chance would have it, Roemer, one of the youngest officers, had been in Hitler's presence only a few weeks before to receive the oak leaf cluster to the chevalier cross from the Fuehrer's hand.

So Hitler was alive! And now this Fuehrer whom Providence had again spared was conferring upon the little major full power over field marshals and generals, over the commanders of the troops that were moving up on Berlin. The Fuehrer was making him responsible for the protection of the capital, for the safety of the Third Reich...

Intuitively, Hitler contrived to enlist the young soldier so cleverly that there was no chance of his defection. Hitler imposed so many responsibilities upon him, so many independent actions, that he had no time for superfluous thought. He was ordered to march to the Bendlerstrasse, to make the approaching companies turn back, to see to the safety of the ministries...

Three quarters of a year later the young major, who had since been promoted to a colonel, committed suicide.

It was fortunate that Helldorf had only prosaic facts to impart to me, not this hair-raising melodrama. His monotonous report, touched with incisive sarcasm and grim humor, was far more affecting than the most imaginatively tragic sketch would have been. His description of events so confused me that I asked one of the most foolish questions that ever passed my lips during my years in the Third Reich: whether we could not intercept Himmler. Would it not be possible to meet him with Helldorf's or Nebe's police officers and shoot down the arch-hangman?

Quite justifiably Helldorf and Nebe repudiated this proposal. When the field marshals had muffed and the generals no longer had any power to command their majors, no policeman could avail.

Nebe dragged me back into reality again. All this time he had allegedly been conducting reconnaissance in Berlin or in police headquarters. Now he must return to his inferno to inform the Cerberus that all the hell-hounds were still properly chained.

I began to feel uncomfortable. At this moment everyone had his place of refuge: Helldorf would go to his police generals; Nebe would fall into the arms of the Gestapists. But where was I to go? A curious sense of pride took possession of me. I declared that I would return to the Bendlerstrasse.

Helldorf dryly remarked that I was out of my mind.

"But what are we to do now? You? Nebe? Myself?"

Helldorf's reply was elementary and disarming. I can still see him standing before me, his expression certainly not that of an idealist and his language not at all appropriate to the gravity of the moment. And yet his tone and his jauntiness were just right; they could no longer save the situation, but they might still save a life. "Now only sheer impudence can help us," he said. "We will deny everything. We'll pretend that nothing happened."

Nebe seconded Helldorf. He himself felt reassured that he had played his game with the Gestapists so adeptly that up to the present moment they had no suspicion of him.

I objected. "Helldorf, you may be able to invent a thousand alibis; Nebe, you can tell the most incredible fairy tales; but how is Government Councilor Gisevius—who at the moment is supposed to be performing his duties as vice-consul at the consulate-general in Switzerland—to explain his presence in the Bendlerstrasse or police headquarters today?"

Helldorf looked at me as if he thought I had lost the last remnants of my reason. "It's simple enough," he said calmly. "Naturally you have to disappear."

Nebe rushed off; Group Leader Mueller must not be permitted to grow suspicious. Helldorf also had to leave in a hurry. I literally plucked at his coat-tails. I needed a car, I said. I could have one, Helldorf said; but I ought not to use it too long.

"No, I'll go no farther than the Bendlerstrasse."

Helldorf stopped short. He turned around to face me once more.

"You're out of your mind."

"Helldorf, I am addressing you now as a Count..."

Helldorf looked at me with an expression almost pitying. Or was he surprised that for the first time I was speaking to him in such a personal vein?

"Helldorf, I ask you as a man of honor: Wouldn't you be thoroughly disgusted with me if I did not return to Beck in the Bendlerstrasse."

I shall never forget the reply I received from this Count, this notable of the Nazi Revolution, because it helped me to overcome many conscientious scruples. In the most vulgar manner imaginable Helldorf answered: "I should say not.

Don't kid yourself, Gisevius. For years these generals have shit all over us. They promised us everything; they've kept not one of their promises. What happened today was right in line with the rest—more of their shit."

I looked inquiringly at Helldorf. I still wondered what I should do, and I was hoping for advice. But Helldorf continued on the same mental track. He merely repeated: "It was all shit, all shit ..."

I found a small police car downstairs and ordered the chauffeur: "To the Bendlerstrasse."

I sat in the car staring dully into space. With part of my consciousness I noticed, as we turned into Unter den Linden, that on all sides troops were marching away. The Wilhelmstrasse was quite free of soldiers; there was no sign of any cordon. In another part of my mind, which seemed to operate quite independently of the observations that my eyes were recording, I was repeating again and again the same foolish, weary refrain: "These generals don't even know how to rebel and now you're riding to suicide ..."

At the Brandenburg Gate I was startled out of my musings. Two martial fellows just like the ones I had met before would not let us through, not even after I showed them my handsome pass. The way to the Bendlerstrasse was blocked. Why? They were not able to say.

I instructed the chauffeur to take the roundabout route. We drove to the Victory Column. On the way I repeated my refrain incessantly: "I am riding to suicide, I am riding to suicide ..."

The more often I repeated it, the more ridiculous I began to seem to myself. One could commit suicide, but one could hardly ride to suicide. My reason intervened and my sense of humor returned. I imagined the astonished expression on

Major Roemer's face if I should appear in the Bendlerstrasse vehemently demanding admission to the doomed circle there.

As we were about to turn left at the Victory Column in order to proceed to Wehrmacht headquarters, two more messengers of destiny stopped us. Again we were not permitted to go on. The sentinels gaped at Stauffenberg's flourishing signature, but they still refused to permit me to continue my ride to suicide.

The chauffeur shifted gears. I shifted plans.

Perhaps Fate would have it that I must deliver my radio address before departing this life. Since there was nothing else to do but to plunge ahead, I directed the chauffeur to drive out to the radio station, which was situated in Charlottenburg, a considerable distance from where we now were.

The farther we drove, the more senseless my situation seemed to me. What did I really have in common with these generals? Was I now to die for them? But no, I did not really have it in mind to die for them. A sense of loyalty made it necessary for me not to desert Beck in his disappointment. Was Beck a general? Just as much and as little a one as Oster. Was Oster a general? Yes and no. Of course he was a general. And yet I could very well understand why he disliked donning his uniform.

As the car left the scene of the drama farther behind, my own situation began to strike me as less dramatic. Suddenly the thought flashed through my mind: You've wanted for a long time to know what an unsuccessful *Putsch* is like; you've really never been able to imagine it. You know an old major who is said to have participated in an unsuccessful *Putsch*, but you've never asked him to tell you why that *Putsch* failed. You weren't interested; it struck you as ancient history.

I recalled the Kapp *Putsch*. I thought of all the grotesque details that had once made it seem so ludicrous. Was it really so ludicrous? Was not any unsuccessful *Putsch* ludicrous? What about the successful ones? Perhaps all uprisings were ludicrous. What could have been more ludicrous than the Eighteenth Brumaire, that textbook model of the successful *Putsch*? I recalled how Napoleon, the great genius, had been anything but a hero on that mad day; it was his reckless brother who virtually pushed him into fame.

We turned into the street on which the radio station was situated. I was very tense, but a glance was enough. There were no military guards, no police protecting the building. As far as the radio station was concerned, the *Putsch* had ended before it began.

At this point my chauffeur suddenly informed me that he could drive me no farther; he would have to hurry back. *Sic transit gloria mundi.* A moment ago I had been the guest of the police chief of the Reich capital and of a police general of the Reich security office. Now this chauffeur refused to transport me any longer. Sadly I watched the vehicle disappear. No doubt that this was the last police automobile I should ride in as a "free" man in the Third Reich. Next time I was given a free ride, the destination would be Gestapo headquarters on the Prinz Albrechtstrasse.

Fortunately, I was now only a short distance from the Reichskanzlerplatz, which was quite near to the Struencks' cellar apartment. As I passed a tall picket fence, I tossed over it the fragments of my handsome pass signed by Colonel Count Klaus von Stauffenberg of the general staff.

The Struencks received me with the tact appropriate for beaten rebels. They asked no questions; my silence was eloquent enough. Obviously they were happy to see me return at all. They had spent the morning and the afternoon in the same torment of waiting as myself. They had to listen to the dreadful radio report. To heighten the piquancy of the situation, they had had the company of one of the future ministers of the new government, Wirmer, the prospective minister of justice, who as yet had no idea of the honor reserved for him. He had received a letter from Goerdeler and had dropped in to see them about it. While having coffee with them, he was surprised by the announcement of the attempted assassination.

I had a hasty bite to eat. Then I repaid their hospitality with an unadorned recital of the facts. But the closer I came to the end of my tale, the more troubled I became. I explained to my friends that I could not possibly leave Beck alone at such a moment as this. Undoubtedly he had long since left for Zossen. Witzleben would have taken Beck with him on his return to the headquarters, and even a Major Roemer would not have barred the way of a field marshal.

In retrospect this line of thought sounds utterly confused. But at the moment I could imagine the end as taking place in no other way: the final battle, I thought, would certainly be fought at Zossen. There, under the command of General Wagner, were enough general staff officers to put up a good fight. Therefore, I wanted to go to Zossen to be with Beck. Beck—not Olbricht, not Stauffenberg, not any of the others, but Beck the "civilian" seemed to me the most tragic figure of the afternoon. Beck was a man—among so many who were mean-spirited.

Actually, Beck's fate had long since been sealed, and that of the others as well. Witzleben alone, who had gone home in a rage, had to wait until early the next morning.

Shortly after eight o'clock the guards battalion, whose arrival Olbricht had so happily announced, surrounded the Wehrmacht headquarters. But there were no arrests. Roemer contented himself with taking the rebels under his "protection." Apparently neither Olbricht nor Stauffenberg nor Merz von Quirnheim, nor any of the others took the obvious step of talking to the major. Had they asked questions, had they personally inquired what had come of the action in the propaganda ministry, they would have found that they were caught in their own "protective custody." Then, by exercise of their authority and their persuasive powers, they might after all have drawn the troops over to their side or at least negotiated a free withdrawal to Zossen. At least they would have been able to load their revolvers...

Instead, for a full hour and a half they did not even realize what was going on. "Orders are orders"; their guard had come, the panzer troops were rolling up; no one was disturbing them; the telephones continued to ring incessantly—what should they distrust?

The *Putsch* continued—a phantom *Putsch*.

At ten o'clock sharp commands suddenly rang out. The guards battalion was being withdrawn. A number of the neutral "putschists"—those officers who had gone along with the revolt in the afternoon and then had got cold feet and had been seeking an escape for hours—understood at once: the SS must be moving up; and they realized that the punishment of the Black hangman would fall upon the just and the unjust alike.

Lieutenant-Colonel von der Heyden, one of these halfhearted rebels, recognized that only one thing could save him and his like-minded fellows. Quickly a group was formed. "Treason!" they cried. They rushed into Stauffenberg's room, and Heyden shot the colonel; but none of these officers could shoot straight today. Stauffenberg was only wounded. Trailing a stream of blood, he ran upstairs to Beck.

Stauffenberg's friends, who were in the room when he was shot, stood around in utter consternation. Not one of them reached for his gun. Or rather one did—the one who described this scene to us—but he found himself too inhibited to shoot;

and the trigger-happy SS men were already approaching to put an end to such poaching in their special field.

Upstairs, Stauffenberg arrived just in time to be in at the finish. Fromm, now "liberated," hastened into his office. "Well, gentlemen," he declared, "now I am going to do to you what you wanted to do to me this afternoon."

What was that? Was he going to lock the rebels in the adjoining room and feed them sandwiches and wine until the storm blew over?

Fromm knew well that such things are done only by men who feel too sure of themselves, who still toy with their fate when the issue is in deadly earnest. He could not afford such sentimental gestures; his own head was at stake. He swung his revolver threateningly. Harshly he barked at the conspirators: "Lay down your weapons."

"None of us had any weapons," said Colonel-General Hoeppner in describing this final scene. I shall continue to quote from his account:

Beck: "I have a pistol here, but I should like to keep it for my private use."

Fromm: "Very well, do so. But at once."

Beck took the pistol and loaded it. Fromm warned Beck not to point it at him. Then Beck said a few words: "At this moment I am thinking of earlier days."

Fromm, interrupting: "We do not wish to go into that now. Will you kindly go ahead!"

Beck said a few more words, put the gun to his head, and shot.

The bullet struck the top of his head. *Beck, reeling:* "Did it fire properly?"

Fromm: "Help the old fellow."

Two officers who were standing on Beck's left went up to him.

Fromm: "Take away his gun."

Beck: "No, no, I want to keep it."

Fromm: "Take the gun away from him; he hasn't the strength."

While the two officers busied themselves with Beck, Fromm turned to Olbricht, Stauffenberg, Merz, and Haeften. "And you, gentlemen, if there is anything you want to put in writing, you still have a few moments."

Olbricht: "I should like to write."

Fromm: "Come over to the round table here, where you always sat opposite me." Olbricht wrote. Fromm went out.

Five minutes later Fromm returned.

Fromm: "Are you finished, gentlemen? Please hurry, so that it will not be too hard for the others. Now, then, in the name of the Fuehrer a court-martial, called by myself, has taken place. The court-martial has condemned four men to death: Colonel of the General Staff Merz von Quirnheim, General of Infantry Olbricht, this colonel whose name I will no longer mention, and this lieutenant." He meant Stauffenberg and Haeften.

Fromm gave the order to a lieutenant standing by: "Take a few men and execute this sentence downstairs in the yard at once."

The four were led away.

Fromm turned to Beck again. "Well, what about it?"

Beck, half-dazed, managed to answer: "Give me another pistol."

One of the men standing by handed a gun to him.

Fromm: "Very well, you have time for a second shot."

Fromm walked to the door and pointed to Hoeppner. "Lead him away."

At that moment a shot rang out.

This was the sum and substance of Hoeppner's account to the People's Court. We can spare ourselves the interjected remarks of Freisler, the president of the court.

Or can we not?

The sound film tells no lies, and this entire court scene was filmed and exhibited. Somehow Hoeppner's further description must be included, his account of how he had objected to his court-martial sentence and had demanded that he be given a chance to be heard. He could "justify" himself, he had said; he was "not a *Schweinehund.*"

"You are not a *Schweinehund?*"

Freisler stretched in his judge's seat and spitefully barked at the defendant: "Well, then, if you don't want to be a *Schweinehund*, tell us what zoological class you consider to be your proper category?"

Hoeppner hesitated briefly. With the sound camera grinding away, Freisler pursued his point.

"Well, what are you?"

"An ass."

Outside the building four salvos boomed.

Olbricht, Merz von Quirnheim, and Haeften died silently. Stauffenberg's last utterance sounded upon the command to fire. "Long live the eternal Germany!" he shouted.

Within the building the small group of arrested men thought the walls would crash from the vibration of the thunderous roar below: "Our Fuehrer, Adolf Hitler—*Sieg Heil! Sieg Heil! Sieg Heil!*..."

About an hour later a large personnel truck circled a nearby cemetery. The driver, an army sergeant, found the gate locked. He learned that the sexton of the church a short distance from the cemetery had the key. The sergeant awakened the sexton from his sleep. There were five bodies in his truck, he said. He had been officially ordered to bury them quietly in this cemetery. The incident must remain absolutely secret, and no one was to know afterward where the grave was situated.

The distracted sexton opened the cemetery gate. He helped to carry the bodies inside the cemetery wall. The sergeant began digging at once. He would have to dig a big grave, he said; thirty more bodies were to follow. The sexton was terrified. He ran to the nearest policeman. Two patrolmen accompanied him back to the cemetery. By light of their pocket torches they examined the bodies: one general, two colonels, a lieutenant, a civilian.

The precinct chief was sent for. Five puzzled men stood around five still-bleeding bodies and conferred. They finally decided it would be best not to do too much thinking. Orders were orders. All five of them began digging. In the morning the precinct chief would make a written report. For a while they kept a death-watch. They were waiting for the remaining thirty bodies; but these did not come, and no one dared to inquire at the headquarters where so many horrors were taking place that night

The grave was closed. Quietly this curious assemblage of grave diggers slunk away.

At dawn the sexton was startled out of his bed again. The SS wanted "their" bodies back: the identification office had to take a few photographs, and then the five dead men were sent off to the crematorium.

Dully, we sat around the radio in the Struencks' apartment. For an hour there had been repeated announcements that Hitler would speak. Again and again the broadcast had been postponed. Consequently, we clung to the faint hope that it was all a fraud, that he was dead after all. If that were the case, who could say that the revolt would not be revived and spread out from Zossen into the rest of the country?

Long after midnight it came at last. The music stopped abruptly. Hans Fritzsche came to the microphone and announced: "The Fuehrer speaks."

We cast questioning glances at one another. Would it really be he? The first few sentences were enough to remove our doubts. It was Hitler—his voice, his coarse speech, the typical Hitlerian vocabulary which was aped by the thousand little Hitlers, but which yet had its own inimitable sound when it came from his own lips. It was Hitler all right, from the inevitable "in the first place" to the equally inevitable "exterminate."

> If I speak to you today, I do so for two special reasons. In the first place, so that you may hear my voice and know that I myself am sound and uninjured; and in the second place, so that you may also hear the particulars about a crime that is without peer in German history.
>
> An extremely small clique of ambitious, conscienceless, and criminal and stupid officers forged a plot to eliminate me and, along with me, to exterminate the staff of officers in actual command of the German Wehrmacht. The bomb, which was planted by Colonel Count von Stauffenberg, burst two yards from my right side. It severely injured several of my colleagues; one of them has died. I myself am wholly unhurt. . . .
>
> The clique of usurpers is, as you may well imagine, very small. It has nothing to do with the German armed forces and above all nothing to do with the German army either. It is an extremely small band of criminal elements who are now being mercilessly exterminated. . . .
>
> I am convinced that with the liquidation of these very small cliques of traitors and conspirators, we are at last creating at

home in the rear the atmosphere that the fighters at the front
need...

This time an accounting will be given such as we National
Socialists are wont to give...

I wish especially to greet you, my old comrades in the struggle, for it has once more been granted me to escape a fate which
holds no terrors for me personally, but which would have
brought terror down upon the heads of the German people. I see
in this another sign from Providence that I must and therefore
shall continue my work.

March music.

On such an occasion Goering, of course, could not hold his
peace. We were revolted by his hypocritical sentimentality.

Comrades of the Luftwaffe! An inconceivably base attempt at
the murder of our Fuehrer was committed today by Colonel
Count von Stauffenberg on the orders of a miserable clique of
one-time generals who, because of their wretched and cowardly
conduct of the war, were driven from their posts. The Fuehrer
was saved as by a miracle

These criminals are now attempting to usurp power and to
sow confusion among the troops by issuing false orders. . . .

Officers and soldiers, no matter what their rank, and civilians
who support these criminals in any manner or who approach you
to win support for their wretched undertaking, are to be seized
and shot at once. Those of you who are called to help exterminate these traitors must act with utter ruthlessness.

These are the same miserable creatures who have tried to
betray and sabotage the front.

Officers who participate in this crime cut themselves off from
their nation, from the Wehrmacht, from all soldierly honor,

from fealty to their oath. Their annihilation will give us new strength.

The Luftwaffe counters this treachery with its sworn loyalty to and fervent love for the Fuehrer and its ruthless devotion to victory.

Long live our Fuehrer whom Almighty God so visibly blessed on this day!

Again a blaring military march. Then it was Doenitz's turn. The supreme commander of the naval forces surpassed himself in superlatives:

Men of the Navy! Holy wrath and immeasurable rage fill our hearts at the criminal assault which was intended to take the life of our beloved Fuehrer. Providence wished to have it otherwise; Providence guarded and protected the Fuehrer; thus Providence did not desert our German Fatherland in its fated hour.

An insanely small clique of generals, who have nothing in common with our brave army, were so cowardly and faithless as to instigate this attempt at murder, thus committing the basest sort of treason to the Fuehrer and the German people. For these scoundrels are no more than the agents of our enemies, whom they serve with their characterless, craven, and perverse cleverness. In actuality their stupidity is boundless...

We will stop these traitors in their tracks. The navy stands true to its oath in tested loyalty to the Fuehrer, absolute in its devotion and readiness to battle...

It will ruthlessly annihilate anyone who is unmasked as a traitor.

Long live our Fuehrer, Adolf Hitler!

The *Putsch* was over.

3

Escape to the Future

SHALL I DENY THAT I SLEPT POORLY THAT NIGHT? Many and variegated were the scenes that whirled before my eyes as I lay dozing: generals, officers, police, civilians, the Bendlerstrasse and Alexanderplatz, an assassin, a radio voice—and how many victims? I felt that the walls of the cellar were about to collapse around me, so oppressed was I by the memory of all the hopes, fears, and disappointments that had engrossed us in our talks within these four walls during the past few days and hours.

The following morning I was impelled to leave the house some time before seven o'clock. I did not breathe easily until I found myself safely inside an overcrowded commuters' train. While standing, I surreptitiously bent my knees—a gymnastic exercise that is quite exhausting after a time. I began cursing all the women who had tried to persuade me that it was wonderful to be so tall. "Don't attract attention"—that is the first command for adventurers who dwell under a system of terror. It is unwise, or at least indiscreet, in revolutionary times to tower a head above one's fellow men.

My goal was Berlin West, where I knew someone whom I had more than once had occasion to help. Recently, when he heard about my being bombed out, he had offered to put me up for the night at his home. But times had changed. When he saw me walking through his garden so early in the morning, he turned pale. He barely had the composure to stammer a greeting; then he at once assured me that his house was oh, so unfortunately overcrowded with guests. Evidently he had a radio.

In such cases it is better to accept the situation with good grace. I drank a cup of coffee and accepted his recommendation that I go to see a neutral diplomat who lived nearby. My friend said he would send another foreign diplomat there, one in whom I placed high hopes. I did not know the gentleman personally, but not long before I had had the opportunity to assist him in a situation that was highly embarrassing for him personally and for his country.

Diplomats hear about everything, and so my host also knew about the events of the day before. Nevertheless, he permitted me to wait in his home until late that afternoon, when he brought with him his colleague whom I wanted to see. The latter's memory needed some jogging before he recalled that it was not some "group" but I, in person, who had given him that needed tip. Then he proved to me that he had the most cogent diplomatic reasons for being cautious. I understood quite well—but earlier, when he had accepted my help with a thousand assurances of gratefulness, he had not turned my messenger away on the ground that he could not violate his country's neutrality.

Both diplomats greedily absorbed my account of the previous day's events. Since Hans Fritzsche had just announced on the radio that only "half a dozen" generals and officers had participated in the *Putsch,* I wished at least to give some publicity to the fact that Field Marshal von Witzleben had been one of the rebels. For all I knew the Nazis might attempt to smother this embarrassing fact in silence.

Then I accepted the diplomat's friendly offer to take me part of my way in his car. I had arranged with the Struencks that we would leave messages and information for one another at the home of our friend, Hans Koch. Since my host was headed for the golf course, Koch's home was on his route. Perhaps Koch would be able to put me up.

I left the diplomat's car at an underpass, and for the next ten minutes I went at a jog-trot. I was in the neighborhood of my former home, which at this particular time, I thought, would undoubtedly exercise a certain attraction for the Gestapo.

There was good news for me at Koch's. The Struencks, thank God had not been picked up, and Koch's reaction was reassuring. He was a rather timid man, circumspect and not overfond of wild ventures, but when he saw me he did not even start back in dismay. I have always felt a particular respect for men on whom nature has conferred a considerable degree of caution—or let us frankly say, timidity—and who nevertheless voluntarily perform acts of great courage. That is a mode of behavior that shows up most vividly under systems of terror.

Hans Koch sheltered me. We arranged an alibi for him in case I should be captured: that I had just arrived from Zurich that morning and had asked him to put me up temporarily since my own home had been destroyed. I did not intend to abuse his hospitality for long.

Weariness soon overwhelmed me. That night I slept splendidly. I forgot everything.

The following morning Frau Koch telephoned the Struencks from a public telephone. Everything appeared to be all right. I sat down with a book on theology to distract my mind. As a matter of fact, I felt that calmness that comes over people who with the best will in the world can no longer think of anything at all to do. For what could I do? Was I to take the next train to the vicinity of the Swiss frontier? During those days there were three separate police authorities checking up on railroad passengers. The military police were looking for deserters, the criminal police for shirking laborers or escaping prisoners of war, and the Gestapo for traitors. Later on perhaps Colonel Hansen would be able to help me, or perhaps some other friend in the Abwehr, or perhaps Nebe.

In order not to endanger Koch unnecessarily, I met the Struencks at a crowded suburban station where we hoped to be lost in the throng. Frau Struenck had meanwhile spoken with Nebe. He had stopped quickly at some street-corner and she had got into his car. Apparently the Gestapo still did not suspect either him or Helldorf. In general, Nebe had said, the Gestapists were not at all certain how they should proceed. They were still shivering from the shock. They felt themselves seriously compromised, for they had been taken by surprise everywhere. In Paris they had put up a particularly poor showing; all the SS leaders had let themselves be arrested without offering the slightest resistance. Himmler and Goebbels would have preferred to cover up this scandal. After all, there was no chance of another *Putsch,* and it seemed to them pointless to let the general public know how widely ramified the conspiracy had been. Kaltenbrunner and Mueller, however, were hot for revenge, but Hitler had not yet made his decision; they still did not know how literally to interpret his threat to "exterminate" the rebels.

Nebe sent word to me that I must on no account travel anywhere by railroad. Remarkably enough, he had not heard my name mentioned by any of the Gestapists as yet. I had to wait for almost ten months before I solved this mystery.

By sheer chance the Gestapo was diverted from my trail for three days which were of inestimable value to me. It seemed that Consistorialist Eugen Gerstenmaier, who for years had been an outspoken opponent of the Confessional Church, had in recent years become a member of the Kreissau circle of the

Opposition, and as it happened, he arrived in Berlin after an absence of a month on the morning of July 20. Hearing the radio report of the unsuccessful attempt at assassination, he had gone to the Bendlerstrasse, arriving there a few minutes after I had left the building. (It was he who later recounted to me the manner of Beck's death.) For once the Gestapists who were invading the building did something that was highly sensible from the point of view of police work. Before they occupied the building, they asked the doormen and the soldiers in the courtyard whom they had seen inside. All answered unanimously that there had been only army officers except for one civilian who had come and gone frequently.

While making their very first arrests in Olbricht's waiting room, they found this "one civilian"—Herr Gerstenmaier. It helped him not at all to insist that he had just arrived in Berlin that morning and had come to the Bendlerstrasse late in the evening. The SS men beat him all the harder for his "lying." Then on the fifth day, they suddenly let him alone; and he, too, had to wait ten months before he found out who it was that competed for his distinction—a distinction for which he had had to pay by enduring so many beatings—of being the sole civilian in the Bendlerstrasse during the *Putsch*. This stouthearted church official had some moments of altogether un-Christian bitterness in May 1945, when I explained to him why the Gestapists had suddenly, after five days, taken his word for it. The flight of Nebe and myself clarified the situation for them.

That came about in the following manner.

Up to Sunday, July 23, everything still seemed to be going well. That morning I had become intensely curious about Helldorf. Boldly I went into the nearest police station—certainly the last place the Gestapo would look for me—and declared it was urgent that I talk to the chief of police over the internal police telephone system. I put over my bluff, and fortunately Helldorf understood at once who the caller was who wanted to discuss the next air-raid drill with him. He asked me to come to his private home at four o'clock—that is, to the ruins that remained of his home.

Since it was Sunday, the streets were almost deserted, nor did I encounter any Gestapo patrols; but in front of Helldorf's door, in an attitude of studied nonchalance, stood his chauffeur who bore the lovely name of Kelch (chalice). The man was deliberately looking away from me, and he held a white handkerchief in his hand. Since he was being so ostentatious about not seeing me, I thought it a signal to continue on my way as fast as I could; but when I surreptitiously looked back, he beckoned to me as if to say that the coast was clear and that I must hurry. Never had I exchanged a word with this man about our *Putsch*—and yet, how many such stout-hearted Kelches must have been secretly in on the conspiracy during all those years.

Helldorf pretended to be perfectly at ease. Nevertheless, I could see by every one of his gestures that he felt dreadfully insecure. Significantly enough, he asked me whether I had heard any details about who was dead and who had been arrested. That was precisely what I had been hoping to hear from him. When I looked my astonishment, he assured me that since our last meeting on the evening of July 20 he had learned nothing, in spite of a number of telephone conversations with Kaltenbrunner and Goebbels. All he knew was of that nocturnal scene at the cemetery, a story he had learned from one of his precinct captains.

Nevertheless, Helldorf put on a good show of assurance. He brushed his hand over his handsome uniform, showed me his chevalier cross, which he had received only a few weeks before, and declared that the system was too shaky for them to dare to take the police chief of the Reich capital to the gallows. We discussed once more our mutual alibis. Then I left.

Near the Grunewald station I met Struenck. He was much more agitated than he had been the day before. He felt that he had to get away. But where to? Colonel Hansen had not yet been heard from, and we felt that we could not leave him in the lurch. If Struenck, his military subordinate, fled prematurely, Hansen would be incriminated. As Struenck left me, I suddenly saw Ambassador Ulrich von Hassell. He seemed to be hurrying like someone who wants to catch a train, and yet I could tell that in reality he was in no haste; but his head was bent in such a curious fashion. It was as if he were trying to hide from some terrible danger that was pursuing him. I involuntarily felt: There goes someone who has death at his heels.

I called out to him in a low voice. He started in fright, then we walked up and down for a while, so that I could tell him about the details of the *Putsch*—the uprising for which he had longed all these many years. He, too, had heard about its failure only over the radio.

As we talked, his posture changed; he stood upright again, as he always had in the past, and showed once more the same impressive bearing and inner strength I had always known him to possess. But the picture of Hassell as he walked, brooding and trying to escape from himself, will always remain with me as one of my most vivid impressions of the days after July 20. Perhaps his complicity would not be discovered by the Gestapo. In that case he must not draw suspicion upon himself by an ill-considered flight. I have already described how I prepared an alibi for my friends. But this alibi would not do for anyone who lived in Germany. How could Hassell—or anyone else—buy his own salvation at the possible cost of the lives of friends and their families?

The real terror of those times is something that cannot be

expressed in abstractions, but only in images. Thus, whenever I think of the abstract problem of "flight under total terror," the image of Hassell rises before my mind's eye. His was the tragic situation of hundreds of thousands (and not only after July 20!); his was the fate of famous and unknown men, of Jews and Christians. The fact simply was that in certain situations there was nothing to do at all. No amount of courage, skill, or force of will could help. Many men simply had to wait for the hangman to come. They could not risk doing anything at all, for fear of endangering their fellows!

That Sunday at the Fuehrer's headquarters the choice was made between prudence and revenge. Kaltenbrunner and his bloodhound, Mueller, won out. Hitler ordered a clean sweep to be made of the Opposition.

On Monday morning Hansen was arrested. He was recalled by telegram from the bedside of his sick wife. Allegedly the matter was one connected with his official duties. He decided to continue in his role of the unsuspecting innocent, and in fact he was received with all due honors at the Gestapo headquarters in the Prinz Albrechtstrasse. In Kaltenbrunner's waiting room, however, the Gestapo thugs were waiting for him. He was handcuffed and his feet were chained, and these fetters were not removed until he was led to the gallows.

Helldorf received a similar friendly invitation from Kaltenbrunner. Again the visitor was received with full honors, and again the Gestapists fell upon the man when his back was turned. Like Hansen, Helldorf bravely kept silent under torture for long days. Their heroism gave the Struencks and myself a head start of about a week.

Nebe now realized that he would have to make haste. Kaltenbrunner, who still did not have a clear view of the extent of our conspiracy, laughingly remarked to him that word was going around that he, Nebe, had been seen frequently in Hell-dorf's company. "If that's the case I'll have to arrest you too," he added.

Nebe did not ask to hear that remark repeated. Returning to his office, he tossed into his car the box containing a civilian suit that he had long had ready and declared that he had to leave on an urgent official mission; he would be gone until the following night. But then came the hitch: the SS man at the gasoline pump, from whom Nebe had always received the fuel for these urgent official missions, refused to issue supplementary cans of gasoline to him. He had strict orders from above that no more than twelve gallons of gasoline should be issued without special permits.

Toward evening Struenck knocked excitedly on our door. He scarcely gave me time to pack my few belongings; then he dragged me along to the next corner, where Nebe's car was waiting. Our small amount of gasoline set narrow limits. We had to eliminate the obvious persons at once because it would have been too easy to trace us. Under a system of total terror a large circle of acquaintances is a luxury that conspirators cannot afford. As long as everything goes well, that is an advantage. The fewer persons one knows, the less there are to betray one later on, under torture, but when it is necessary to flee, one becomes conscious of the disadvantages of such caution, for suddenly the small group of friends and acquaintances are all on the same blacklist. It becomes quite a problem to find someone whom one knows well enough to ask for refuge and who is at the same time not suspect.

I recalled that Hans Asmussen, one of the leaders of the Confessional Church, had spoken to me years ago about a pastor in the provinces who would be able to hide me with his peasants if need be. While Nebe and Struenck drove off to pick

up Frau Struenck, I looked up another pastor I knew and
obtained the address and a note of introduction.

It was late at night when we finally left the city. Our destination was a village about sixty miles beyond Potsdam. Finding our way in the blackout was extremely difficult. Again and
again we had to get out of the car to check the roads. Above us
the bombers roared to drop their cargoes on Berlin. We sent up
to them our pious wishes that they might score a direct hit on
the Prinz Albrechtstrasse.

En route we were stopped dozens of times by police patrols
or militia units. Fortunately, Nebe's uniform of an SS group
leader still merited respect, but I was given a good lesson on
how limited were the chances for escape by automobile in
wartime. Who had sufficient gasoline? Who had permission to
travel beyond the narrowest local limits? Who would be permitted to take unknown passengers in his car? Only a high-
ranking leader of the SS could meet all such requirements, and
by tomorrow noon at the latest, by which time the warrant
would have been wirelessed and telegraphed throughout the
country, even Nebe's precious papers would be valueless ...

In a dictatorship even the so-called "big shots" could be
reduced overnight to insignificance. In the face of omnipotent
terror, everything is fictional. That was why so many had hastened to hide behind the saving mask—a title, a membership
book in the Nazi Party, a uniform; that was why so few people
dared to go along without such camouflage, even long after
they had with horror recognized the true nature of the Nazi
criminals—and of themselves.

We must not make the error of thinking that all those who
eat the bread of dictatorship are evil from the first; but they
must necessarily become evil. Other systems of government,
including democracy, may have their faults; but so long as they
permit the possibility of free choice between good and evil,

defects can be remedied and the crooked made straight. The curse of a system of terror is that there is no turning back; neither in the large realm of policies nor the "smaller" realm of everyday human relationships is it possible for men to retrace their steps.

It was past midnight when we knocked on the door of the parsonage. Frau Struenck had some difficulty persuading the pastor that we were neither robbers nor Gestapo officers, but people who needed help. But we had no luck. In his whole parish he no longer knew anyone who would be willing to run such a risk. The people in the villages were no longer by themselves. Everywhere bombed-out refugees were being quartered, and all of them were intensely suspicious of one another. Every prefect or gendarme was required to report immediately the presence of unannounced visitors, and in wartime men fit for military service were not usually seen playing cards at a village tavern.

"I implore you for the sake of my wife and children not to come here again," the pastor had called after us as we left. He had already had more than one run-in with the Gestapo. He had, however, mentioned to us a remote village. His colleague there would certainly be able to help us, he thought. Only recently he had hidden a number of Jews.

Over deserted back roads we made our way toward the village. It was already dawn when we knocked again. The pastor and his wife were friendly and invited us into their tiny little parsonage. Yes, of course, he had concealed a number of Jews. But naturally he could not endanger them for our sakes.

We ourselves realized that this splendid man had done what he could—indeed, had outdone himself. We were really at a loss now. We still had half a gallon of gasoline. What should we do with the car? Finally we decided to hide the car in the dense underbrush of a forest. Then we returned to the parsonage. On the way, Nebe demonstrated to me the correct technique for concealing our trail from bloodhounds. In this at least we were successful, for two days later, when the car was found and a grand search was organized, dozens of police dogs passed by the parsonage without pausing.

In the laundry-room we burned Nebe's uniform. For another twenty-four hours we wandered around this vicinity. Then hunger and closed doors convinced us that it was all in vain. Finally I insisted on my old thesis, that in such dangerous times there is only one relatively safe refuge—in the lions' den.

The ride back to Berlin was sheer torment. For we had to change trains five times. I felt immensely relieved when we at last reached the center of Berlin.

The Struencks went their own ways. We had made arrangements for keeping in touch with one another. At first Nebe and I tried our luck together, but after a few hours we realized that two was too many: we also would have to separate.

As we were walking through the streets of Berlin West in search of a mutual acquaintance, Nebe and I suddenly felt ourselves observed by persons in a car parked nearby. Quickly we vanished into the entrance of a building. Fortunately the spies were interested in their own special task. They were watching the chief provost marshal of the army, Doctor Sack, who lived there. Sack came home a moment later. Not suspecting that it was by pure chance that we had encountered him here, he assumed we had come to meet him. I shall never forget the tense warning spoken by this noble man: "Clear out; I am under observation; the Gestapo is at my heels."

The scene was one that is possible only in revolutionary times and that an outsider will scarcely understand. Here was the chief of military justice, the man who at the moment was entrusted with the judicial investigation of the events of July

20, giving a warning to two fugitives, while outside the spies set to watch him were waiting. Moreover, Sack continued in his position for at least another week! Then the ring had closed so tightly around him that it left space only for a cell in the Prinz Albrechtstrasse. There he sat close by his fellow fighters and fellow sufferers whom he had protected and to some extent prosecuted. Together with them he died courageously the death of a believing Christian.

On August 30, Struenck was picked up. Twenty days later his brave wife was taken. A full five months more passed before the Gestapo ferreted out Nebe in his hiding-place. A few days later, when they raided my last hiding-place (they threw a cordon around several street blocks and several dozens of them swarmed into the house), they found that the bird had flown. My rescuers had forestalled them by a few days.

I am loath to recount the details of this game of hide-and-seek. Those who have had luck ought not to boast about it. I say "luck" because I cannot dare speak of skill or intelligence; I was aided at dramatic moments by too many strange chances and coincidences. The lucky ones must be grateful for their luck and must look upon their furlough from death as imposing a mission upon them: to speak of the struggles and sufferings of their dead friends.

I shall mention only three examples. The brave man who concealed Nebe was killed, his family was arrested and his property was confiscated. My friend, Otto Huebner, the insurance man, who was a real "plutocrat" and might have escaped to the safety of some Bavarian village, lost his life in the very last days of the Nazi regime because he had sheltered two fleeing French officers. And on my account more than a dozen men and women were thrown into the Gestapo cellars because they had really or allegedly hidden me. I thank God that "only" one of them had to sacrifice his life, my faithful friend and helper Hans Koch.

But of what importance are these personal difficulties compared to the torture of those who suffered in the Gestapo cellar? For day and night, even when they ate, even when they walked to the scaffold, they were fettered hand and foot. They were not fed so well or treated so carefully as the Nuremberg war criminals. Their cell doors always stood open; two SS men stared continually at them. Their food was insufficient for living and too much for dying.... But it is not possible to describe the kind of "interrogation" that was practiced in the Prinz Albrechtstrasse. We do know one thing, however, from the records that were found and from the accounts of the few survivors: those martyred men heroically kept silence.

When the storm was over, some persons in their initial flurry leveled the accusation that this one or that one had talked too much, but, as I have said earlier in connection with Goerdeler, resistance to interrogation, or to the chemical preparations that were mixed with the prisoners' food, is not primarily a matter of character but of physical constitution. Some resisted, some talked, and some—made mistakes.

Since I was spared by the kindness of destiny from "softening up" or from making such "mistakes," I have the right to give myself as an example. Every day that I continued to "enjoy" my freedom, I considered anew the burning question: What will you say if the police come this minute? The longer I remained at liberty and the more I heard of others who had already been tried, the more opportunities I had to judge what the Gestapo knew and what it did not know, and the more simple my situation appeared to me. After about four months I said to myself: Now they know everything. Consequently I may as well die with dignity. I would openly hurl defiance into their faces. Yes, I would say, I thought so and so, those men were my friends, these were my deeds.

When everything was over, I was shocked that I had ever had such thoughts. I learned how many of my friends had preserved their secrets unto death. Goerdeler and Schlabrendorff sat in adjoining cells, but in the presence of the Gestapists they did not admit to knowing one another. The 1943 plans for assassination were never revealed. Oster, Struenck, and Canaris sat in adjoining cells—and yet the Gestapo never learned how far their collaboration had gone. Almost the entire *fronde* were gathered in cells within a few yards of one another, and yet, up to the very last, the Gestapo tortured "only a few" to death and never grasped the full extent of the conspiracy. What would have happened if at the end of 1944 or the beginning of 1945 I had joined this company of martyrs who were heroically concealing the truth and if I had "bravely" and "honestly" confessed the truth? Perhaps my court record would read more nobly today than the statements of the others in which the defendants portrayed their friends, if not themselves, as hundred-percent Nazis and patriots. It may be argued that in the end almost all were executed, but I should nevertheless have been the one who provided the final evidence the Gestapo needed, the final pretext they desired, for incredible as it may seem, even in 1945 murder was still being done "legally." Even while millions of Jews were being killed without any judicial proceedings, Freisler, the president of the revolutionary tribunal, insisted upon having "proofs" or a "confession."

It is tragic, indeed, to suffer martyrdom without having said a last word of self-justification, but how terrible a torment of conscience would it have been to know, as one mounted the scaffold, that a hasty word had meant the deaths of friends or relations!

Afterward Frau Struenck told me that immediately following her arrest she was mockingly informed that I had long been in the hands of the Gestapo. To prove it to her and to make it easier for her to confess, she was read pages of statements that I had allegedly made on the subject of our joint treasonous activities. This stratagem restored Frau Struenck's composure, for she knew definitely that I was still at liberty. What would have happened if, months later, I had been read the confessions of Goerdeler, Oster, Canaris, Struenck, or Nebe? In truth, perhaps the greatest perversion of human nature that takes place under a system of terror is that more character is needed, more courage required, to lie than to confess the truth.

Not only did those men and women keep their secrets bravely; they died even more bravely. Both men and women went to the scaffold with a bearing and courage for which no tribute is too high. I know that for many the end was certainly not the worst, not so tormenting as the interrogations, not so wearing as the waiting. When the hoarse, harsh cry came: "Number 27, finish him off, quick, quick . . ." there may have been some to whom it meant release.

Nevertheless, it could not be easy to die amid the mocking laughter of Gestapo men.

In mid-October I sent word to Hans Koch from my hiding-place that I thought the coast was clear and could responsibly ask him to pay me a visit. He came the following night. I was happy to see him again and to find him looking well. But before I could say a word about this, he took my hand and said: "Forgive me; please don't say anything; I've simply been too cowardly to come..."

What could I say to him? My friend was the father of five children. In 1934 he had been thrown into the Gestapo cellar for the first time because he attempted to save a Jew's property. Then he had courageously defended Niemoeller at his trial.

In hundreds of cases he had quietly contributed his help, and always he had gone his own straight way. Without quavering he had concealed me during the first days after July 20. And now he was apologizing because he had, out of a perfectly reasonable sense of caution, kept away for a few months. To such behavior this man, who for years had been oppressed by premonitions of a violent death, gave the name of "cowardice."

Moreover, Koch had not been inactive during this time. He had gathered a great deal of information, although in times of terror mere curiosity can prove fatal and is certainly unwise when a man has something to conceal. Koch had nevertheless found out that for weeks after Struenck's arrest the Gestapo had posted five men in Struenck's house and garden in case I should turn up there. They were still paying visits to the place at regular intervals.

Hans Koch also had news of my sister. In mid-August the Gestapo had located her in the country. Since then she had vanished without a trace. Apparently one hostage was not enough for them. I had succeeded in getting my mother safely into Switzerland before it was too late. Determined to have their revenge, they sent a special plane to arrest a cousin of mine who was at the moment fighting on the Baltic front. "Arrest of kin," this was called; it was the latest Gestapo accomplishment. Until the day the American army in South Tyrol liberated my sister, together with other "prominent" persons—Leon Blum, Schuschnigg, Martin Niemoeller, the family of Goerdeler, and many, many others of almost every nation—no one had any idea where these unfortunates were. They were not permitted to send to their relations any indication that they were still alive. They themselves were not even allowed to know where they were being kept. It created a sensation among them one day when they found a name engraved on the underside of a chair in their quarters—the name: Buchenwald Concentration Camp.

Was torment of the prisoners the only motive? Not at all. On the one hand, the Nazis wanted to hold hostages for the future, so that they could buy themselves free. On the other hand, they deliberately spread the word that all relations of traitors were being executed. They knew very well the panicky terror this would create among all those who had ever had oppositional ideas. Everyone has the moral right to risk his own life, but can he justify himself before God and man if he also hazards the lives of his wife and children?

The rest of what Koch had to tell was equally crushing. Almost all our friends were under arrest, but Koch had a horrible story to tell about them. Many of these men, especially the prominent ones, were still alive. Condemned to death by Nazi justice and long ago hanged according to the reports of the grapevine or of official sources, they were till dragging out a shadow existence in the Gestapo cellars. The technicians of torture and drugs still hoped to squeeze some more information out of their living corpses . . .

Around the time of Koch's visit some good news came from Switzerland for me personally. Help was on the way. I had friends there—and friends helped. A "book" given to intermediaries was to serve as a confirmation to me that I could trust the messenger. A week passed—two, three, four. Then at last it came. I read every page over twice, three times, to see whether the text contained some hidden message; I tore open the binding; I guessed and puzzled and reasoned; but I learned nothing beyond what the accompanying written note had told me, that a further message would be forthcoming "shortly."

"Shortly." I have sworn eternal enmity with that word. At first I smiled with the knowingness of an old hand at conspiracy. Splendid! Now they have determined that the coast is clear and that I am still here, I thought. Tomorrow they'll certainly send their promised additional message. "Shortly."

Next day I waited till darkness fell. Of course, how could I have been so foolish as to expect them at once? They must have spent the day making sure that the house was not surrounded by the Gestapo. I gave them two days more. I suddenly had an inspiration. "Shortly" must certainly mean the next change in the phase of the moon. How could I expect them to come for me during nights such as these when the moon was so bright that I, tall as I was, would easily be recognized against the bright background of snow?

The moonless nights approached closer and closer, and they passed; but for all my looking out of the window and satisfying myself as to the blackness of the night, nothing came of the promised "shortly." Again imagination came to my rescue. How could I have made such a mistake? I asked myself. In order for us to find our way through underbrush and swamps to the border, some natural light was needed. Not, of course, bright sunlight, but on the contrary the full moon that so many lyric poets have justly praised. The message had been smuggled to me at the time of the last full moon. When the next came...

The moon swelled; then it began to diminish again; and "shortly" was still not yet. Twice more I waited for the dark of the moon, twice more for the full moon. In vain.

Meanwhile Christmas came. What a fool I had been! I told myself. Shouldn't I have realized from the first that they would have chosen the peace of Christmas Eve for my rescue? On that night even the Gestapo patrols stayed at home. Which would it be—Christmas Eve or Christmas Night?

When these last illusions proved false, I decided now that I definitely knew what "shortly" must mean. One thing was clear, I thought, and that was that half a year of hiding had utterly dulled my mind. After all, my rescuers would have realized that all the customs officials and border guards in the world would want to drink to the New Year. Undoubtedly "shortly" must mean New Year's Eve.

By the middle of January, I gave up hoping. Something must have gone wrong. Well, what did it matter; the rescue probably would not have worked successfully anyway. Nature, too, went on strike. For a week I lay in bed with a severe case of grippe. I ran a dangerously high fever. Was it that I knew intuitively that Nebe had just been arrested and that the search for me was being renewed with fresh intensity? Or was I disturbed by an official announcement that after January 21 there would be no more trains for civilian passengers and all travelers would have to obtain special permits from the police?

On Saturday, January 20, Koch intended to visit me. But he did not turn up. Around eight o'clock in the evening I had a sudden attack of nervousness. It was pitch-dark outside, and so I ventured out and ran to a coin telephone. My friend did not answer. He had gone out a few hours ago, an unknown voice informed me. I imagined that the person who answered must have been some tenant in his house.

Then he must be on his way to see me, I thought. I hastened back in order not to miss him, and I did not have long to wait, for soon the bell rang. But it was not Koch. The woman who had brought me the book months ago—I will call her Miss "Shortly"—stood at the door and breathlessly asked me whether everything was all right. When I said yes, she vanished into the darkness.

Dramatic! But what did this strange visit mean?

A few moments later there was another ring. I rushed outside, only to hear a blacked-out automobile driving away.

But there was a fat envelope in the mailbox. The first thing that fell into my hand was a thick metal badge—the well-known badge of executive officers of the Gestapo. Then I unfolded an official German passport with a picture of myself. I found that my name was Hoffmann and that I was a high-ranking functionary of the Gestapo. There was a special pass and a letter from Gestapo headquarters instructing all officials of the government and the Nazi Party to assist me in my secret mission to Switzerland.

My jubilation was mingled with a little alarm. It had been a point of pride with me that none of the many offices in which I had worked in the Third Reich possessed any picture of me. I knew that the Gestapo had been compelled to work with an old passport picture dating from 1932. They had even sent a "good friend" to visit my mother in her peaceful room in Zurich in order to secure a picture. Only a few weeks before they had at last found a photograph—not a passport photo, but an almost full-length portrait, and this very portrait now looked at me out of the passport. My friends had done an artistic job of reducing its size, but for that very reason it was all the more likely to attract attention. The Gestapo passport office generally used the ordinary type of police photograph, showing only the head and shoulders.

Moreover, there was no railroad ticket. I hoped Hans Koch would obtain one for me. Still he did not come. Finally I went to the telephone again. This time I was more tenacious. When the unknown voice informed me that he was "away on a trip," I asked for Frau Koch. Although it was just before the time for an air-raid alarm, she had gone out. I asked for the oldest daughter. She also was not there. Then I knew what had happened.

There was nothing for me to do but to buy the ticket myself. I thought it would be better to get it at night than in broad daylight on the morrow. Unfortunately, it was too late for me to walk all the way to the railroad station. For good or ill I would have to venture the subway. The worst of that was that the subway stations and trains were illuminated, but there was no help for it. At the railroad terminal the ticket agent looked critically at my pass, and then he handed me my ticket.

I stood for a while in front of the blacked-out station wondering whether I ought to return to my hideout at all. How long would Koch resist the torture? Had he made agreements with his wife and daughter beforehand on what they would say? Many months later I learned that all three of them had heroically refused to talk, but the Gestapo placed in Frau Koch's cell a woman spy who alleged that she was about to be released and offered to help in any way she could. Frau Koch was convinced of her sincerity, and in order to warn me she gave the woman my address. In the meantime I had made good my escape.

Those last hours seemed an eternity to me. The train was scheduled to leave at six P.M. I would have to be at the station by five at the latest in order to get a seat. That meant that I would have to leave my hideout in broad daylight.

Nevertheless, I reached the railroad terminal safely. There was a double platform; on one side stood my own train, which was bound for Stuttgart, and on the other side the Vienna Express. On the other side of the platform I saw a line of SS guards and a host of SS officers and adjutants. As I found out a little later, Kaltenbrunner was taking a trip to his native Austria. Perhaps that was my salvation. Everyone's attention was concentrated upon this Gestapo chief and no one regarded his subordinate, "Doctor Hoffmann."

I wanted to jump right into the first car and disappear amid the crowd, but it was impossible. Probably the train had been jammed for hours with people who wanted to take advantage of this last opportunity for civilian travel.

In despair I walked up front to the locomotive. I thought of bribing the engineer to give me a place. Just then I heard a furious out burst of cursing and screeching from the dense crowd around the baggage car. The conductor and the baggage-master were trying to get into their baggage car, but the crowd had stormed it and filled it to overflowing. The two railroad officials stood on the platform gesticulating wildly. In front of them was a huge crowd of people who also wanted to get in.

The saving idea flashed through my mind. Pure chance had thrust me into my life's adventure in 1933, when I suddenly found myself a member of the newly established Gestapo. Since I had witnessed the beginnings of that noble institution, I ought to help its unpopularity along a bit, now that it was in its death-throes.

I took out my Gestapo badge. With a few vigorous thrusts of arms and elbows I worked my way through the shouting, pushing throng and in a moment had reached the two excited officials. "Gestapo!" I barked. And I offered to help them clear the car.

And I did clear it.

I proved, however, to be a very mild-mannered Gestapist. As soon as I had worked my way into the car and had reached the conductor's seat, my officious zeal suddenly faded. Behind me the crowd poured into the car again. I myself sat down and took two small children on my knee—hiding my face behind them. I paid no attention when I heard the two railroad officials despairingly call out for the police officer who had just promised to help them. Let them find me in this mob!

At last the train was ready to depart. Slowly it began to move, and the bombers, too, spared us this time. We emerged safely from the city, and the trip went much faster than I had expected. We were only twelve hours late!

There were a few more agitating intermezzos. As we left the bombed areas behind, the conductor regained control of his baggage car. I had several run-ins with him because, peculiar Gestapo man that I was, I absolutely refused to go forward where a special compartment was reserved for government officials.

My destination was the little border station of St. Margrethen. But instead the train was routed to Constance. Perhaps this was lucky for me. I went on foot to the tiny border crossing in Kreuzlingen.

Hungry, thirsty, and exhausted by my illness and the strain of the journey, I entered the little waiting room of the frontier post January 23, 1945, at six o'clock in the morning. The two officials, the Gestapo man and the customs officer, rubbed their eyes sleepily. It was rare for them to have travelers at such an early hour, particularly a traveler from Berlin and a high functionary of the Gestapo. Chills ran down my spine as they stood looking searchingly at me.

Certainly my physical and sartorial appearance had not improved in the past six months. I had worn my suit continuously since July 20 and it badly needed a pressing. My light spring coat was dirty and torn. I had given my own hat to Nebe when we parted. However, I had "borrowed" another from someone during the railroad journey. It did not fit too well, but at least it covered my thick head of hair, which was fortunate. When for a whole year you have been your own barber and have had to snip away at your hair with a nail scissors, your hair is not likely to be cut according to the correct, close-cropped SS pattern. My fleece-lined high shoes looked none too appropriate to my thin summer suit, but I had had to wear them because my other shoes were so worn that they would have done little credit to a Gestapo agent. In short, my appearance was not one to inspire confidence.

Perhaps it was for that very reason that they let me cross the border. They may have assumed that I had been carefully costumed for this particular expedition, so that, once across the border, I would be able to work as a member of the Fifth Column. They opened the border gate. I raised my arm limply in response to their greeting, for the two of them stood stiffly to see me out of the Gestapo's Germany.

And then I was free!

What was I to do now? If I reported myself to the Swiss frontier police as a political refugee, I would probably have been quarantined for several days and afterward interned. Therefore, I again drew out my forged passport. It had certainly been fabricated well. The Swiss officials looked crossly at this Doctor Hoffmann who wanted to go to the German embassy, but they let him pass.

I rushed to a telephone. My friends were overjoyed, for I was days overdue and they had already given me up for lost.

A few hours later I reached Zurich. Eddi Waetjen was there to meet me at the station, and in his excitement and joy he kissed not me but my mother. Then Gero von Gaevernitz joined us. He was too modest to listen to my thanks for all his efforts. Instead he told me the story of my "shortly."

Allen Dulles had quickly obtained from his superiors permission to help me. Thereupon Gero had personally gone to the London office of the OSS. My friends in the German embassy in Berne had supplied him with several models of passports. By October my papers were ready. But the OSS was careful. An important stamp had not been printed clearly, and if they were going to assist the Gestapo in issuing passports, they were determined to have the documents correct to the last dot over the last "i"; and so the passport had been sent back to London. In order to speed matters, it had been given to an Allied official who was flying to London. At the Paris airport the American military police had asked him whether he had

any written matter with him. The man had innocently said yes
and taken out my Gestapo passport.

I understood that this little incident produced something
of a delay!

When the passport was ultimately returned to Berne, they
still had to make sure of their courier connection with Berlin.
The Hamburg publisher, Henry Goverts, had undertaken this
most difficult and most courageous part of the task. Twice he
went to Constance to meet the messenger, who was to smuggle the forged passport over the border, and twice he missed
him.

But at last the rendezvous was made. With this dangerous
paper in his pocket, Goverts entered his hotel in Constance.
He intended to return to Hamburg and then go on to Berlin to
deliver the papers to me. Had he done so, he would have arrived
too late. But again chance came to my rescue.

In the hotel lobby Goverts encountered an acquaintance
who inquisitively asked what Goverts was doing there. This
man knew that Goverts traveled about as a liaison officer for
the Abwehr—for he was the new chief of the Abwehr, the
notorious SS General Schellenberg. The shock of this
encounter made Goverts decide to get rid of his perilous papers
at once. He took the fastest train to Berlin, and thus arrived
just in time.

Gero and Eddi ran through a hasty summary of this story.
Then I went straight to the barber's. The barber proved to be
an amateur detective. He glanced expertly at my hair and
informed me that I had just come from Germany. He said no
more, but his manner told me the state of my hair had convinced him that Germany was at last collapsing.

In the evening I called on Allen Dulles in the Herrengasse
in Berne. The servant led me to the club room that was so
familiar to me. I settled into the handsome red easy-chair by

the fireplace where we had so often chatted. I felt as if my pil-grimage through the Nazi millennium was over at last. I was deeply moved, profoundly grateful. I thought of my friends, of the dead, of the living.

Allen came in. I held out both hands.

"Thank you," I said. And for a long time I could say no more.

At last I began to talk. I recounted my experiences of the past six months. And the more I talked, the less oppressed my heart felt. I stopped thinking of the bitter end and began to hope for a new and better beginning.

Epilogue

NOW THAT MY STORY IS FINISHED, I must ask my readers to pause for a moment's reflection. No one can accuse me of having written a book containing facile apologies for Germany. Indeed, many of my German countrymen have accused me of disloyalty; they say that I should never have revealed my knowledge of so many shameful lacks and defects. In reply to them I have written a different final chapter for the German edition of this book, a chapter entitled *On Guilt*.

But I should also like to clear up all doubts in the minds of my readers abroad. Unfortunately, the phrase "collective guilt" has been abused with evil intent and ill results in recent years. Generalizations are never salutary. Often their effect is the opposite of the intended one, for after a time the pendulum swings in the other direction—and again swings too far. Then it is said that everything is relative, everything is destined; what could we "little people" do to stop the daemonic forces? And in fact the killing, the pillaging, the cynicism were so monstrous that we often ask whether real men were capable of these things or whether altogether inhuman forces were not behind them. Not the individual criminals but the extent of their crimes assume, to our horrified eyes, superhuman proportions. Nevertheless, at the present moment nothing would be more dangerous than to blur over the personal responsibility—and therefore the guilt—of every individual.

This is not a matter of pharasaical sitting in judgment; what we are aiming at is a vital and generally valid political lesson, and for this reason we are in duty bound not to conceal or cover up what went on in Germany during the past twelve years. Above all, we must understand the inherent logic of events; we must see why things had to happen—and to end— as they did. Today the Germans can no longer recognize themselves. The Nazi epoch seems to them a confused nightmare which they try irritably to shake off in order to clear the mind for a fresh day's work. Best of all, they would like to forget the whole diabolic business. Is it really sheer hypocrisy when they advance a thousand-and-one reasons to "explain" all the incomprehensible facts?

We ought to consider carefully and not satisfy ourselves with the simple answer that the Germans were or are a nation of devils. The self-enslavement of sixty or eighty million people remains an historic phenomenon of tremendous importance, and in the age of the atomic bomb it is a phenomenon that must be disquieting for all non-Germans as well. It is incontrovertible that there existed in Germany a class of moral and honorable men of the highest quality. The obvious question is: How could such men permit themselves to be overrun by the Nazi usurpers without offering resistance? Is the civilization of all other nations impregnably fortified against similar outbreaks of imminent evil?

The Nazi catastrophe began against the background of a slow—and often initially unperceived—growth of complicity. [There were] plain signposts along the precipitous road to revolutionary totality. Each event provided in itself a clear, definite set of facts. To be entirely candid, however, we must admit that, in spite of the clarity of the facts, there remain elements that are mysterious, opaque, and bewildering for foreign observers as well. A small group of men on top appeared guilty or responsible, and below them were millions who either were unsuspecting or without influence. In the beginning the latter did not at all perceive what responsibility they were being forced to share. Their real guilt began when they did recognize the crimes being committed in their name, and neglected to oppose them; that is to say, their duty to oppose the regime really began at a stage when effective opposition had become immeasurably more difficult.

From the middle of 1938 on, the direction in which things were headed became terrifyingly clear even to those far removed from the centers of government. From month to month the outline of things to come grew more and more distinct. It was clear that "this man Hitler" wanted "his" war. The history of all revolutions was being repeated: first terror raged at home; then an adventure abroad was embarked upon. By that time, however, too many people were already caught in their own trap. Is it not altogether uncanny the way these ministers, economists, scholars, and bishops, and above all the hesitant generals, acted again and again against their better judgment? With open eyes they let themselves be dragged down into a general and a personal disaster.

These psychological or political considerations must not divert us from the question of guilt. Rather, they should lead us to consider that question more profoundly and more honestly. Naturally no serious-minded person can pronounce all Germans guilty in the criminal sense. We have seen how careful the Nuremberg judges were, even with so prominent a group of persons as the members of the Reich government. But when such a calamity descends upon a civilized nation, and when for twelve years that nation is incapable of throwing off the shame that burdens it, it goes against the sound ethical instinct of people to cast all the blame upon a clique of leaders, no matter whether that clique is numbered in the dozens, the hundreds, or the thousands. When such a disaster takes place, there must have been something wrong with those who were led or misled.

What is that thing? One of the vital lessons that we must learn from the German disaster is the ease with which a people can be sucked down into the morass of inaction; let them as individuals fall prey to overcleverness, opportunism, or cowardliness and they are irrevocably lost. In this mass epoch it is by no means a settled thing that acts alone make for guilt. Passive acceptance, intellectual subservience, or, in religious terms, failure to pray against the evil, may constitute a kind of silent support for authoritarian rule. Once the system of terror has been installed, however, there is only one course remaining to each individual and to all individuals collectively: to fight the terrorists with the same courage and tenacity, with the same willingness to take risks, that they employ in wartime under "orders" when they fight against the "enemy."

There are some Germans who mistakenly examine the history of the Nazi Revolution in search of "daemonic forces" or other alibis. Everyone knows that terrorism and Gestapo methods existed in other places—and still exist. No one will attempt to deny that others were also guilty—and still are. In the final analysis there were millions of unteachable persons throughout the world who made a pact with the forces of Revolution and only came to their senses when the Revolution swallowed them alive. These provisos may assert many psychological or political truths; they may serve to warn the rest of the world against hasty or one-sided condemnation; but they do not excuse the Germans.

I have not, in this book, had the intention of clapping myself or my friends on the shoulder and saying: "At least we did what we could." The "success" of our oppositional efforts proves that we should have done much more. So far as my dead friends are concerned, I should be dishonoring the memory of their sacrifices were I to assert that in all their actions they behaved without hesitation and without error. Of myself I can only say that every page of this book has given me cause to reflect on how frequently I thought wrongly or acted wrongly. I know that I am responsible for these mistakes, and that is why, out of my experience with twelve years of Nazism, I cannot help maintaining that German guilt does exist; it is a reality. It cannot be cast off upon a collective group, so that each individual need bear only a millionth part of the weight of guilt. All of us, and not alone the Nazis, strayed into dangerous, evil ways. We were guilty of failure to understand, of willful blindness, of misguided obedience, of paltry compromising, of exaggerated caution or of persistent shirking of the logical conclusions. In these turbulent times only those who courageously face the fact of personal guilt will be saved from going astray again in the future.

Nowadays—in practice if not in words—fatalism is the fashion. People wait for orders from above, or take refuge by invoking political necessity; or they ask: What can one individual do to oppose the course of "destiny"? It is precisely because I do literally believe in daemonic evil forces that I do not wish to amalgamate two elements which should be kept strictly apart in any factual report on the Nazi régime. Without doubt there existed the incomprehensible and irrational element, the eruptiveness, the temper of the times, or whatever else we choose to call it; but there is also no doubt that on the other hand there existed the distinctly concrete reaction of responsible men to demands or necessities.

We must once more clearly delimit responsibilities, and what persons have more right to lead the way in such an endeavor than those who died fighting, not against any "destiny," but for their sincerest convictions? Few ages have produced so many martyrs as ours, and in time to come countless Germans will also be included in the roll of honor of those who perished for freedom and a better future. It is my duty, at the end of this book, to pay this tribute to my dead friends.

This homage is directed, not alone to those whose story I tell in this book; if it were I should tremble to think of how many names I have omitted. The world feels a justified sense of outrage at what happened in Germany and because of Germany during those terrible years of tyranny. Let us not forget, however, that long before the first foreigner was murdered by the SS killers, hundreds of thousands of Germans had died. Let us leave to those whose ashes have been scattered at least their undefiled faith in a better world. Let us leave to them their last despairing hope that the world would be startled out of its slumber by their lonely cries of agony and would not wait for the thunder of Hitler's cannon.

Index